LAMENT For
SIAVASH

ON DEATH & RESURRECTION

Shahrokh Meskoob

Translated from the Persian by
Mahasti Afshar

Foreword
Abbas Milani

MAGE PUBLISHERS

This book is part of a series of Iranian Studies publications made possible by the Hamid and Christina Moghadam Program in Iranian Studies at Stanford University.

MAGE PUBLISHERS INC
WWW.MAGE.COM

LIBRARY OF CONGRESS CATALOGING-IN-PUBLICATION DATA
Available at the Library of Congress

FIRST HARDCOVER EDITION
ISBN: 978-1-949445-76-3

VISIT MAGE ONLINE: WWW.MAGE.COM
EMAIL: AS@MAGE.COM

To my loving son Dadali
in memory of our beloved Hossein

CONTENTS

FOREWORD

The *Shahnameh* is a majestic monument of Iranian literature, a pillar of the Persian language, a beacon of rationality, a celebration of women's assertive presence in pre-Islamic Iran, and the mytho-history of the country's great ancient civilization.

Yet, for much of the twentieth century, all too many Iranian public intellectuals, literary critics, and cultural activists chose to ignore, dismiss, even disparage the text for its incongruence with their creed. The secular left and the religious right, both keen on purveying their dogmatic certitudes, shared a distaste for Ferdowsi. The left erroneously regarded it as a panegyric of kings or overly nationalistic, while Islamist foes of Ferdowsi were correctly wary of it as an unmistakably secular, even un-Islamic text. Shahrokh Meskoob was among the most appreciative and prolific exceptions to this damaging politics of exclusion.

He began his long and luminous intellectual odyssey as a communist and ended it as a relentless advocate of secular democracy, literary and cultural criticism shorn of shibboleths of the left and right, of unflinching honesty, integrity and impartiality in his examination of Iran's cultural history. Even when he was a member of a party whose literary taste was shaped by Stalin and Zhedanov's mantra of "socialist realism," Meskoob voraciously devoured Iranian classical texts as well as classics of the Western canon. He spent much of his lifetime studying the *Shahnameh*, excavating its genealogy, comparing it with other mythologies, and expounding its philosophical and existential foundations and its narrative tropes. In everything he wrote, including his much acclaimed literary texts, his uniquely pithy, parsimonious, and often poetic prose is as much worthy of scrutiny and praise as the ideas and insights he articulated. His form was, in short, part of his content. Meskoob's papers, now at Stanford, include the detailed notes he wrote on his comparative studies of myths and of the *Shahnameh* as well as the extensive correspondence he had with fellow academics, artists and past comrades. Included in the collection is the full text of his daily journals. A heavily edited version of these journals—tailored perhaps to ensure the book adhered to the Procrustean pathologies of Iranian censorship—has been published in Persian, but, hopefully, an unexpurgated edition, worthy of Meskoob's iconoclasm, will eventually be published.

In celebration of the arrival of this important collection at Stanford, we organized a daylong conference to discuss the many facets of Meskoob's intellectual journey. The collected papers of that conference were published in 2022 (*A Scholar for Our Times: A Celebration of the Life and Work of Shahrokh Meskoob*). The book is part of an ongoing series called Stanford Iranian Studies.

An alchemist of words and ideas, an erudite explorer of myth and history, an astute observer of the interplay of literature and politics, Meskoob has found in Mahasti Afshar a masterful translator of equal erudition and perception, with a keen sense of the precision, power, and beauty of words and their infinite potential. Her extraordinary skill in conveying Meskoob's linguistic virtuosity, in selecting words in English with all the cultural and emotional resonance of the original Persian, has created a work of art in itself.

We are fortunate in having Mage as the publishers of this exceptional translation of a seminal work of Iranian scholarship. They have spared no effort in helping to bring to publication a book that gives the English-language reader as authentic an insight into Meskoob's masterpiece as is possible.

Abbas Milani

TRANSLATOR'S NOTE

Lament for Siavash is an almost literal translation of Shahrokh Meskoob's *Sūg-e Siavash*, Tehran: Kharazmi, Tir 1351 (June 1972). Knowing the author's distaste for editorialized reproductions of his writings, I have replicated his choice of words and phraseology wherever possible, plus his liberal use of alliteration, assonance, repetition of words in the same passage, and the many original verbs and compound nouns he formed to convey his thoughts in terse, stylized, and complex prose-poetic constructs.

Indeed, *Lament* self-consciously elevates prose to the level of poetry, a style that I believe reflects Meskoob's singular admiration for the prose account of the trials and tribulations of Hasanak-e Vazir in Beyhaqi's *History* on the one hand, and Ferdowsi's versification of Iranian storytelling traditions in the *Shahnameh* on the other, both of which date from the 11th century. He avoids superfluous words at all costs.

That is not to say that the purity, exactitude, and economy of Meskoob's language do not pose certain challenges for the reader, for much of his vocabulary is loaded with layers of meaning and symbolic referents. Thus, while the thinking behind his writing is lucid, it at times requires parsing to be grasped, particularly given the complex mixture of religious, literary, and historical elements involved. Moreover, his presentation does not unfold in a linear fashion but in a three-dimensional pointillist matrix of themes and motifs derived from varied sources—Avestan, Pahlavi, and New Persian—and related scholarship. Nor do the three main chapters, "Twilight," "Night," and "Dawn" follow the timeline that is given in the "Prelude" in shorthand but instead draw parallel themes from different eras and sources to bear on a point. The complexity is a work of art and, as such, demanding. To ease the load, I have taken the liberty of inserting some connective tissue where warranted.

For the reader who may be unfamiliar with some of the uncited material, I have also added informational footnotes duly marked "Trans." and provided a "Glossary of Names." The many uncited *Shahnameh* verses or phrases that are embedded in the text remain in quotation marks as in the original, and without a gloss; where the author has paraphrased dialogues from the *Shahnameh* in prose, they are presented in single quotation marks to distinguish them from direct quotes.

I owe *Lament* entirely to two people, Professor Abbas Milani, who suggested the translation be included in the Stanford Iranian Studies series and continued to encourage me as I worked away, and Mohmmad Batmanglij of Mage Publishers without whose critical review of my initial drafts the quality of my work would have greatly suffered. Translation is not my métier though the subject of *Lament* is, so their support mattered. Last but not least, I owe endless gratitude to Kate Parker, the remarkable copyeditor who helped fine-tune my work with her faultless commentary, questions, and apropos suggestions. I am in awe of her standards. Given that I lack any talent for poetry, however, I should add that despite everyone's best efforts, my renditions of the *Shahnameh* verses—some rhymed, others not—remain adequate at best. For that, I apologize to Ferdowsi and Meskoob and beg the reader's mercy.

Finally, a note on transliteration where there are no hard and fast rules for rendering foreign names in English. My challenge began with the Book of Kings, which I have rendered as *Shahnameh* given that it ends in a silent é, instead of the academically established, but audibly misleading *Shahnama*; fortunately, my preference conforms with related titles by Mage Publishers. Elsewhere, I have used diacritic marks only where essential, notably in the long vowels, ā, ī, ū, and the occasional ē, ō, and č, for (ch), š (sh), and ž (zh), but to satisfy the specialists, I have applied diacritics in the "Glossary of Names."

Standard abbreviations apply here: Av. (Avestan); Gk (Greek); MP (Middle Persian); NP (New Persian); OP (Old Persian); *GBd* (Iranian/Greater Bundahišn); and *Yt* (Yašt). For abbreviated references to the Moscow and the Borukhim editions of the *Shahnameh*, see Bibliography, Sources in Persian, p. 209.

Mahasti Afshar

PRELUDE

Siavash was the son of Kay Kāvus, the son of Kay Qobād. Kāvus was the king of Iran. He entrusted his son to the great hero Rostam-e Dastān, who took him away to Sistan to teach him the art of chivalry, war, hunting, and feasting.

Seven years later, Siavash surpassed all his peers in battle and banqueting, and Rostam brought him back to the court of Kāvus.

Kāvus had a wife named Sudabeh, the daughter of the king of Hāmāvarān. Sudabeh fell in love with and coveted Siavash, for none in the world surpassed him in beauty. He was the epitome of physical perfection. But Siavash spurned the queen's love. Sudabeh's stratagems to net him failed. For Siavash was also the epitome of spiritual purity.

Sudabeh felt her love was unrequited and feared exposure. She alleged, 'Siavash tried to lie with me who am his stepmother.' Of course, Siavash did not concede to the lie.

Kāvus was oblivious and obsessed with Sudabeh; though he knew Siavash bore no blame, he did not know what to do. At his wife's urging, he ultimately agreed that Siavash should undergo the ordeal of trial by fire to prove his innocence. For fire does not catch on to the pure.

Siavash duly complied and rode through extended mountainous fires and emerged on the other side unscathed. Sudabeh's transgression was proven and so Kāvus opted to kill her. Siavash knew his father was enamored of the woman and would someday feel regret, so he intervened. He implored Kāvus to refrain from seeking retribution, and the king refrained.

Meanwhile, Afrasiyab, the king of Turan, attacked Iran and crossed the river Oxus bordering the two lands. Siavash petitioned Kāvus to send him to fight the foe, wishing to go away and be freed from both Sudabeh and his father. Kāvus agreed. Siavash left, along with Rostam, and leading the army fought and captured Balkh. The Turanians fled. The prince penned a victory writ and asked Kāvus for a decree to attack Turan. The king did not issue a decree and said, 'Do not go beyond the Oxus; wait for Afrasiyab to advance.'

Afrasiyab was assembling troops when he had an ominous dream; terrified, he sued for peace and as a guarantee that he would uphold his oath dispatched a hundred kinsmen to Siavash to be held hostage, and Siavash affirmed the pact.

But Kāvus changed his mind. He sent a message to Siavash to dispatch the hostages to his court, saying, 'I'll kill them; then you break the oath and attack Turan.'

Siavash refused, which barred his return to Iran. He asked Afrasiyab for safe passage through Turan instead.

Afrasiyab had a wise and gracious general and adviser named Piran. He sought his counsel about Siavash's request and consequently invited the Iranian prince to come and stay and never depart from Turan. Siavash went and stayed.

Afrasiyab loved Siavash as would any father and cherished him dearly. He gave him his daughter Farangis in marriage and granted him a province in Khotan where he built Siavashgerd and Kangdež and prospered as king.

Afrasiyab had a brother named Garsivaz. This Garsivaz was a jealous man. He assumed people would never consider him noteworthy if Siavash continued to be universally favored. Therefore, resorting to lies and calumny, he made Afrasiyab and Siavash suspicious of one another: the king of Turan came to believe that the Iranian prince intended to seize his land and crown and Siavash believed that Afrasiyab intended to kill him without cause.

In the end, Afrasiyab killed Siavash, but with Piran's mediation abstained from killing his wife, his own daughter Farangis. Before long, Farangis gave birth to Kay Khosrow. Piran placed Kay Khosrow in the care of shepherds to keep him away from the king's court, and safe. For Afrasiyab lived in fear that Siavash's offspring might someday kill him to avenge his father.

When news of Siavash's slaying reached Iran, Rostam slew Sudadeh in revenge and attacked Turan and for several years pillaged and slaughtered and torched the land before returning to his native Zābolestan.

Then Afrasiyab attacked Iran. For seven years, the country was beset by drought and devastation until the Iranian hero Gudarz saw the divine Sorūsh in a dream who told him, 'Send your son Gīv to Turan to look for Kay Khosrow; he is the only one who can find him and bring him back.' Gīv searched for Kay Khosrow for seven years until he found him. Then, together with Farangis and aided by the horse and armor that Siavash had left Kay Khosrow, they battled their way out of Turan and returned to Iran. Kay Khosrow went to Kāvus who, as recounted in the *Shahnameh*, crowned him king of Iran.

The deadliest wars of vengeance between Iran and Turan over Siavash occurred during Kay Khosrow's reign. He led the final battles himself. In the end, the Turanians were defeated; Afrasiyab and Garsivaz fled and were captured and killed.

Kay Khosrow had a sixty-year reign marked by justice and fairness and prosperity. He then stepped down from the throne, appointed

Lohrāsp as king, turned his back on the world, and went to the heavenly sphere.

This book is an account and a commentary on the twilight of the father and the dawn of the son, the killing of Siavash in the days of Afrasiyab and Kāvus, and the kingship of Kay Khosrow—of death and resurrection.

TWILIGHT

"In the beginning the twin spirits of good and evil revealed themselves in better and poorer thoughts, words, and deeds. Between these two, the wise chose rightly, the unwise not so."[1]

In the beginning was Ahura Mazda and Ahriman and the world of light and the world of darkness, each distinct from the other. When night was not yet and day was not yet, one "day" Ahriman emerged from the dark depths and saw light; it was beautiful. He coveted it and when he attacked, the cosmic battle between good and evil erupted. At first, victory was Ahriman's. To save light and goodness, Ahura Mazda created this world—the earth—to be his ally in battle. But the earth was lifeless, the stars dull, and the sun and the moon stationery, and the waters still and the plants fallow. How could such a dispirited somnolent do battle?! Thereupon, Ahura Mazda uttered a prayer to the ethereal spirits of human beings, "O *faravahar*s of the righteous, come to my aid."[2] The *faravahar*s complied and came and by their grace

---

1. *Yasnā* 30:3, in Pourdavoud, trans., *Gāthā*, 80.

2. On the contested etymology and nature of the *faravahar*s (Av. *fravaši*, OP *fravarti*, MP *frawahr, frōhar, frawaš*), see Mary Boyce, "Fravaši," *Encyclopædia Iranica*, 2000/2012. Trans.

the stars shone, and the sun and the moon moved along their paths and the waters flowed and the plants grew. Humankind is the life of the earth without whose intervention the earth would have lain dead. Light issued from righteous humans, absent whom Ahriman would have triumphed.

> From time immemorial Hormozd lay amid light and Ahriman amid darkness. Hormozd knew Ahriman would one day rise to do battle with him and prepared munitions for such an event. He created the world in a *mēnōg* (celestial/spiritual, holy, embryonic) state. Three thousand years later, Ahriman fell upon a ray of light by chance and became aware of his adversary's creation. He longed to possess it. Thereupon Hormozd created finite space and time and by reciting the sacred prayer Ahunvar (Av. *Yata ahu vairyo*), prescribed the outcome of the battle ... Ahriman was locked in the sky unable to escape to his abode in the depths of darkness ... On learning that he had no choice but to fight until his annihilation, Ahriman sank into a stupor for three thousand years. Hormozd carried on, regardless, and transformed his creation into a *gētīg* (earthly and corporeal) state. Once Ahriman rose from his stupor, he charged. He slew Geush, the primordial Bull, and thirty years later Kiumars, the first human. He corrupted creation. War raged for another six thousand years during which Zoroaster was born."[3]

The purpose of the creation and descent of the spirits, the *faravahars*, to earth—as us, humans—is to fight Ahriman and defeat him. The genesis of the world and of humanity has a purpose, which is to be achieved within a prescribed period. To that end, the cosmic battle unfolds through time, which is why it is sometimes said that the first thing Ahura created was Time so that the end may be known in the beginning.

---

3. Molé, "La naissance du monde," 302. [NP Kiumars, Av. Gayō.maretan, "mortal life."—Trans.]

Thus, the earth has a celestial history with a known beginning and end spanning three ages of spirituality, mixture, and unification. Each age lasts three thousand years. In the first age, good and evil are separate, darkness has not mingled with light, and Ahriman has not assailed Ahura Mazda. All is primal paradise. Next comes Ahriman's assault and the age of the mixture of good and evil. Zoroaster was born during that age, which at the outset was more favorable to Ahriman. The last three thousand years see the rise of the savior-figure *Sūshiyāns* sons of Zoroaster and other immortals and the separation of good and evil up to the advent of Renovation when all turns into light, and all is eternal paradise.

During the Spiritual Age, light is shielded from the bane of evil; it is one with itself and whole, and being discrete from darkness, is of its own essence and nature. The primordial spirits of humankind and the entire Good Existence that has not yet become existent are contained in Ahura Mazda's "omniscient mind"; he embodies them all. Ahura Mazda is the thought of the thinker and the goodness of a cogitated reality. He is singular, whole, and undivided. Such is the spiritual world in the incorporeal age. But the totality of existence is a bipartite and binary dyad. For Ahriman also exists, together with his host of demons and fiends, consistent with his nature, in the depths of darkness. When he assailed light to draw it unto himself, darkness and light, Ahrimanic and Ahuric entities, intermingled. The battle between good and evil and the three-thousand-year age of mixture began. As Ahriman ravaged the sky and Ahura Mazda's creation, he corrupted everything and cried out:

> "My victory is complete, for I ruptured the sky, sullied it with
> gloom and turned it into my fortress; I polluted the waters
> and opened the earth wide and covered it with darkness.
> I desiccated the plants and brought death upon the Bull
> and sickness upon Kiumars . . . I attained to sovereignty.

> Nothing stands at Ahura's flank in battle except human
> beings. And what can humans do, isolated and alone?[4]

During this era, collectivity and unity, Ahura and the good creation, are in turmoil. Ahriman and the demons ravage the world and, like filth seeping into water, infiltrate humans and heaven and earth. The chaos that ensues is a transitory phenomenon, however, and does not lead to its total disintegration as, by the grace of his "omniscient wisdom," Ahura Mazda is wise to his final victory. By the grace of *daena*—conscience, faith, the sublime, incorporeal self [5]—humanity, too, is aware of its own wholeness and the attacks directed at it, and that awareness is an agency that prevents humans from becoming detached from their essence or becoming alienated or uprooted from their Ahuric source.

In this sorry age of thwarted hopes, of Zahhāk's and Afrasiyab's rapacity, every human is engaged in a battle to overcome the evil beings, demons, and agents of obstruction in order to recover their essence, each according to the strength of their own spirit. Thus, individual human victory in the microcosm replicates Ahura Mazda's universal victory in the macrocosm; the one is not possible without the other.

The battle between good and evil in both the human and cosmic sphere lasts six thousand years. Zoroaster is born at the end of this age of mixture. In the ensuing three millennia that culminate in Renovation, God and humans recover their wholeness. God safeguards paradise, *Garōdmān* ("House of Song"), from Ahrimanic elements. Upon deliverance, humans join the domain of light and song—that is, the essence of Ahura Mazda.

The *faravahar* of humans subscribed to donning a corporeal garb, and humankind was born into this world to fight Ahriman. But once Ahriman is annihilated, humans will regain their spiritual form. The *faravahar* in Ahura Mazda is as radiance in light, and Ahura Mazda without the *faravahar*s of humankind is light without radiance. Humanity

---

4. *Zādspram* 4:3, quoted in Zaehner, *Dawn and Twilight*, 264.

5. Corbin, *Corps spirituel*, 68–9.

descends from the heavens to earth, accomplishes its mission, and returns to heaven. Humanity reunites with itself, with the world and with God, and creature and creator become one.

In primal time, there was Ahura Mazda and Ahriman; the essence of existence was binary. But when the cosmic battle ends and Ahriman is annihilated, duality is eliminated and existence becomes one with itself; Ahura Mazda who was potentially omnipotent in the past becomes so in actuality.

Each of the two ages of mixture and unification in the spiritual history of the universe is subdivided into millenary stages,[6] culminating in the birth of the three sons of Zoroaster, each a thousand years apart, in the age of unification.

The Age of Mixture

- Creation of Geush Urvan (the "guardian angel" of animals) up to the kingship of Kiumars and Jamshid

- Kingship of Zahhāk

- Kingship of Fereidun and Manuchehr; Afrasiyab's vices; kingship of Goshtāsp

- Birth of Zoroaster

- Alexander's invasion and the restoration of the Good Religion

- The Arabs' religious conquest; liberation of land and religion by King Kay Bahram and Pashūtan

---

6. *GBd* 33, in Duchesne-Guillemin, *La religion de l'Iran ancien*, 55–6, and *Farvardin Yt*, in Pourdavoud, trans., *Yašthā*, vol. 2, 100. Accounts of the creation of the world, the cosmic battle, and Resurrection/Renovation vary, some postulate three periods of three thousand years each, others four periods of three thousand years—which may be a Zurvanite tradition (see Widengren, *Les religions de l'Iran*, 316). The order of the millenary periods also varies, though all are cyclical.

The Age of Unification

- Birth of Hūshidar, the first son of Zoroaster; the winter
  of Malkūs; repopulation of the world from Jamshid's
  var, the subterranean enclosure built to preserve
  human, animal, and plant life from the fatal winter.

- Birth of Hūshidar-Māh, the second son of Zoroaster;
  Zahhāk unchained; rise of Garshāsp, Kay Khosrow,
  and the other immortals, culminating in the:

- Birth and kingship of Sūshiyāns, the third son of Zoroaster;
  the resurrection, Renovation (frašegird, "making
  excellent/brilliant") and salvation of the world.

The world begins on a cyclical trajectory with the rule of Ahura
Mazda, and following various fated fluctuations ends with his victory.
Existence integrates within itself at the end of a nine- or twelve-thou-
sand-year closed cycle and reclaims its original state. From the beginning,
the goal is the return to the beginning.

In the end, time ends. The purpose of creation has been achieved.

In the age of mixture when darkness has supremacy, two millennial
periods are rounded off by solar kings, Jamshid and Kay Khosrow.
Jamshid is "vigilant, like the sun" or "omniscient, like the sun."[7] He and
Kay Khosrow are each the sun at its summit. Jamshid rescues the world
from primeval disorder and chaos by civilizing it, and Kay Khosrow
liberates it from Afrasiyab's tyranny. Both figures possess the *Jām-e
Jahān-namā*, the "world-revealing cup," an allusion to the omniscient
sun, which is to say that as kings whose essence is of radiance and light,

---

7. In Carnoy, *Asātīr-e Irani*, trans. Tabatabaie, 77: "One may in general conclude
that the Indian Yama and his Iranian counterpart Yima [Jamshid] are the
luminous sun . . . In Iran, the sun and Jam are more closely identified . . .
Jamshid is regularly called *xšaeta* (shining and bright), which is the most
common epithet of the sun. Jamshid is moreover called supremely glorious and
resplendent and sunlike."

they both hold the sun in their hands. Each appears once in a thousand years and draws one age to its close.

Zoroaster himself, the nexus of the sphere of existence, appears in the middle of the cosmic battle between good and evil at the end of the age of mixture and the start of the age of unification.[8]

Renovation, set in motion by Hūshidar and Hūshidar-Māh, and sealed by Sūshiyāns, occurs in the age of unification. In the first millennium of that age, canon and country are still in the grip of Ahriman. Then Hūshidar eradicates tyrannical kingship. At the end of Hūshidar's millennium, plants and animals have been cleansed of all Ahrimanic elements that had been ravaged by the winter of Malkūs. The Ahuric plants and animals that Jamshid had selected for his secret mythical *var*, have escaped the sting of Ahriman and may now proliferate across the earth. Following the advent of Hūshidar-Māh, Sūshiyāns' final act of renovation purifies the world. Demons and reprobates will be undone, resurrected human beings will wade through molten metal, the last vestiges of sin will be wiped from them, body and soul, and the universe will be reborn anew. "The people of the world shall become one in thought, speech, and deed . . . all shall pass through molten metal and become clear and radiant and pure as the luminous sun."[9]

When each of Zoroaster's offspring emerge, the noonday sun hangs in the middle of the sky and shines upon the seven climes of the earth and cleanses impurities. The sun signals the arrival of these sacred beings—or they themselves are the sun, come to expel darkness. Once every thousand years.[10]

Such is the *mēnōg*, or spiritual, history of *gētī*, the earth—with the participation of Ahura Mazda and Ahriman and humankind and

---

8. Pahlavi literature refers to the entire era of the cosmic battle as "the age of mixture." But two periods may be singled out in the six-thousand-year era: the first marks Ahriman's victory and the second ushers in his defeat.

9. Hedayat, trans., "Yādgār i Jāmāspi," *Sokhan* 1:4–5.

10. *Farvardin Yt* 27–8/128–9, in Pourdavoud, trans., *Yaŝthā*, vol. 2, 100–101, and Bahar, "Joqrāfiyā-ye Asātiri," 93.

the "cosmos." The earth is a singular workshop where each entity has a task to perform.

Such an understanding of the history of the world is circular.

Observing the movements of the sun, moon, and the stars around the earth, the succession of night and day, the waxing and waning of the moon, and the rise of the seasons, gave birth to the notion of time. The cosmos encircles the earth like a ring and in this ring each luminous orb returns to its homestead at a specific time. The changing seasons and the growth of vegetation and the harvesting of crops are sequential and repeated at regular intervals. Every night and every day, every season and every year, the sun, the moon, and nature begin life anew and everything starts over.

On the other hand, time is not merely an abstract and mental concept for it is intertwined with the movement of the stars and the transformations of humanity's natural habitat. Time is not separate from the cradle of time. The signifiers of time having a circular movement, time itself is therefore conceived of as circular, or, given that spring and autumn and the growth and withering of vegetation and the waxing and waning of the moon are cyclical, time is also conceived of as cyclical.[11] Time is itself a circle that initiates everything and after a circular course returns them to their starting point. It follows that whatever unfolds in time, or that time unfolds in, is cyclical. That includes humanity, which time lowers from above in an unbroken continuum and returns to the heavens after a while, just like the sun's passage from dawn to dusk and a return to radiance. Or, put differently, the history of the earth and its return to a spiritual state after nine thousand years is, like fertility and pregnancy, to pass nine months in the dark of the womb, followed by birth and emergence into the light. The birth of the world and humanity are analogous; each return to their essence, one after Renovation and the other after death.

---

11. Duchesne-Guillemain, "Espace et temps," 268, 272–3, and Corbin, *Corps spirituel*, 40. In Iranian mythology the sky (*sepehr*) is also circular and rotates like time, Bahar, "Joqrāfiyā-ye Asātiri," 93.

The history of the earth is preordained. Whatever happens in this world is otherworldly. But if everything in this workshop is prefabricated, why has transient humanity been tossed into the fray? The answer is, not only is creation made possible with the help of humanity but the war between good and evil ends in God's victory because humans join the battle. Instead of staying in the sky and abiding in safety, the *faravahars become earthly* so they can fight. It is thanks to them that the cosmic battle and Ahura Mazda's victory become possible.

> Sky, wind, water, and earth, and the movement of the sun
> and the moon and the stars are owed to the *faravahars'*
> radiance and *farr*. The righteous *faravahar* is more powerful
> than all created beings. Just as humankind is supreme
> among earthly beings and is their chief, the *faravahars'*
> superior power in the heavens also informs earthlings.[12]

When Ahriman first attacked Ahura Mazda in the spiritual world, the *faravahar*s surrounded him like a battalion and shielded him from harm. On earth, humankind likewise commands and leads all fighting forces. People thus have a task to perform in the cosmic order and in the battle between good and evil. In Pahlavi, this task and its performance is called *xwēškārīh*, "self-purpose,"[13] which is the precise and clear translation of *xwarrah* (*farr*), the "numinous force."[14]

> The Creator created creatures to accomplish a mission and
> they are at the service of the Creator. Their work, *kār*, is

---

12. *Dēnkard*, quoted in Molé, *Culte, mythe et cosmologie*, 393.

13. NP *khīsh-kāri*, from *khīsh*, "self," and *kār*, which can translate into "work, purpose, duty, or function" depending on the context.—Trans.

14. Zaehner, *Dawn and Twilight*, 151. [Farr, commonly translated as "glory," is a force possessed by divinities and royalty (*Farreh-ye īzadi/Kiani*); but it also manifests in less notable humans, hence, a more inclusive translation here as the "numinous force."—Trans.]

accomplished through *farr* and self-purpose. Self-purpose
is to obey *farr*. By applying self-purpose, the Creator's work
is done, and His wish is thus fulfilled. But if they controvert
self-purpose, they have reviled *farr* and the Creator's
mission; His wish is not fulfilled, and harm shall follow.[15]

When an individual applies themselves to a task for which they
were born, the Creator is gratified. An individual's work is God's work.[16]

In the vicissitudes of time, people may disengage from their self-purpose, as did Jamshid. He became estranged from his spiritual fate; *farr*
abandoned him and Zahhāk tore him in half. All who neglect their
self-purpose are torn up; they take in evil and thereby gratify Ahriman.

Self-purpose is not a blind, cruel fate; it does not accost and oppose
individuals but is in alignment and solidarity with them; it is a mission
preconceived by God and its conscious and voluntary performance—the
harmony and the unity between the two. Self-purpose does not help
expedite Renovation and salvation. The earth's timeline has a fixed
duration and that fate rules the earth just as death rules the body. Thanks
to the primary *faravahar*s humans join forces with Ahura Mazda and
victory becomes possible; self-purpose hauls the limited time (nine
or twelve thousand years) *triumphantly* to its limit. It is also by virtue
of self-purpose that an individual embraces the depth of their soul.

Self-purpose drives the earth toward a coveted end, and humanity
toward the heavens. The perfectly purposeful individual is one with the
Creator and creation. Self-purpose is thus humanity's coveted, spiritual
fate. By virtue of self-purpose, every human is a *Sūshiyāns*, a Renovator
and bringer of salvation, for each person has a hand in Renovation and
salvation and whoever is more self-purposeful has more of a hand in

---

15. *Dēnkard*, quoted in Molé, *Culte, mythe et cosmologie*, 434.

16. *Yasnā* 33:2: "The person who opposes an errant, whether in speech, in
thought or in action, or who teaches their associates goodness, such people
have gratified Ahura Mazda and accomplished his will."

the process and whoever is unified with it is sacred and spiritual. The perfectly self-purposeful individual is the perfect soul.

Enacting self-purpose is a covenant with the world, oneself, and God. Whoever rejoins their spiritual self through self-purpose *here on earth* has transcended the mixture of good and evil and is unified with God.

Siavash, the son of Kāvus, the son of Kay Qobād, is such a man. He ranks among the righteous who appear from time to time to lead this troubled world to a transcendent order.

> He created the triumphant and valiant *faravahar*s of the righteous for the visible cloak—the visible earth. *He decreed that they assimilate their essence from time to time and don earthly cloaks and join the cohort of humans. A handful of perfect ones were thus born to accomplish the purpose of their particular time*—the highly fecund Fravāk; the Pīshdād-to-be Hūshang; the dragon-slayer Tahmuras; the *farr*-sated Jamshid, the healer Fereidun; he of twofold wisdom, the righteous Manuchehr; the mighty Garshāsp; the descendant of a *farr*-endowed race, Kay Qobād; the very wise Oshnar; the noble Siavash; the man of action Kay Khosrow; the one of bold horses, the exalted Kay Vishtāsp, and the most benevolent and just Zoroaster; the patron of world order Pashūtan; the proponent of religion Āturpāt; the *mānsrīk* (exponent of sacred narratives) Hūshidar; the *dātīk* (exponent of laws) Hūshidar-Māh; the ultimate *gāsānīk* (exponent of spiritual knowledge and ethics) Sūshiyāns. There will be among them several immortals of glorious deeds, hallowed and of good governance, created to vanquish *Druj* ("the Lie") and gratify the Creator.[17]

---

17. *Dādestān-i Dēnīg* 3, quoted in Molé, *Culte, mythe et cosmologie*, 403, and 63, "Zoroastrian texts are of three kinds: *Gāsān* (the *Gāthās*), which is mostly about the heavens; *Dāt*, which is mostly about the earth; and *Hātmansr*, which is mostly about interactions between the two."

"Noble Siavash" is among the perfect souls who embraced his essence. He is as self-purposeful as he is passionate about alignment with God and the world. Such a man is incapable of countering self-purpose and violating an oath. Because Mehr, "the stout-armed gallant warrior,"[18] the divinity of light and contracts, rises before dawn, and with his thousand watchful eyes and a thousand ears that cannot be tricked, drives his chariot across every land to observe all that transpires above and below and to destroy liars and those who violate their oaths, because oath-breakers and liars bring ruin across the land. Oaths should not and may not be violated even if made with the deceitful.[19] Nor will Siavash betray his oath to that disciple of the Lie Afrasiyab. Kāvus sent Siavash to combat Afrasiyab; following a battle, the enemy retreated to the Oxus, the Iran–Turan border. When Siavash prepared to lead an attack across the river and rout them, Kāvus wrote him to not march on the host, saying that if Afrasiyab crosses over into Iran, his blood will be on his own hands.

But Afrasiyab had an ominous dream and sued for peace. He dispatched his brother Garsivaz to Siavash with gifts and glad tidings, handmaidens and slaves, and valuables and coins. The two were mutually respectful as was proper. But both the prince and the leonine paladin Tahamtan (Rostam), his companion and counselor in the military campaign, suspected that their rival's proposed cure may be laced with venom. They therefore demanded that Afrasiyab withdraw from all Iranian territory as a condition of peace and stay on the other side of the Oxus, and to bolster the pact send a hundred kinsmen and relatives to Siavash as hostages. The prince and the paladin hoped that once King Kāvus received that bundle, he would shed his grudge. Afrasiyab accepted Siavash's terms and sent him the hostages as Rostam had demanded. The peace pact was concluded.

---

18. *Mehr Yt* 7:25. The god's many other epithets include, "the lord of vast pastures, cognizant of true speech, the speaker who has one thousand ears, sleepless and ever awake, the incarnate Word of God . . ."

19. *Mehr Yt*, in Pourdavoud, trans., *Yašthā*, vol. 1, 422–503.

But Kāvus was a rash king prone to changing course on a whim. When Rostam brought him the message of victory and peace, he became enraged and overwrought. He ordered that Siavash build a large fire and burn Afrasiyab's gifts and to dispatch the hostages to him where he would kill them, and for Rostam to then attack Afrasiyab and pillage and scorch his land. The wise Rostam's words did not sway Kāvus: 'Your Majesty, you yourself ordered us to not rush to war and to not cross the river; now Afrasiyab has agreed to peace on our terms, and you have all that you desired. Oath-breaking is unbecoming of royalty.'

> *I speak plainly and tell you the truth,*
> *Siavash shall never betray his word.*
> *The scheme envisaged by the king*
> *Shall vex and plague the storied lord.*
>
> (M3: 63)

Even foes know that oath-breaking is not the Iranian way. Gudarz and Piran had sworn an oath that should Piran be killed, the Turanians would not be hounded but be allowed to return to their homeland. Later, when Piran is killed, Turanian generals declare:

> *Iranians do not betray their oaths,*
> *There is no chance we will be harmed.*
>
> (M5: 210)

And when an oath was betrayed, a Rostam turned wretched and a Sohrab returned to dust.

So, what says Kāvus? A vengeful king loses his mind for victory has come too easily. He tells Siavash what he wants in a letter: Hostages, wealth, war, people's lives and livelihood, and the world's demise. Siavash dissents. Rostam is wise, and Kāvus is a fool to expect the impossible.

In an epic whose fabric is woven out of the wars between Iran and Turan, a prince who is the best and first among men flees Iran and takes refuge in Turan. That is an anti-heroic act suited to cowed souls who are content to make it for another day or two, and are perhaps happier that way.

But what does that sorry scheme have to do with the noble Siavash? Well, he has come to achieve the purpose of his time, and his purpose is to beget the wonder-worker Kay Khosrow, then die and consequently bring about Afrasiyab's end.

When the ambitious Kāvus flew up to the sky to assume lordship of the heavens, the divine messenger Nēryōsang was wont to end the king's life.

> The *faravashi* [spiritual form] of Kay Khosrow who had not yet been born of a mother . . . said, "O Nēryōsang, do not kill Kāvus because if you take his life *one of the chief vanquishers of Turan will not emerge*, for Siavash is to be sired by this man and I will be sired by Siavash, I, who am Khosrow, I who shall reclaim him from Turan, he who is the most gallant, he who is the greatest vanquisher of warriors and armies."[20]

> *The world did not slay him out of wonder,*
> *For he carried within one yet to be born.*
> *It is from him that Siavash shall emerge.*
> *Today, one must linger and idle a while.*

>   (M2: 4)

Thus, Kāvus survived so Siavash might come and be slain.

> *The World-creator, such He willed,*
> *Turan is where he shall be killed.*

>   (M3: 41)

And when Afrasiyab dipped his hands in Siavash's hot blood, he destroyed his own kingship.

---

20. *Dēnkard*, quoted in Christensen, *Kiāniān*, trans. Safa, 118.

The Creator thought that if He stopped Ahriman from assailing the world of light, *Druj* would linger at the border, undefeated forever, and the created world's anguish and dread would wax eternal. At the same time, attacking *Druj* before she assailed the Ahuric luminaries would contravene the justice and equity that are the essence of His creation. So, it is only after *Druj* attacked the created world that Ahura ordered His host to defeat her and protect the world of light. For being struck in return is the price paid by one who strikes, and vengefulness is punishment for the vengeful, and extinction is retribution for sinful aggressors.[21]

In myth and epic, in the Avesta and the *Shahnameh,* the Ahuric and the Iranians do not initiate carnage; but once warmongers strike, eradicating them is a matter of truth and justice, the order and the honor of existence. By killing Siavash, Afrasiyab kills himself.

> For Siavash's blood, water shall wear black,
> And deluge Afrasiyab with a flood of curses.

> (M3: 150)

The world and humanity cannot endure his death, and there is no escape for his killer. The setting of that sun is the rise of another that will be the undoing of darkness.

Such is the mournful purpose of that noble Siavash in the world and in bringing Time to a close. He is a man of "ill fortune," *bakht-e bad,* and himself states, "Much harm has come upon *my body* due to ill fortune" (M3: 67).

The spiritual and eternal fate of every individual is a function of their personal "duty," their "self-purpose." But fortune—a person's fate on earth—is not in their hands. The wheel of time has pre-designed and shaped humanity's earthly fate. "Fortune" is the sum of the vicissitudes

---

21. *Dādestān-i Dēnīg* 16, quoted in Molé, *Culte, mythe et cosmologie,* 401.

of life, the societal shell, and one's lot and share on earth; there is no trace of that in one's spiritual (*mēnōg*) existence. For the "earth is by fortune and the sky by action."[22] "Fortune and action coupled are like body and soul, for a body without a soul is an inutile corpse and a soul without a body is an insensate breath, but when they cohere, they are strong and highly beneficial."[23]

The harmony and conjunction of fortune and action are the source of "strength and profit," but the features of fortune cannot be manipulated by "purpose." One flounces about the field of fortune, at times losing a gain by transgressing and at times averting misfortune by exercising piety, but it is the congruence of "fortune and action" that forges humanity's eternal salvation. In this paradigm, humanity is governed by subjection on earth and liberty above. In the human journey from sky to earth and from earth to sky, time is bounded in the exigent closed circle; in liberty, it is unbound.

In the case of Siavash, he is a man with a scourged "fortune" and a sublime "purpose" that drive him toward Afrasiyab's kingdom and to death.

Siavash feels tormented because the king wants him to break his oath.

> Brazenly he urges and exhorts me to fight,
> Dread be the day that an oath I may slight.
>
> (M3: 68)

He has no hesitation in upholding an oath and accepts all the consequences. To deliver hostages to someone waiting to kill them and then fight pacific innocents is to break an oath, and Siavash knows that God condones neither action.

---

22. *Vendidad*, quoted in Zaehner, *Zurvan*, 406.

23. *Yādgār-i Bozorgmehr*, quoted in ibid., 225.

To turn and fight, tread on my conscience,
Turn my back on the heavens and earth,
How would God be pleased with my act?
How would the times reward me for that?

   (M3: 68)

If Siavash breaks his oath and resolves on war, he has parted from *dēn*, "faith"—God's moral truth and its practice; he has defied sky and earth and the entire benevolent world and challenged the demanding but well-destined wheel of time. And none of that pleases God. For God upholds this Ahriman-trapped earth with *dad*, "justice"—the order and well-being of things, the cosmic law that governs the earth's movements and by which the heavens and earth are harmonized and dualistic existence is unified. Justice is to live by that universal law and apply it. If the *faravahar*s volunteered and promised to come down to earth, then breaking a promise and betraying an oath is *bīdād*, "injustice," the disruption of God's "law." Siavash is not a man of "injustice," not even when Afrasiyab is about to kill him:

Siavash by the oath he'd sworn
Did not reach for sword or spear,
Ordered none among his troops
To step forth in battle gear.

   (B: 656)

Without a fight, he surrenders to "fortune" so as not to break his oath with Afrasiyab, for in his mind to break an oath is to leave the path of the wending world; it is enmity with the whole of nature, with sky and earth, with fire and water. He will not spurn noble conduct, the God-oriented mission, and the grace of the living world; he will not kill the spirit of the world inside him, he will not gratify Ahriman. With the clairvoyance of a holy man, he envisages what may issue from Kāvus' intent:

> *He shall strip me of the two worlds,*
> *Ahriman's heart shall swell content.*

> (M3: 67)

Whoever loses the two worlds has also lost themselves. An Ahriman-hearted individual has become detached from their *faravahar* and is not what they should be but is what he should not; he lacks a self, and the duality of darkness and light has penetrated him. Such a man is torn and confused. Therefore, in response to his counselors Bahrām and Zangeh who urge him to yield to his father and break his oath, he states that though king Kāvus' command towers above Sun and Moon,

> *Against the will of the gallant God,*
> *Elephants, lions, nor dust can rise.*
> *Whoever defies God's command,*
> **Frenzied, cannot find his self.**

> (M3: 70)

Siavash stays true to his selfhood. During "his time," he is the leader and commander of the host of the righteous. The Ahuric universe has manifested in this Ahuric being, the macrocosm has merged with the microcosm. With Siavash's "self-purpose," the microcosm is also distributed across the macrocosm. When he was killed, the universe teemed with Siavash, his blood streamed through the earth's veins. Because he honored the oath with the Ahrimanic Afrasiyab, the "function" or the self-purpose of his time inevitably seeped into the Ahuric world and disrupted Afrisiyab's reign.

Siavash sent a message to the king of Turan, saying:

> *I shall not turn my head from the oath,*
> *Though it means forsaking the crown.*

> (M3: 71)

And because there was no way out of his predicament, he asked Afrasiyab to grant him safe passage through Turan. For return to Iran was out of the question. Having defied Kāvus' command, he had no recourse to the king. Sudabeh holds the reins of that captive's mind in her grip with an insane, indiscriminate passion, a delirious, aching desire, and now a ruinous rancor. Siavash had left to fight Afrasiyab so he could be away from that couple and their court for a while. He could not humor the king's weakness before Sudabeh, or the vindictiveness of that frustrated stepmother, the schemes concocted by her acolytes, or the insidious air that pervaded Kāvus' court. Hoping to get away from such a place,

> *"I'll head out to war," he mused to himself.*
> *"I'll speak with passion, plead with the king.*
> *Perchance the Lord shall grant me freedom*
> *From the blather of Sudabeh and Father."*

>   (M3: 40)

And he sued to leave and battle Afrasiyab. He had grown tired of the foxes' covert games, of his father's ineptitude and his "blatherings," and went to war so as not to be. Siavash is not a rebel, but he does not condone his father's ineptness and lifestyle or his duplicitous milieu. In the house of that monarch, lies and slander rule supreme. Siyavash's departure is to turn his back on Kāvus' world: a world of paltry trivia, fickle friendships, folly, rage, intrigue, reprisal, and a misguided, oath-breaking king, a wolf friendly with fools and frauds.

> *Imagine how I feel at this hour,*
> *Suffering as I must inhuman stables.*[24]

---

24. Sa'di/Ganjoor, *Golestān* 2: "The Morals of Dervishes," Story No. 31, in which a man bemoans the fact that having left his friends in Damascus to keep company with animals in the deserts of Jerusalem, he is now held captive by Christians and doing slave labor digging mud with Jews in Tripoli. "Inhuman," *nā-mardomi*, refers to the condition of slaves.—Trans.

Such a world is internally congruent and orderly. All its varied parts intertwined in complex relationships repel the outsider as when a foreign germ enters the body. Whoever wishes to stay in such a world must learn the ins and outs of its relationships and be prepared to play different roles at given moments. Siavash is exhausted from the start; he feels disgusted.

But flouting such a world when it is one's nest will end in solitude and eventually to death. Siavash is Ferdowsi's solitary prince, "like a flower in the grass" (M3: 92). His soul is detached from malice. He who is weary of wickedness and aspires to something else renounces the Kāvus-like life, and by doing so kills "Kāvus' Siavash" and resigns to die to rescue the oath that God and the world have stamped on him. For he is the meeting place between what has been and the passageway on the trajectory of the earth. His flight from Kāvus is leaving the world to save the universe, and repairing to Turan is resigning to die to be saved from death.

Even when about to march out the army, when father and son bid each other goodbye,

> His heart warned that leaving now
> Will mean no more meeting then.
>> (M3: 43)

And leaving Iran behind is not an easy task. With dead ends on all sides, it is hard for a human to hold onto their humanity.

> Would that my mother had not begot me,
> Or if she did bear me, I would have died.
>> (M3: 68)

The passage to Turan marks the climax in the drama of Siavash's quest for transcendence and his heroic demeanor.

Resigning oneself to reality is one thing; accepting it in one's heart is a different matter. So many things agitate us inside like a chronic infirmity and we ourselves get through a day or two in an infirm society. Our aspirations are always out of reach; the instant we take a step, they have already leapt farther away—a body that is a captive of time and space and a mind that's quick to take flight! We live in real time and are preoccupied with our livelihood; we eat and sleep and wearily do unwanted chores, perpetuate the relentless eating and sleeping and repeat the vicious circle, then, "Suddenly came a cry, the don is dead!"[25]—that passing twister that has no end!

Not that Siavash does not love this world. Like every epic hero, he is a friend of the sword and of wine, of the wide expanse that is the terrain of hunting and battle and the breeding ground of men of action, and of the rising sun that arouses the human will, the will that gravitates to action! Hustling for glory! The epic life is worth living. Siavash is the friend of such a life. But merely pluck at its aimless course? That, he does not want. Nor is he an ascetic who renounces the world with solely the hereafter on mind. But his ethos cannot humor trivial pursuits. In his mind,

> Eat and sleep is the way of the wild,
> A way that solely a fool may abide.[26]

So, he does not sink into the floating swamp of life and does not conform to its pettiness. For conforming to such realities, being receptive to them, retreating from every lofty, sublime goal and the allure of aspirational notions, is to plunge the spirit into the abyss of that same viscous, onerous course; thus, no thoughts and wants other than these

---

25. A line originally composed by Sharif Razi (b. 970 CE) as a title for Wisdom #372 in his Persian translation of Imam Ali's *Nahj ul-Balāqeh*. It is commonly attributed to Sa'di, who two centuries later popularized it in an ode: "*Āvāz dar sarāy oftād ke khajeh mord / Va'z bam o zīr, khāneh por āh o faqān shaved.*" See Sa'di/Ganjoor, *Maāvez, Ghasideh* #24:21.—Trans.

26. Sa'di/Ganjoor, *Būstan* 6:1: "On Contentment."—Trans.

will remain. Siavash is too free to remain pinned in the stranglehold of triviality. He has a body on earth and a soul in the stars. He came to earth from the beyond; now it is from earth that he goes to the beyond.

Not breaking an oath, not fighting Afrasiyab, not dispatching the hostages, not repairing to Kāvus, and not returning to Iran, all tangle in a knot along the string of his life, and he tries to avert all that is misguided with a willpower not granted to everyone. As such, his heroic act, the resolve that moves from potentiality to actuality and leaves its irreversible imprint on the world, is passive; it's in not doing and not becoming that his self-purpose is achieved—indirectly and invertedly. A man like him must first plunge into the sea of death and, like the sun, sink from the bright day into the dark night so he may re-emerge after his journey.

Siavash is unrivalled in the world in thought and deed.

> *I have heard in all the world*
> *He's nonpareil among the great*
> *In form and mien and poise,*
> *In learning, mind, and merit.*
>
>   (M3: 72)

He is a perfect man who looks ahead to perfection; he lives in the transitory world, which is on a transcendent path, and he has come to help it in that transcendental journey. Humanity and the world are fellow travelers. Just as the sky and earth share a harmonious end, so there is unity between human beings on earth and their *faravahar* and between body and soul, which partake of the same essence, for

> *Your soul is a wonder, your body a wonder,*
> *The self is the scale for gauging all measures.*
>
>   (M4: 302)

Siavash's perfection is not in the superiority of a soul that considers the body inferior. The body is the *faravahar* incarnate. That spiritual essence must inhabit a home undamaged by Ahriman. Evil, ugliness, weakness, and deformity are the scourges of Ahriman. Siavash's body is pure, beautiful, and well-built.

> *The sages did not overstate when they said,*
> *The bodies of the pure are lucid as their soul.*[27]

Kāvus' son Siavash is a prince endowed with the divine glory. As for his body, in his own words to Sudabeh,

> *The Creator indeed, O most fair mistress,*
> *Fashioned me before from His own farr.*
>
> (M3: 23)

When he arrived in Turan, Afrasiyab

> *Cast an eye on his visage and said,*
> *There is no match for him on earth.*
> *None are like him in the world,*
> *In features, form, and great glory.*
>
> (M3: 83)

In the Avesta, age fifteen represents physical maturity. The god of victory reveals himself to Zoroaster as a fifteen-year-old youth and the angel of rain flies in daylight like a fifteen-year-old, "resplendent, with light eyes, towering, and very strong."[28] In the paradisical period of Jamshid's kingship where heat and cold and old age and death did not exist, both father and son looked fifteen.[29]

---

27. Nicholson, ed., *The Mathnawi of Rumi*, 121.

28. *Tīr Yt* 13, quoted in Pourdavoud, trans., *Yaśthā*, vol. 1, 345.

29. "Jamshid," in ibid., 181 and 168, n. 3.

In transitioning from childhood to maturity, the body is ready for the soul and can assume the burden of good and evil. At fifteen, youth wearing the *kustī* girdle and dressed in a white shirt, *sadreh*,[30] were admitted into the Zoroastrian faith and their initiation became official.

"Fifteen is the age of maturity, and the possibility of transgression starts from that age."[31] It is from that moment that an individual's *faravahar* undertakes its "work"—self-purpose—on earth and the body that is the spirit's cloak and earthly form becomes beautiful. For it is from age fifteen that a human being enters the battlefield of good and evil *like a warrior*. Ahura Mazda created Kiumars "as a fifteen-year-old youth, towering, radiant, majestic, and with a fair complexion;"[32] God created the first human as a youth from the outset so his *faravahar* might immediately begin to do the earth's "work."

The body would be perfected once the spirit had a chance to begin enacting its cosmic purpose inside it; that blessed event allowed the individual's face and form to achieve perfection. For it is only in such a state of being that the body can acquire its raison d'être and the corporeal form could become ethereal.

For humans, the waxing and waning of the moon was the clearest sign of the continuous flow of time. For fourteen nights the moon gradually fills up and on the last night is saturated and complete. The fifteenth night is the start of the incline, and it gradually wanes.

> Objects that lie beneath the sphere of the moon and the stars
> and are encircled by the cosmos do not remain stationery;
> their state changes as well . . . There is no end to anything, and
> if anything has an end there is again a beginning, meaning
> that at the end of the cycle of the moon everything attains its
> perfection and anything that attains its perfection is the end of

---

30. *Tīr Yt* 14, in ibid., 347 and n. 1.

31. Widengren, *Les religions de l'Iran*, 389.

32. *GBd*, quoted in Carnoy, *Asātīr-e Irani*, trans. Tabatabaie, 51.

that thing; and again, at the beginning of the next cycle everything has a beginning until it gradually attains its perfection.[33]

If in mystical thought the phases of the moon are correlated with the cosmic order and may be taken as the model of the transfiguration of all things below its sphere, it is no surprise that others should have likened the human condition to that of the moon and taken the effect of time on humans as mirroring its effect on the moon. That is how a mythical conception of time came to inform our worldview. Drawing a parallel between the full moon on the fourteenth night and human maturity and adulthood at age fourteen to fifteen may have also helped associate the perfection of the moon with the perfection of the human body. The body, which is the invisible cradle of time, was taken to resemble the moon, which is time's visible cradle.

In Persian literature, the ideal symbolic age—fifteen in the Avesta— is fourteen. Thus, while as in earlier times it is at fifteen that Zoroaster is portrayed as devout, wise, and in constant contemplation of God, his divine glory appears in a dream to Zoroaster's mother as a "youth like the moon at two fives and four" and vanquishes demons.[34] His divine glory is a youth that resembles the moon on night fourteen, full and perfect.[35]

Ferdowsi's Siavash is likewise "aged fourteen" at the time he leads the army. Having seen him in a dream to be no more than fourteen, Afrasiyab tells the dream exegetes:

> *There stood like the moon a lucent throne,*

---

33. Nasafi, *Kitāb al-Insān ul-Kāmil*, ed. Molé, 30, 34.

34. Pazhdo, *Zarātušt-nāmeh*, ed. Dabir-Siaghi, 7:96; 10:145; 25:387.

35. In a similar vein, Nezami tells his fourteen-year-old son to open his eyes wide and go build his own family, and refers to Bahram's slave girl whose beauty is perfect as "a moon at two weeks." Likewise, a "fourteen-year-old lover" and "two-year-old wine" are the long and the short of what Hafez longs for . . .

Aloft on the seat, Kāvus' son prone.
Though only two weeks he spanned in age,
I stood there before him bound like a page.
He gave out a cry, roaring like thunder,
And his sword forthwith split me asunder.

(M3: 50)

As if the *Shahnameh's* fourteen-year-old were the fifteen-year-old Bahrām of the Avesta.

But at this point Siavash is older than fourteen. He was likely at least seven years old when he was entrusted to Rostam's care.[36] Tahamtan taught him riding and archery and feasting and military leadership and the principles of nobility, and all that takes more than a year or two's work. Kāvus then tested him for seven years before appointing him king of a region (M3: 10 and 13). Thus, Siavash is not "twice seven years" but a moon at two-weeks seated on a throne as brilliant as the moon. In Tabari's account, when Siavash was brought back to his father, he was twenty.[37] It was soon afterward that Sudabeh fell in love at first sight.

Siavash was entrusted to Rostam's care so the guardian would bring him up like himself. Rostam was an arch hero. If they put Siavash in his care, it was so another champion would arise—so that the apprentice would grow and soar like his master. When Rostam brought him back to Iran, the prince was a full-fledged sophic hero whom everyone held in awe. In the battle against Turan, the victorious general was not Rostam but Siavash. Praising his merits, Afrasiyab observes:

None in the world can pass his test,
When bow and arrow brace his chest.

---

36. Widengren, *Les religions de l'Iran*, 389: It was customary to remove male children at age seven from female caregivers and put them in the care of educators.

37. Bahar and Gonabadi, eds., *Tārīkh-e Balʿami*, 596.

(M3: 88)

No one had the strength to bend his bow and string it. When it came to grandstanding, he lifted five interlaced suits of chain mail off the ground with his spear, his arrowhead pierced four inviolable Gilani shields, he grabbed four riders off their horses and threw them to the ground . . . and did this, that, and the other.

> *A chorus rang out: "Ne'er did we see*
> *One astride a saddle as skilled as he."*
>
> (M3: 87)

Siavash was not only handsome and heroic, he was also immaculate. His body was as pure as the fiber of fire and thus could not be scathed by it.

Because Sudabeh said that Siavash wanted to lie with her, the prince told the king he would ride through a mountain of fire so others would know he was innocent.

> *A headful of shame and sanction is mine,*
> *Or if I'm innocent, then freedom is mine.*
> *Should I prove guilty of any such fault,*
> *My life the Creator shall bring to a halt.*
>
> (M3: 35)

Thus, he entered the fire and emerged unscathed. In purity and innocence, his body is like Zoroaster's who also endured an ordeal by fire so that his message might be believed.[38]

The Avesta enumerates five types of fire: The first is the one found in temples and in daily life; the next three are the types of fire found in humans and animals, in plants, and in clouds, in that order; while the

---

38. Pazhdo, *Zarātusht-nāmeh*, ed. Dabir-Siaghi, 37.

fifth burns in paradise and is equated with Ahura Mazda.[39] The spiritual fire is the protector of living beings.[40] Fire is purgative and consumes evil and sin. At the end of the world, all human beings will walk over molten metal —which acts like fire—and good and evil beings will be rewarded with either peace or punishment.[41]

Fire is the corporeal form of *aša*, "truth"—cosmic order, and justice. Truth is the order of integrity and harmony, the way things should be, and justice protects that order, or establishes it in the aftermath of chaos.[42]

Truth, *aša*, is the offspring of Ahura Mazda[43] and of the same essence as fire. Given that the self-purpose of both Zoroaster and Siavash embodies truth and cosmic order, not only does fire not harm either one, but it is their ally and protector.

Because "the constitution of Iranian kings is celestial fire (*āzaraxš*, lightning), they cannot be harmed by fire, as they are innately of fire."[44] The essence of kings is the *fire in clouds*, and their glory, *farr*, is "evidently the earthly symbol of the fire that is in heaven."[45]

> Rain did not fall during the time of Pīrūz, Anushirvan's ancestor, and the people in Iran suffered droughts . . . Pīrūz went to the *Āzarxwarrah* fire temple . . . and prayed and prostrated himself and implored God to lift this plague from living beings on earth. He then approached the fire vessel

---

39. Christensen, *Iran dar Zamān-e Sāsānian*, trans. Yasami, 91-2. [The five types of fire in ascending order of status are: *berezi.savah*, "of high benefit" (in temples and daily life); *vohu.fryāna*, "caring for the good" (in humans and animals); *urvāzišta*, "the most joyful" (in plants); *vazišta*, "the swiftest" (in clouds); *spēništa* "the most sacred" (in heaven).—Trans.

40. *Zādspram*, in Molé, *Culte, mythe et cosmologie*, 93.

41. *Yasnā* 32:7 and 51:9, in Pourdavoud, trans., *Gāthā*, 102 and 200.

42. Molé, *Culte, mythe et cosmologie*, 207, and Zaehner, *Zurvan*, 61, 101.

43. *Yasnā* 44:3, in Poudavoud, trans., *Gāthā*, 138.

44. Widengren, *Les religions de l'Iran*, 350.

45. Christensen, *Iran dar Zamān-e Sāsānian*, trans. Yasami, 91-2.

... and moved his arms and hands over the fire and three
times laid the fire on his chest like a friend tightly clasping a
friend; the flame caught his beard but did not burn it.[46]

Sasanian kings, who by virtue of their innate fiery force were associated with the celestial kings—divinities—were protected from fire
unless they deviated from truth—fire—and, neglecting their self-purpose, practiced injustice; in such an event, *farr* abandoned them.

Siavash's royal essence is of the fire in lightning, and the fire of
heaven resides in him as *farreh*. His life is the paragon of truth, meaning
it follows the creed of fire, Ahura Mazda's offspring: A man with a
body and soul of the nature of fire. Thus, when passing through fire,
this personification of truth is passing through himself; being of the
same nature, they cannot do each other harm. His physical body is
spiritual. Siavash's earth is heavenly. That is how, with truth for an ally
and aligned with nature, he subsumes the world. The particular human
turns into the universal human.

But this spiritual body is in fact a corporeal spirit, union of the
cradle and the cradled. His response to Sudabeh shows that his spirit,
like his body, is as pure as fire.

Kāvus' wife is a "paradise resplendent with color and scent" who
offers her "precious body and soul" to Siavash to give and take pleasure.
The prince dreads her passion.

> *"From the demon's tricks,"* he prayed,
> *"May I be spared by the Lord on high.*
> *That I do not betray my father,*
> *That I do not befriend the Lie."*

> (M3: 23)

---

46. Biruni, *Āthār ul-Bāghiya*, trans. Dānāseresht, 261–2.

Accepting this woman's love would be to break an unspoken vow between father and son; it would be disloyal and a rejection of chivalry and wisdom (M3: 25). Here, disloyalty would not only be to invade the father's private domain and damage him but to embrace the world of Ahriman and be transformed. So, for the first and last time, the otherwise "serene, unvengeful" prince shows "rage and aggression" and repels Sudabeh.

Both Sudabeh and Kāvus—each with a different motive—want one thing from Siavash: that he should break an oath, one with Kāvus, the other with Afrasiyab. We know Siavash's response. His respect for covenants and his sense of loyalty is immutable and all-embracing.

Siavash does not think much of Kāvus' harem girls either and does not care for them; he is a man who repels women. A hero is actionable willpower. Once love conquers, it imposes its will until the conqueror and the conquered, lover and beloved, become one, the duality of will is eliminated, and the goal of love is squarely the lover. Such an internal and emotional sensibility belongs to romantic epic and to later literary genres; it is alien to heroic epic, where the protagonist is oblivious to it. An all-embracing love that consumes the lover's soul has no place in heroic epic. Here, love is an incidental and passing matter, like the love between Rudabeh and Zāl, and Tahmineh and Rostam; it shows up in the throes of the story and fades out, and note that in Kāvus' all-consuming love for Sudabeh, to be discussed in the next section, he is not the main protagonist—Siavash is. And where a drawn-out, all-out romance appears in epic, as in Bižan and Manižeh, heroes encounter love in the course of heroic exploits, and love is a pretext for a series of other heroic deeds. The warrior has to gallop across fields of battle; to him, being stuck at home and resting next to women is beneath him. In Esfandiyar's words:

> When a man lingers with women at home,
> His fiber is subdued, his spirit is forlorn.

> (M6: 229)

Thus, in response to Kāvus who wants his son to join the company of women and girls, Siavash says, 'I need the conversation of wise men and warriors; I need a mace and a bow and battle; I need the ways of royalty and wining and feasting. What do I have to do with women?!'

> *In the king's harem what will I learn?*
> *Could ever a woman teach to discern?*
>
> (M3: 15)

Discernment is God's first and greatest blessing, and falling in love is to relinquish reason. Rudabeh is one example:

> *Her heart filled with passion for Zāl,*
> *Poise, peace, and zeal abandoned her.*
> *Her learning overcome by longing,*
> *Her thinking, ways, and temper turned.*
>
> (M1: 160)

And enamored of Rostam, Tahmineh confesses:

> *Having turned such as I have toward you,*
> *I have smothered reason in favor of love.*
>
> (M2: 175)

So, women, who are the cradle of love, cannot teach reason and learning that are its fruit.

Of course, heroes tend to fancy, and are partial to feasting. But such feasts are held before or after battle or another weighty undertaking for diversion. It is chiefly by token of their children that we know heroes have loved. Nor have they lain with women as smitten lovers but as paladins who must produce other men. A woman is for begetting a child.

> *Once a seemly son is born,*
> *Heart from woman must be torn.*

    (M3: 39)

It is required of a son to grow up brave and battle-hungry; praise is due women for nurturing such progeny.

Abstinence from women is thus a virtue of the "female-free" epic hero. For him, abstinence means being mentally self-sufficient and physically free. As to Siavash's marriage, Piran arranges everything, and Siavash does nothing. The Turanian general offers him both his own and Afrasiyab's daughter. Siavash merely accepts them; he does not choose them himself.

The prince is a timid man. The women in his life are unrewarded vis-à-vis Forūd and rewarded with Kay Khosrow. Forūd, the son of Siavash and Farangis, is killed young and has no chance to shine. We meet his mother Jarireh, who is praised as pure-blooded and prestigious, only when she marries and gives birth and when she kills herself over his corpse. As a wife and mother, she is only mentioned in connection with Siavash and Forūd.

But because Kay Khosrow is out to avenge his father's blood and is an agent of cosmic transfiguration, his mother Farangis continues to play an important role in the story and in the workings of the world until her son reaches Iran. Siavash knows that the son born of this woman is destined to destroy Afrasiyab's kingship. Thus, the purpose of "love" is to achieve the "purpose" of the time. Union with women is not for love's sake.

Deprived of the fervor and passion of love, Siavash is unacquainted with its agony and ecstasy. His body lives for a different end; his is the body of a holy man, not of a hero. Zoroaster prays that like Siavash, his patron King Goshtāsp may be "beautiful-bodied and immaculate,"[47] as if the prophet knows no one purer than the hero. Likewise, Afrasiyab

---

47. *Visperad, Āfrin-i Zartosht* 3 ("Zoroaster's Prayer"), quoted in Pourdavoud, trans., *Yašthā*, vol. 2, 234.

knows no one worthier than Siavash, declaring he had never seen anyone
his equal and that the father who was weary of such a son was not wise.

> *Afrasiyab fell for him head over heels,*
> *Unable to repose without Siavash.*
>
> > (M3: 84)

Even the unwise Kāvus had told his son:

> *God created you limpid as light,*
> *All who see you love you on sight.*
>
> > (M3: 15)

"So, salutations to the supreme Creator," for "God is beautiful and
loves beauty."[48] The prince's body and soul rendered everyone covetous
and captivated, including Zoroaster and Afrasiyab. Thanks to Siavash,
hope for friendship, peace, and tranquility enfolded even the battle
hawks for a time. On first encountering him, Afrasiyab proclaimed:

> *No more war now, no more welter.*
> *Tiger and lamb together shall shelter.*
> *Feuds across two lands without cease*
> *The world abided, oblivious to peace.*
> *By you the times shall now be tamed,*
> *Warring lost and calmness gained.*
>
> > (M3: 83)

The mythic duality dissolved in epic for a while and the whole
world converged in the prince and looked to the light aided by that
source of the sun.

---

48. *Inna 'llāha jamīlun wa-yuhibbu 'l-jamāl.* [Hadith No. 6906 in *al-Muʿjam
al-Awsat*, a collection of more than 9,500 reports on the prophet Mohammad
by Abu'l-Qasim Tabarani (874-971 CE).—Trans.]

Afrasiyab was kind to Siavash for a long time. The Turanian king felt joyful in soul and spirit. In turn, Siavash surpassed the bounds of goodness and breached Afrasiyab's dark heart with the light of truth.

By doing good, he had an impact on evil. If he was able to distinguish between the two, it is because he was wise. For in the age of mixture, the world overflows with truth and lies. Thus, the soul's foremost task is to be conscious of the two. The virtue that helps one distinguish between good and evil, that is, the eye of the soul, is called wisdom. Such wisdom is the essence and the truth of Mazdayasna.[49]

In the *Shahnameh*, wisdom is God's greatest blessing and humanity's finest virtue. Ferdowsi opens his book with, "In the name of the God of the soul and wisdom," the God who gave life and set wisdom as its guide so humans may understand their actions. Next follows a section in praise of wisdom saying it was created before all else. Then comes the birth of the world and humans and words of praise for the prophet. Throughout the *Shahnameh*, the poet names wisdom as the first blessing. While the heroes in his book do not owe their greatness solely to wisdom, in the case of Siavash and the holy Kay Khosrow wisdom is unquestionably king. In Siavash, the beauty of his countenance and the perfection of his conduct are conjoint. When he comes before his father for the first time, Kāvus

> *Gazing upon him, awed by his sight,*
> *Over and over, he called upon God:*
> *He is so young and yet so wise,*
> *As if his soul nurtures wisdom.*

>   (M3: 12)

Every person's mind reflects their soul, and Siavash's soul is such that it appears as if he himself breeds and propagates wisdom. Piran, too, tells Afrasiyab:

---

49. Mazdayasna, literally, "adulation of wisdom."—Trans.

Should Sorūsh himself from the heavens alight,
In glory and aura wouldn't reach such a height.

(M3: 116)

Now, what path does that wisdom point to, and how does that wise one act before the world?

The function of wisdom is for Siavash to recognize his time as it had been shaped in God's thought, and his self-purpose is to execute that thought. The effective scope of his wisdom is the entire cosmos, to free the hero from his confined body and soul and release him into the universe.

Siavash's conduct intimates a somewhat gnostic understanding of the perfect man; he has a grasp of the trajectory of existence and an awareness of transcendence and the attainment of godhood.

> Now know that despite his perfection and magnitude, the perfect man is powerless; he lives unrequited and merely tries to cope. He is perfect in knowledge and morality but wanting in power and victory.[50]

Should a mystic enter the territory of epic, which is the land of willpower and action, he is more powerless and less victorious. Siavash perceives the arc of time with the lucidity of a sage, yet that same perception paralyzes his arms. He knows that the revolving sky does not favor him, that he will be killed in enemy territory at their hands. But such is God's "justice" (M3: 41 and 142), meaning to establish and maintain order and harmonize and better the world requires injustice against Siavash. That is how the world will proceed from injustice to justice, from turmoil to tranquility, and from war to peace. Siavash knows that. If that is God's will, then manliness and exertion is futile (M5: 145)—death is nigh.

---

50. Nasafi, *Kitāb al-Insān ul-Kāmil*, ed. Molé, 4–5.

> *No one seeks light in the night*
> *If endowed with clear insight.*

>   (M5: 141)

He does not heed Farangis' advice to flee Turan but submits to destiny. Siavash is a fatalist; he believes what must happen, will.

From one point of view, it could be said that Siavash is a "Zurvanite."[51] He holds fast to the belief in the vicissitudes of life, in the blind fate born from the motion of absolute time, and in the futility of human endeavor. The *Shahnameh* is weighted with Zurvanite thought and Siavash's response to Garsivaz and Afrasiyab intimates a Zurvanite apostle.

Zurvanite thought was popular and widespread in the Sasanian period. That potentially strong yet effectively weak and despairing prince is the product of that insular, demoralizing society. In a despotic society, a man with a noble spirit is often incapacitated in thought and action, forced to turn inward, away from the outer world. Introversion and surrender to the course of life, that resigned worldview, reaches its peak in Siavash. But unlike mystics, his dejection is far from the mystic's ecstasy and ardor, for unlike them, he does not underrate the body in order to liberate the soul. There is no duality or conflict here between body and soul. To him, the body—though mortal—is as exalted as the soul, meaning that a man who surrenders his body to Ahrimanic forces effectively cedes his soul. That is perhaps why Siavash—though

---

51. Zurvanite thought, which developed in early Sasanian times, does not represent a heretical sect but an alternative cosmogony and theological account of the age of "mixture" that lends itself to fatalism. According to the myth, which is not found in Iranian but in Armenian, Syriac, Greek, Arabic, and other sources, the pre-existent god Zurvan ("Time," a minor deity in the Avesta and in Manichaean texts) offered up sacrifices for a thousand years to conceive a son. He then begat the twin spirits of good and evil, Ahura Mazda and Ahriman, the latter resulting from the doubt that had entered his mind at the last moment.—Trans.

too late and in vain—confronts Afrasiyab and is destroyed together with his companions.

Without overthinking what is involved, epic heroes demand light from darkness with such a relentless will and chase their impossible quest so arduously as to fall. Siavash, on the other hand, has an anti-heroic posture in the face of death. He is "duly endowed" with knowledge and understands the futility of action. In him, knowledge is powerlessness. At last, the fear of death, a fear such as may grip any wretched soul, lodges in his body. At that point, the "lion-clawed hero" is "quivering atremble, his mien turned pale." He does not welcome his ill "fortune" but accepts it exigently. There is, between his wish and the will of the world, a sharp and divisive dichotomy. He wishes to stay alive, while the cosmic wheel, or the Creator, wants him dead.

> *An innocent man if the cosmic wheel*
> *Wants by wicked men to bring to keel,*
> *It is not manliness to raise up a horde,*
> *And oppose in battle the Almighty Lord.*

> (M3: 145)

This is one of the rare instances in which the *Shahnameh* equates the cosmic wheel, the universe, or the indiscriminate, fate-forging times with God, the creator of discernment.

In Zurvanite thought, Ahura and Ahriman are born of Zurvan— infinite Time. Therefore, both good and evil were procreated by him. "Zurvan is equally the father of good as of evil; just as Zurvan is substantially day *and* night, morally, too, it is good *and* evil."[52] Zurvan, Time—the World, the whirling wheel, the universe, life—does not know good and evil; it is the natural law and the lord of destiny and death,"[53] which "is never obscured and cannot be cured. When someone's

---

52. Zaehner, *Zurvan*, 61.
53. Ibid., 239.

time comes, there is nothing one can do."[54] In death—in the time—of Siavash, the Zurvanite whirling wheel and the Mazdayasnian Creator have the same disposition; Siavash knows there is nothing he can do, and this very knowledge has defeated him.

On the other hand, the world is ruled by "Fortune" and once this mortal body falls and a human's earthly life ends, fate loses its dominion. As soon as Siavash's blood was spilled, his wretched death grew as magnificent as the cosmos and his life reclaimed its meaning. This noble spirit who had withdrawn into solitude spread across the universe and that celestial glory that had been tethered to earth seeped into the body of the earth.

Toward the end of his days, Siavash becomes a fatalist and a Zurvanite. His power is released after death, and it is Afrasiyab who liberates him unwittingly. Evil is the enabler of good and inadvertently drives the world toward deliverance.

Siavash's worldview is the source of disillusionment; when night falls, he does not seek light, but then when the day dawns, he believes that darkness is forever banished:

> Wherever the truth is exposed to light,
> The luster of lies is dimmed to sight.
> An open heart to Afrasiyab I'll show,
> Brighter than sun in the sky it'll glow.

(M3: 133)

And yet, fate does what it must; the moment the truth shines out, the glow of the lie should dim. But it does not dim.

Such a perception of truth is itself a lie, for the "Lie" was Ahriman's mightiest creation, and in essence aggressive and extremely cunning. The essence of Siavash's worldview is stasis and inertia. Thus, his knowledge

---

54. Ibid., 90, referring to *Pahlavi Texts* and *Jāmāsp-nāmeh*.

does not break out of its shell as action; it does not move from potentiality to actuality. He is cognizant but not powerful, for his thought does not crystallize into action. Good and evil function independently of the cognizant man who himself is an outlying entity, an object that is utilized by the world. Given his kind of wisdom, Siavash has in effect a passive existence. Not that his self-purpose is not achieved. In fact, "injustice" reveals his raison d'être, for his martyrdom becomes the catalyst for wars that render the world active and effectual and propel the "history" of life on earth toward its ultimate destination.

Siavash remains oblivious to the thousand-fold twists and turns of Ahriman's ways. He is in fact a prisoner of the purity of his own heart, as if he were a pure light that wherever it is there is no darkness, such that he only perceives his own brightness. He knows about darkness but does not know its duplicity. With his farsighted vision he sees the future, and though he knows and tells Piran that he is doomed to fall by his ill-wishers' chicanery (M3: 109), he fails to see Garsivaz' schemes before his very eyes (M3: 141). His eyes are open to distant horizons yet blind to nearby dead ends.

Garsivaz knows that as well and tells Siavash that despite your "learning and keen insight and lofty vision," you cannot tell affectation from affection (M3: 133). Only once did the barb of suspicion prick at Siavash's heart, and then it vanished, "like a stain dissolved before settling" (M3: 130). Though he had a dream where he was caught between a fire and a flood unleashed by Garsivaz, he did not heed the ethereal warning and caved in to Garsivaz again.

Siavash is not a capricious man. His artlessness touches on naïveté, making it impossible for him to fathom frivolous flimflam. He judges others by his own standards and his standards are of a different order. In this age of mixture, a man of unadulterated goodness cannot defeat evil with sheer kindness. One must, like Kay Khosrow, hold Ahriman-bred vengeance fast in one's heart and confront evil. Siavash expects, on the strength of truth, to be protected from liars, from Sudabeh and Garsivaz and Afrasiyab. Fair Siavash's purity and grace feed a gentle heart and arms that he does not raise in protestation; he does not revolt, for he expects goodness from evil until death. Though he does not covet Sudabeh's love, he does not tell her he feels outraged. It is as if he lacks the courage to scold. Instead, he praises Sudabeh, saying, "You deserve the king; it's better if I should want your daughter and not you" (M3: 23). He somehow tries to not hurt her feelings but being a man in the action-laden realm of epic, it is impossible for him to evade danger by gentleness. Siavash has a justification for gentility. 'If I treat this shameless woman coldly,' he reflects, 'she will harden the king's heart toward me.' Such muddled calculations may ease the plight of petty, ignoble men, but they trample the noble underfoot. Indeed, living by the side of Sudabeh and Kāvus, tolerating them while being of unlike nature, is to walk a tightrope with dire consequences. It is only when he has no other choice that Siavash brushes Sudabeh off harshly in anger, though at the eleventh hour he acts as a mediator to save her life. In every instance, he seeks a solution to avert any harm. In the same vein, he does not recognize Garsivaz' duplicity and cherishes that adversary more than anyone. Siavash who refuses to fight Afrasiyab when his own life is imperiled tells Garsivaz, "Should the king of Turan harm you, I will fight him on your behalf" (M3: 136). Siavash is not to be believed, of course; he does not have the gall to fight Afrasiyab, but caring and sympathy forces the "quiet, docile" soul to act out of character. In the face of Garsivaz' ruses, "his wakeful soul slumbers" (M3: 136).

So, all the virtues that formed the bedrock of Siavash's perfection are themselves the source of his shortcomings and weakness. Reared by the greatest of heroes, this perfect man is wide of perfection and disabled by his innocent deficiencies.

A prince of such attributes and demeanor is burdened with a great "task" in a landscape permeated with lies and greed and injustice. Siavash does not know the world around him. It is as if a baffled alien has fallen from lofty heights into the abyss below. He is "present in the crowd and his heart is elsewhere."[55] So, he does not know confrontation

---

55. Sa'di/Ganjoor, Qazaliyāt #63: "Hargez vojūd-e hāzer-e qāyeb shenideh-i? / Man dar miyān-e jam' o delam jāy-e dīgar ast."—Trans.

and conflict, and cannot. The world and the living drive him toward death, and whatever he does without wishing to ends in annihilating his earthly form—as if he cannot liberate the soul without sacrificing the body. And in Iranian mythology and epic, this is a critical weakness.

Among those that drive Siavash toward death, Sudabeh is the first. She drives Siavash from Iran. Of course, the prince's heading for Turan had a deeper motive, but Sudabeh had so designed Kāvus' court that it could not accommodate Siavash. Her presence was one of the reasons for Siavash's flight and eventual death.

In the land of Turan, too, another enemy is lying in wait for Siavash. The "ensnarer" Garsivaz is jealous of Siavash; to kill him, he creates a false premise whereby friends, oblivious and unwittingly, face off, each with a dagger at the other's throat. In the machinations of Sudabeh and Garsivaz, the kings of Iran and Turan give succor to the Ahrimanic pair, each for a reason.

But how can an individual repel the fate that awaits them? Is it not the case that the schemes concocted by Siavash's killers to save themselves are all for naught and that they all lose their lives because of his death?! Besides, not just this or that individual but the world drives Siavash to his death; the individuals are the tools of death. Siavash flees from Kāvus to Afrasiyab, from Iran to Turan. The longstanding enmity between these two countries has fertilized the soil of our epic lays like seed and rain. By crossing the Iranian frontier into Turan, Siavash has flung himself between two crushing boulders, between two thrashing storms; in vain did he imagine he would pull away to safety from their midst.

> *Two lands, one fire, the other water,*
> *Each one eager to conquer the other.*
> *To hope into one the two to unite*
> *Is trying to nail the wind in midflight.*

> (M3: 125)

The battle between Ahura Mazda and Ahriman in myth is translated into enmity between Iran and Turan in epic, one country depicted as good, and the other as evil. On that battlefield, Siavash's blood is the stormy spring of wars that end in Turanian defeat and Afrasiyab's death. That spiritual "purpose" is achieved in an epic landscape. In Iranian mythology, human action is in essence heroic. The *faravahar*s choose goodness by volition and turn earthly. They volunteer, and through war turn goodness from potentiality to actuality. In the lament (*sūg*) for Siavash, that heroic essence assumes an epic garb and Siavash's "purpose" (*kār*) morphs into the revenge (*kēn*) for Siavash.

In this epic lamentation, a collective drives Siavash to his death. In the land of Afrasiyab, he is aware of the wheel of life's secret design. When he erects the paradisical fortress of Kang[56] and is at his most privileged, he tells Piran that it will not be long before he, despite being innocent, will be slain by the king owing to his ill-wishers' murmurings and his own ill-fortune. When saying farewell to Farangis, he tells her how they will come in search of their son and what that son will do to Afrasiyab and what Farangis must do as the turmoil unfolds. He even whispers into the ear of his stallion, Shabrang-e Behzād, telling him where to wait for Kay Khosrow who will come and mount him and escape to Iran. Siavash is a man of secrets. He has knowledge of "spiritual history" and knows how and where his death will lead it.

> From Iran and Turan shall break out a roar,
> Thereby my blood shall boil the earth's core.

(M3: 109)

---

56. Mistakenly inscribed as Gang in some *Shahnameh* editions, the correct form is Kang, from Av. *kan-*, "to dig" (NP *kandan*). In *Ābān Yt* 14:54, Tūs invokes Aredvī Sūrā Anāhitā above the "soaring, sacred" *Kangha* to overcome the *Tūirya* (Turanians). As a place name, Kang is also applied to Siavash's paradisical fort (See Kangdež in the "Glossary of Names") and to Afrasiyab's underground fortification, *Hang-e Afrasiyab* (*Hankana* in *GBd* 32.6, 13, and *Yasnā* 11:7). As a common noun, it is applied to the mountain-top "pit" or "cave" where Afrasiyab hides before he is killed.—Trans.

A man achieves the "purpose" of his time by living and dying, or the "purpose" of his time demands such living and dying. Divine providence unites with that man's unintended intent. Though Siavash begrudges death, his ethos does not choose a way and behavior contrary to his essence to escape death and protect his body from harm.

That death reveals its true meaning in the course of the history of the earth. With such a mythical and metaphysical understanding of history, Siavash is both a man of history and its architect. He is one of the few who are most instrumental in destroying the kingdom of the Lie, and that mission is accomplished when his blood is spilled. Thus, his death turns into martyrdom, for it is an act to release God and save the world, with a rigor and a power that was absent in his life. The clamor in this death accounts for the inertia of that life.

On discovering that her father is bent on destroying Siavash, Farangis is distraught:

> *A curse on his spirit for months and all years,*
> *Who batters your body and brings you to tears.*
>
> (M3: 139)

Farangis' curse afflicts.

All who have had enough of the reign of the Lie rise to wipe Siavash's killer off the face of the earth. And so, death expands. A prince who in life was a solitary outlier becomes present in everyone; that is an imperative. The world is now infused with him. Every person needs to decide whose side to take in regard to that spilled blood—the side of the killer or the killed. And that injustice weighs very heavy on everyone and everything. The moment Siavash is slain,

> *At once a wild wind whirled a raging gust,*
> *Hiding Sun and Moon behind a black dust.*
> *No man could behold another man's face,*
> *They all darted Gerūy a murderer's curse.*

Crown and country forced of their king free,
The sun was no more, nor the cypress tree.[57]

(M3: 153)

Nature is distraught and the light is dimmed. Everyone bewails in the dark and curses the executioner. These grief-stricken people trapped in darkness despise the light and the living. A world voided of Siavash, may that world itself not exist! The earth is grieving for a despairing man, and a man at the height of desperation has left the earth. But humanity is not a shooting star lost in a dark night; it is a part of a coherent and interconnected universal order. When destruction and injustice permeate the world, the Earth (Spandārmaz, daughter of Ahura Mazda) cries out to her father: "I shall not suffer this violence. I shall quake and I shall make these people quake. They defile fire and water with inebriety (abuse and torture) and injustice."[58]

There is a communion between the earth and whatever grows out of it and flourishes; it is not as if anyone may do as they please without any accountability or punishment! The divinity of Earth, compassionate and forbearing as she may be, is the enemy of the unjust and will not drink the blood of the oppressed until such time as the oppressor is punished. Afrasiyab knows that, too, as he says, "kill," but

Let the blood of Siavash the earth not smell,
For vengeance shall from it sprout and swell.

(M3: 151)

---

57. Luke 23:44–46: "From about the sixth hour to the ninth hour darkness came over the whole world because of the eclipse of the sun. Then the veil of the temple was torn down the middle. Jesus cried out in a loud voice, "Father, into your hands I commend my spirit"; and when he had said this, he breathed his last."

58. Hedayat, trans., "Yādgār i Jāmāspi," *Sokhan* 1:3.

For should his blood spill on the soil, it shall boil forever; the earth shall not let it seep below, even years after Afrasiyab's death. When Alexander reached Siavashgerd,[59] "he forthwith repaired to Siavash's resting place. When he arrived, he thought it was paradise. He walked to his gravesite. The soil was red. There he beheld fresh blood boiling, and in that warm blood a plant sprouted green."[60] That is *parsiavashān*.[61] When Gerūy cut off Siavash's head, his blood spilled on the ground and

> *From the blood forthwith sprouted a plant,*
> *On the spot where bowl tipped to a slant.*
> *I'll show you the seed that was then sown,*
> *As Blood o' Siavashān the plant is known.*[62]

Parsiyāvashān sprouts afresh no matter how often it is hacked back. The plant is a sign of Siavash's life after death and encodes the perpetuity of his existence.

In mythopoeic thought, if the thread of a life is brutally cut, it is certain to return in a new form and begin life afresh.[63] So, too, in Iranian mythology, when Ahriman slew the First Man, his semen fell on the

---

59. Siavash's city in Khotan where he resides until his death.

60. Afshar, ed., *Eskandar-nāmeh*, 243.

61. A fern that grows in moist habitats and reproduces via spores and has no seeds nor flowers. *See parsiāvašān* in *Loqat-nāmeh-ye Dehkhoda* for the plant's medicinal properties.—Trans.

62. These verses cited from B: 664 are relegated to a footnote in the Moscow *Shahnameh*. But they cannot be later additions, for a plant springing from the blood of Siavash is integral to his myth. The theme also appears in Bundari Isfahani's Arabic translation of the *Shahnameh* in the early thirteenth century, published in Cairo, 1350/1932, vol. 2, 37, where Afrasiyab kills Nozar, the captive king of Iran. In mourning him, Iranians lament: "Your head from earth does seek its crown, / The earth smells the royal blood dripped down. / The plant that sprouts in that land and domain / Makes the sun hang its head low in shame."

63. Eliade, *L'éternel retour*, 257.

ground; the earth preserved it, and after forty years a plant sprouted from it that resembled two stalks of celery. From these two stalks, a male and a female human came to be. Thus, by the grace of Mother Earth and vegetation, humankind began life afresh. Likewise, Siavash is killed, but when his blood spills upon the soil, it does not end. Here, death and extinction are strangers to one another.

The essence of every human is primeval and will abide eternally; it is only during its personal time that it crosses the path of death. If a person performs the "purpose" of their time in this world well, they will, even before bounded time reaches its end, join unbounded time and Ahura Mazda's infinity and wax eternal. By that percept, death kills Siavash but does not extinguish him, for while his form is finite, his being is eternal. Death is an external phenomenon that appears on a person's journey at the right time, and though it transforms their condition, it cannot affect their essence. Death is not malicious, fundamentally: it does not wish anyone ill; it merely brings humans closer to their essence. The existence that follows death is more complete and more axiomatic.

Today, which is a different world with different precepts, existence in and of itself is the axiom underlying all principles; living is the opposite of nonbeing and death lies at the border of presence and absence. Life is no longer a "bridge on the road to the afterlife," something that the wise should not prize.[64] Many believe that what is here is all there is and that each beginning ends in death and that the soul perishes with the body. Today, existence is considered an accident, and every human is alone; a person is prey and a passive agent before death. In the end, the act of death will befall them; one day death will come and haul them away whole. Even in times past, there were nonbelievers who proclaimed, "There is no returning; once you're gone, you're gone."[65]

---

64. Sa'di/Ganjoor, *Qazaliyāt* #60: "Life is a bridge on the road to the afterlife. / The wise do not erect their house upon a bridge."—Trans.

65. Omar Khayyam/Ganjoor, *Couplets* #160: *Bāz-āmadanat nīst, cho raftī raftī.*—Trans.

Such sore suspicions could not, however, rattle everyone's inner serenity, hurling them like a speck of nothingness into a void of nothingness. Even Job found a way out of blasphemy to belief, and "repented in dust and ashes."[66] Repentance reunited a human being with God and His creation. There was always a path to atonement in bygone days, and existence had a rationale beyond itself. Existence, which today is considered an end, was, whether good or bad, merely a means. Today, death targets the end; in the past, it only ended the means. If it ravaged the body of martyrs, which housed their soul, and took away their life—which materialized their metaphysical essence—they would pass into the bodies and lives of countless others and slip under the skin of the world and run through its veins.

The Siavashes of our times are no different. When someone turns the truth of their time into reality at the cost of their own life, death is not the beginning of nothingness; it's a current that flows in others, especially if the death is a signifier of oppression—when the dead is a martyr and has died for a truth. But truth is a universal event that requires a referent in a group or a community to be grasped. The more universal the truth, the more widely and potently martyrdom demands justice!

For someone run aground in an oppressive world and society, someone at the mercy of poverty and loss, what could be more potent than the injustice assailing them from every angle—for someone who has failed to achieve anything they want, and whatever they have achieved is perhaps not what they wanted? A human is a stubborn creature; oppression gnaws at their marrow. For such a person, what enterprise could be more inescapable and potent than accosting the world and oppressors? Martyrs invariably rank among the oppressed, and anyone who has tasted the venom of injustice, if not joining their voice with martyrs out of fear, shares their secret at heart.

---

66. Job 42:6.

Martyrs are the product of despotic times and societies. In a utopian society of the free-spirited, should it ever exist, there is no need for martyrdom. The story of Siavash is not the product of noble times, but it was produced by free spirits, or those seeking freedom in times of slavery. The epic tale of Siavash as told in the *Shahnameh* is the legacy of the despotic Sasanian society; in Avestan mythology, by contrast, Siavash likewise dies in enemy territory, but absent sorrowful intonations.

Heroic tales in the *Shahnameh* are the product of the fusion of Avestan mythological characters with Parthian historical figures and times informed by a Sasanian worldview. The fusion and alignment of the diverse elements occurred toward the end of that period. In the final years of the Sasanian monarchy, people lived in an insular and exacting society. Next to the royal dynasty, power is yielded by *mobeds*—priests—military chiefs, and scribes. The rural and laboring hordes have no social awareness and do not stand to benefit from imperial societal advantages, being deprived of such privileges. They make do within the confines of the class structure, the four "estates," and know that they cannot escape it. Negative awareness of their position, or awareness of the negative attributes of their position, prevents them from taking action. Birth determines their social coordinates and circumscribes their choice of trade and community. A wish to improve or transform one's life seems prohibitive and does not translate into a will that might actualize a potentiality. Wishes are not activated and hover on the segregated horizon.

> The [Sasanian] King of Kings . . . established a clear and
> choate distinction between the estates of the nobility and
> the commoners as regards horses and clothing and home
> and garden and women and servants. In addition, for the
> ranked nobility he established protocols for reception,
> assembly, feasting, comportment, appearance, accoutrements,
> and residence, so each might manage their household
> according to their status and uphold their proper station
> so that no commoner might socialize with them, and

prohibited kinship and marriage between the two estates
... He forbade individual commoners from purchasing
land from the nobility and underscored the matter so
that each would hold a specific rank and standing.[67]

Even the privileged have restricted and constrained privileges.
For even they may not violate the framework of their "estate." Society
acquires a closed and curbed structure based on the exacting privileges
of the upper classes that constrains those classes as well and does not
exempt them from the injustices born of the monopoly of privileges.
Their future secured within the limits of the binding rules of privilege,
they are well nourished and indulgent prisoners in the self-constructed
citadels of their own class. For the "free" nobility, *āzādan*, leaving their
own class and joining another is a nearly impossible concept. There
is minimal variation in their social life and exerting individual will is
prohibitive. In a brutal society, even tyrants are not safe.

That is not to say that the "free" in Sasanian society did not enjoy
freedom in its more current sense—which is the aspiration of today's
society—yet the notion of freedom as such never occurred to anyone in
those days. Absent such a notion, the mere awareness of the restrictions
and constraints in an archaic society prevents even the "free" from
exercising their will and freely indulging their ego. The free are not free.
They play a meek and repetitious social role in a confined playing field.

There is no room in that society to evolve toward perfection and
salvation and the hereafter. The social superiority of the aristocracy and
the grandees even transfers to their afterlife. Miscellaneous Zoroastrian
texts opine that propertied people of great wealth are similarly privileged in the next world.[68] The poor have no hope for riches in the next
world, while affluence is fated for the wealthy in both. Stasis and inertia
constitute the essence of social and even metasocial life. "The worst

---

67. Minovi and Rezvani, eds., *Nāmeh-ye Tansar*, 19.

68. Zaehner, *Zurvan*, 258–60.

sin is for someone to kill their master or to leave them malcontent. Whoever leaves their master malcontent has no place in radiant heaven."[69]

A member of such a society must accept the status quo and abandon the thought of transforming social life; otherwise, it is feared society's rigid and dry skeleton might fracture and fall apart. Indeed, religion and state are fast interlocked. Religion is national and governmental; any opposition and attempt to overturn its mandates means enmity with Iranians and the Sasanian empire. Likewise, the state is religious and any opposition to it means refuting the Mazdaean faith. Furthermore, religion and state are stewards and guardians of society's internal divisions, both spiritual and material. Challenging these divisions is to assail religion and state, Ahura Mazda, and the king. For several years, religion and stated collaborated in quashing social, religious, and political rebellions and court conspiracies. Whenever cracks appeared in social cohesiveness prompting fears of the prevailing class structure collapsing at the expense of the "free," or when the privileges and the social status of a powerful body such as the clergy was threatened and the king was reluctant to react or favored a rival sect, priests and generals would declare the king "impious" and take whatever steps they could that might benefit them.

From the very first half of the Sasanian period, people turned to Manichaean, Buddhist, and Christian creeds. Zurvanite and Mazdakite beliefs and Neoplatonist philosophy spread wide and took root. All the new faiths and doctrines other than Zurvanism were introspective and asocial; they considered retreat from society and the worldly life and cultivating the soul and cleansing the ego as the means to deliverance. A sclerotic society that had blocked intellectual and practical paths to freedom became an open field for novel thoughts that assuaged the citizenry's antisocial conscience and sanctioned their conduct in defiance of the social system.

---

69. Ibid., 398, quoting *Pahlavi Texts*.

While spurning the social structure was anathema to a devout Zoroastrian, to someone of a different faith the system not only lacked a sacred and divine nature but was a profane and likely evil design whose destruction would usher in the dawn of deliverance. No doubt, for Manichaeans and Christians and Buddhists, submitting and conforming to a polity that chained them to the earth and the body would not lead to salvation and nirvana. Non-Zoroastrians were outsiders in the empire and were not subsumed in the social system. From the point of view of the ruling establishment any form of opposition was a manifestation of evil-worship, *dīv-yasna*, and an Ahrimanic intent that had to be crushed with the utmost force.

Such a view of social life is extremely conservative and reactionary; it constantly looks to the past to decipher the present and avert the slightest deviation.

In such a suffocating environment where every organism withers in its shell, those who turn to new ideas and religions find a newfangled intellectual freedom. If they are circumscribed in action over here, they are free in thought over there.

Zurvanite thought does not feature a god concerned with humanity's fortunes and misfortunes. Unbounded Time, *Zurvan Akarana*, has predetermined everyone's fate, and no one can alter that. A Zurvanite dictate governs social life. In such a hostile world, many are martyred. Aspirations and actions aligned with the logic of individual hearts and minds are regularly crushed so that whatever aligns with the logic of social imperatives may soar. In such a workshop where humans are molded as clay into bricks, martyrdom is a stalwart shade tree. A troubled soul finds at least some solace in that shade.

A prince of such a body and soul, with faultless talents and character, a young man of extreme beauty inside and out, falls and turns insubstantial, but under the auspices of his death, the wrongdoer's life is also ruined. Now all who are weary of this life and of that death have a share in Siavash's thwarted hopes and his world-changing "self-purpose." By converging their frustrations on a single moment in Siavash's life, like rays of light concentrated on one spot, they grasp the essence and manifestation of their own earthly existence; if Siavash's death is not for naught, then the death of all who live a similar life is not in vain. Every thwarted soul is a *Sūshiyāns*, a savior figure of their time, each according to their own "self-purpose," and thanks to Siavash also grasps the truth of otherworldly life.

In Siavash's life, his gifts and virtues are stifled by those on the outside—the world and society. But by his death, the same gifts and virtues transfigure the wheel of time. Here, death is more powerful than life.

A thirst for death if quenched by the wellspring of faith blunts the hardships of life. Life will then have a dour look but a kind heart. So, better to transcribe the miseries of this ephemeral life onto the lasting comforts of the afterlife, and if it is not possible to "cast a new design"[70] today, appreciate the unseen yet to come.

Until such time as society's proclivities are in control of personal aspirations and the polity and individuals are unequal opponents the martyr is a hero, for even when they do not revolt against the order, at least they reject it. At any rate, a martyr must be deserving of life so that killing them in whatever manner and by whomever will feel unjust, and elicit sympathy. A man like Siavash is not merely a victim of society and those around him; he is the victim of a universal order where society itself is its tool.

Although after the fall of the Sasanians the social fabric, class relations, and the perception of the physical and the metaphysical world changed radically and a different order became dominant, life's injustices and societal oppression continued to dominate human life. Thus, it is not only thanks to the *Shahnameh* that the story of Siavash has lived on; the "injustice to Siavash has collared the king of the

---

70. After the opening line of Hafez/Ganjoor, *Qazal* #374 that, evoking the rebirth of nature in spring, calls for breaking the heavenly ceiling and undertaking a "redesign."—Trans.

Turks."[71] For the soil of our conscience never sought Siavash's blood
and never tasted it.

> The inhabitants of Bokhara know strange songs about the
> slaying of Siavash and minstrels call those songs *Lament
> for Siavash* . . . The people of Bokhara know dirges about
> the slaying of Siavash that are popular in every province,
> and minstrels have turned them into songs and chant
> them and bards call them the *Wailing of the Magi*, and
> this account is more than three thousand years old.[72]

Even today, Siavash stands for the proverbial martyr in some
far-flung corners, his fate a token of the injustices that beset people.
"In mourning rituals in Kohkiluyeh[73] as well, there are women who
sing very old songs with plaintive tunes, and moan and wail. They call
this performance *Sūsiyūsh* ['Lament for Siavash']"[74]

The grief of loss invades us, and we find solace in the song of
Siavash's death, which is the most undeserved death of a man most
deserving of life. Where such injustice is brought upon such a noble
man, what right do the likes of you and me have to complain?

> *The world's seen many like you and me,*
> *It spares no one to live a life carefree.*
>
> (M5: 203)

---

71. Citing Hafez/Ganjoor, *Qazal* #105: "The king of the Turks hears the
plaintiffs; may he regret the injustice to Siavash."—Trans.

72. Narshakhi, *Tārīkh-e Bokhārā*, ed. Razavi, 20 and 28.

73. The Kohgiluyeh and Boyer-Ahmad province lies in southwestern Iran, west
of Esfahan and Fars, north of Bushehr. It is home to Mount Dena, a peak in the
Alborz range where Kay Khosrow is said to have gone into occultation.—Trans.

74. Hedayat, "Tarānehāye Āmiyaneh." *Majalleh-ye Musīghī*, 1:7.

Martyrdom is a sacred event and therefore intertwined with religious beliefs. The life and religion of Iranian people changed after Islam, but many ancient socio-religious principles that had settled deep in their subconscious endured. As time passed, some principles were forgotten while others blended with their altered way of life and produced new beliefs and perspectives.

The story of Siavash's martyrdom was of the enduring kind, and it endured. However, in as much as a martyr is a sacred hero, the converted needed a martyr from among the holy figures of their new religion. True, Siavash's martyrdom is also associated with the divine, but he could not be the harbinger of salvation in the mind of a devout Muslim. For every religion promises a final blessing to its followers based on its own tenets and expects it to be achieved by its own illustrious and hallowed figures. From the standpoint of a Muslim Iranian, the story of that unrequited soul of old is a warning and a lesson, a sign of the tyranny of affluent men of power and the victimized pure, and of the final triumph of truth over falsehood. The mortal world is Afrasiyab's paradise and Siavash's hell, and the eternal world the opposite. Nevertheless, they no longer regard him as the chosen figure with a divine mission to transform the world.

A Muslim Iranian who grows up steeped in their national mythological traditions may conceivably *sense* Siavash in such a capacity. It is possible for such an unconscious image to lie behind a conscious perception of myth. But that sense cannot enter the consciousness of a Muslim, for although the Magians are acknowledged as 'a People of the Book,' the two creeds' beliefs about resurrection and salvation diverge. "When a different world is created, a different human must be created."[75]

And that different human is Hossein-e Ali, the martyr of Karbela. The supernal Siavash relegated his place to him and the Shi'ite passion play or *ta'ziyeh* replaced *Lament for Siavash*.

---

75. Hafez/Ganjoor, *Qazal* #470: *Ālami dīgar bebāyad sākht va'z no ādami.*—Trans.

Martyrdom is the province of Shi'ites, who while Muslim were outsiders to the Baghdad caliphate. At a time when being a Muslim was cognate with Arab ethnicity and culture, the *'Ajam*, or Iranians, who did not relinquish their culture persisted as a different nation. They were not assimilated into the Arabs pursuant to Islam. For them, therefore, the caliph in Baghdad was the ruler of a different nation.

In Islamic Iran, nationality was not a sign of unity or foreignness as such. Islam was a thread that connected all believers. Whoever was a Muslim was considered an insider and whoever was not, depending on their faith, was an outsider to a greater or lesser extent. Muslims were brothers, Iranian Muslims stepbrothers. The Sh'ite sect accentuated the sense of foreignness. If religion was the common denominator among the populace, then deviating from it and following another creed was a cause for discord and disunity.

Thus, Iranian Shi'ite considered the caliphate despotic and their rule as unjust and from an ethnic and religious standpoint, believed themselves to be rightful and oppressed. The ancillary belief in being oppressed connected them to other oppressed groups, to the household of Ali. The Shi'a were partisans of the latter's creed and, in their animosity toward the caliphs in Damascus and Baghdad, sympathizers of other oppressed groups.

The martyrdom of Hossein and his companions represents, for Shi'ite as well as for other justice-loving Muslims, the conflict between truth-seekers and avaricious perverts.[76] When Hasanak-e Vazir is being led to his death, he states with the martyr of Karbela on his mind, that "I had plenitude and did plenty; the fate of mankind is death; if today my end has come, none can stop them from hanging me or otherwise, for I am no greater than Hossein-e Ali."[77] Hasanak was accused of being a

---

76. Yaqmaie, ed., *Tafsīr-e Tabari*, vol. 5, 1386 ff.

77. Fayyāz, ed., *Tārīkh-e Beyhaqi*, 184. For an English translation, see *The History of Beyhaqi*, trans. C.E. Bosworth, rev. M. Ashtiāny (Boston, MA: Ilex Foundation, 2011), vol. 1, 277.—Trans.

Qarmati,[78] but given his denial and Abu'l-Fazl Beyhaqi's words, it appears that the Shi'a label was merely a pretext for killing him. Thus, in the opinion of the Sunni speaker and writer, the third Imam's martyrdom exemplifies a most vicious and unjust death. Imagine the opinion of Shi'a devotees of that eminence.

In any event, the tradition of the martyrdom and lamentation for Siavash noted in *Tārīkh-e Bokhārā* could not have provided a better vessel for the story of Hossein.[79] Whatever was incompatible with the new religious ideology was forgotten and whatever endured produced the myth of the martyrdom of Imam Hossein and his companions in fusion with historical events and another tale. The dynamics of that development was unconscious and buried deep in the pith of the faithful's mind. That is why related records in Iranian languages and literature, written or oral, and among religious sects, is extremely rare. Examples are found in the religious songs of the Yārsān[80] where the supreme soul of the mendicant Abel penetrates Jamshid and from him to Iraj and Siavash and Imam Hossein, and thereafter to Baba Taher and others . . .[81]

---

78. A militant sect of Sevener Isma'ili Shi'ites that flourished in the 9th c., with a network of missionaries and activists expanding from S. Iran and Bahrain to Iraq, E. Arabia, Yemen, Egypt and Syria, that revolted against the Fatimid and Abbasid Caliphates. See Farhad Daftari, "Carmatians," *Encyclopedia Iranica.*— Trans.

79. Quoting Soheili Khansari, ed., *Khosrow Nāmeh-ye Attār*, 25, "On the virtues of the Commander of the Faithful, Hossein, *peace be upon him*": "The opprobrious have shed much blood. / Nor shall it clot till Judgment Day. / Any blood shed on the dial of time / Disappears from sight and turns eternal. / Since that Sun of the faith disappeared / The times circle in his blood compass-like."

80. Mokri, ed., *Shahnameh-ye Haqiqat*, vol. 1, Introduction, 3: "The songs of the Yārsān belong to the followers of Ahl-e Haqq ('People of the Truth'). The religion, or the sect, of Ahl-e Haqq is a branch of Shi'ism. It constitutes a collection of beliefs and unique religious practices intermixed with pre-Islamic Iranian spiritual traditions and extremist post-Islamic sectarian creeds that are especially widespread in western Iran."

81. To paraphrase Suri, trans., *Yārsān*, 89–95, according to the Yārsān, humans

1. Āw[82] golden bowl

2. Three dūnam chin[83] Āw golden bowl

3. First Siavaxš, second Yahyā

4. Third Hossein, son of the King of Kings

5. Gilding the bowl, my quarry

6. Beheading my illuminator[84]

7. Propagator of every religion, chief leader of kings

8. Jamshid of the Jam-band, guardian of the paths (of solitude)

9. (You are) Iraj, Yahya, Siavash Kay

10. (Then in the form of) Hossein you were killed in Karbela

11. ʿĀli Qalandar, Taher Qalandar

12. What more shall I tell (you), son of Alexander?[85]

---

are endowed with a ray of God's light . . . And ibid., 176: These divine rays always circulate in the body of the pure and the select. Yārsān call this penetration metempsychosis, *dūnādūn*. A *dūn* signifies a select one into whom God's essence has transmigrated.

82. *Āw*, "That."

83. *chin*, "departed." (See n. 81 for *dūn*).

84. Idem: 102, excerpt from Song No. 4, referring to Yahyā (Saint John the Baptist). The myth of Siavash's blood has intertwined with the martyrdom of Yahyā. In the *Taʿziyeh of the Martyrdom of Yahyā* (unpublished MS #4816, Malek Library, Tehran), the sage says (to the king): "This is my counsel, O king of the heavenly throne, / Listen to it and take my words to heart. / Now that the ship of Yahyā is on your mind, / Know that I have seen it written in histories / That should a drop of his blood fall to earth, / Plants shall grow no more; that is a certainty. / Think about a way, O attentive Lord, / For his blood not to drip on earth in any way." In Yaqmaie, ed., *Tafsīr-e Tabari*, vol. 1, 210: "Where they had killed Yahyā, his blood kept boiling, and no matter how much earth they poured on, the blood percolated up and continued boiling. News of his blood spread across the world; people were saying, 'King Herod joined the congregation, and they killed Yahyā, and his blood never rests and keeps boiling.'"

85. Idem: 150, excerpts of Song #8.

Thus, Hossein ibn Ali appears after Siavash and Yahyā/John the Baptist and others[86] and his martyrdom is another iteration of their death. The new martyr does not obliterate his predecessors but coalesces with them. The essence of God transmigrates to a select few, and, these same chosen ones are also martyred. It is as if the earthly world cannot suffer their existence, and though this world cannot touch God's essence, it destroys the chosen one's body. Perchance such continuous metempsychosis means the earth shall never lack a leader and a savior shall exist in every period.

In any event, wailing over the dead was an age-old custom. The Avesta proscribed it but that did not stop believers from continuing to weep over the loss of loved ones. For many years after adopting Islam, Iranians continued to mourn Siavash of the bygone religion and myth in chants and sanctioned rituals. There is evidence of wailing and chanting not only in Bokhara but in Marv as well,[87] and furthermore, "chanting laments for the dead was always a collective ritual among the Dailamian."[88]

Dailamestan was an unruly region that was late to fall into Arab hands and blended little with their mores and customs, while the caliph was never able to govern the land with ease. These were simple

---

86. In *ta'ziyeh*, Hossein's martyrdom also recalls Yahyā (*Ta'ziyeh-ye Ashura: Shahādat-e Imam Hossein*, MS, Mushqin Village, Qazvin). Zainab says of her brother: "I have wept for a while by Yahyā's side. / Now to fetch him a water bowl, / Collect his pure rose blood . . ." And shortly afterward in a different gathering in the same *ta'ziyeh*, she says: "Let me come to the slaughterhouse awhile / Color my head-covering with this blood / Shame if they should spill your blood on earth. / My Yahyā! Let me fetch a bowl."

87. Bahar, *Sabk-Shenāsi*, vol. 1, 21.

88. Minorsky, "La domination des Dailamites," 19. [A province on the southwest coast of the Caspian Sea, Dailam was inhabited by warlike Iranian peoples that the Arabs were unable to conquer in the 7th c. In time, they adopted Shi'ite Zaidi Islam and Nizari Isma'ilism. The Dailamite Būyid dynasty, Āl-e Būyeh, controlled most of Iran in the 930s until the Seljuk invasion in the mid eleventh century.—Trans.]

people that gained kingship, the progeny of Būyeh the fisherman. So, their customs and practices were authentic and not borrowings or products of contact with other cultures. The Dailamian mourned for Imam Hossein in Baghdad.

> On the 10th of Muharram of the current year, Moʿez ud-Dowleh Dailami ordered people to close their shops for Hossein-e Ali and shut down the bazaars and undertake no transactions and to sing dirges and wear black outfits of rough cloth, and for the women to let their hair down and blacken their face and tear their frocks and chant dirges and walk through the city and slap their faces, and that is what people did. And owing to the excessive number of the Shiʿite and because the king accompanied them, the Sunnis were powerless to stop that.[89]

The Shiʿi Dailamites mourned the martyr of Karbela according to their own customs. This is the first large religious "troupe," *dasteh*, that we know of, and we know that here, too, as in the plaintive elegies of old, they chanted dirges and wept for the dead.

The traditional mourning ritual was used to elegize the new martyr. A mythical figure relegated his place to a historical man so that he, too, may in time lodge at the nebulous border between myth and history. Mourning ritual was then embellished and refined, and the "chanting and the wailing of the Magi" developed into dirge-and-troupe formations, which culminated in *taʿziyeh*.

What we know about *taʿziyeh* dates from recent times, but what it looked like in the Qajar period that is known to us—its popularity, the texts, the staging, and the sets—could not have been born and matured overnight. Although the past is obscure, that evolution is likely the outcome of a long life.

Nor did the perception of martyrdom, like its customs and rituals, remain uniform. Until his last breath, Siavash is a fated man who does

---

89. Rohani, trans., *Ibn Athīr*, events of the year 352 AH.

not run from whatever destiny has in store or what may befall him until death alters all the equations, including himself. The Shi'ites' Hossein, on the other hand, though fully cognizant of his imminent fate and destiny, has a quarrel with it and fights. He knows the outcome of the battle and when he is killed, he wins, because he is able to sacrifice the temporal present for the atemporal future and release his soul by parting with his body, and by standing before the tyranny of the worldly, become a guardian of heavenly justice on earth.

In those days of rebellions by Bābak and Ya'qūb and the strident and riotous poetry of Nāsser Khosrow, the Rāfezi, Qarmati, Isma'ili and sundry other Shit'ites that contested the caliphate reflected on the martyrdom of Hossein and perhaps others and learned the art of life from death. For the restless, the martyr of Karbela was, as it were, the hero who even after death appeared on horseback among his men and was the source of their fearlessness.[90]

For a few hundred years up to a little before Shi'ism became our official religion, we had a chaotic society and a turbulent and unstable community life; the nation's spiritual life was in distress. Earlier losses and bloodbaths were had left their mark. Our struggles in the first centuries of Islam and the heavy toll we paid fighting the Omayyad and Abbasid caliphates failed, and in the end, Khājeh Nasīr-e Tūsi went to Baghdad not on behalf of Hasan Sabbāh's heirs but to ride alongside a Mongol lord, ambitious for political power.[91]

---

90. Cf. El Cid, the celebrated Spaniard crusader and national hero who battled the Arabs rode his horse among the generals and the soldiers even after death, which gave them courage and victory. See Guerber, *Myths and Legends*, 366–7.

91. Khājeh Nasīr-al-Din (1201–74) was a polymath born in Tūs, Khorasan. He is celebrated for his contributions to astronomy, biology and chemistry, mathematics, medicine, mysticism, philosophy, and theology. He was a militant Nizāri Isma'ili, a Shi'a sect (the Assassins, so-called) founded by Hasan Sabbāh (d. 1124) and in their state employ at Alamūt in Dailam. On capturing the castle in 1256, Hulagu Khan appointed him scientific adviser to the Mongol court. In early 1258, Khājeh Nasīr accompanied Hulagu on his thirteen-day siege of Baghdad, seat of the Abbasid Caliphate, where most of

As a sense of impotence before native and foreign rulers—Iranian, Arab, and Turkish—and displeasure with the outside world increased over time, taking refuge in the inner world and union with the beyond seeped into the collective and generated a culture of its own. In the beginning, Sanā'ie and Nasser Khosrow, Manuchehri and Attār, interfused in a way and like a multifaceted but unified and harmonious culture, merged in the people's soul. But in the wake of all the disillusionments, the Mongol invasion sealed the message of Sufis and mystics. Now it was the words of Azizeddin Nasafi[92] that appealed, not those of Unsur al-Ma'āli.[93] The self-reflective and aspirational thinking of Hafez flowed through the spirit's veins, but as to standards by which to live, what coagulated was *Golestan*'s crafty morality, which endures to this day: the posture of the devious effete before despotic strongmen. And a panegyrist called Anvari who considered begging to be the axiom of poetry[94] was judged to be a prophet of poetry along with Ferdowsi.

---

the population was massacred. He then became the financial administrator of religious foundations and a fervent proselytizer of Twelver Shi'ism.—Trans.

92. Aziz ibn Mohammad Nasafi, born in late twelfth century in Nasaf (Nakhshab, in present-day Uzbekistan), was a Sunni exponent of mysticism with Isma'ili leanings. He authored many widely popular works in Persian, including *Kitāb al-Insān ul-Kāmil* (the "Perfect Man," referenced in nn. 33 and 50 above), which he began in Bokhara in 1261–2 and was still writing in Abarqū in 1292 where he had settled after sojourns in Kerman, Esfahan, and Shiraz.—Trans.

93. Kay Kāvus b. Iskandar b. Qābus, *Unsur al-Ma'āli* (b. 1021), was a Ziyarid prince and author of a work dedicated to his son, Gilanshah that was later named *Qābūs-nāmeh*. The book is one of the earliest and most distinctive examples of wisdom literature (*andarz-nāmeh*) popular in Pahlavi writings. Composed in a simple Persian prose with a mix of anecdotes, poems, and proverbs, it is a 44-chapter manual on ethical principles and the proper conduct of a prince, the arts, good governance, and military leadership.—Trans.

94. Nafisi, ed., *Dīvān-e Anvari*, 29: "Begging is the canon, shari'at, of poetry." [Ali ibn Mahmud Anvari, born in Balkh in 1126, was an astronomer and a famed poet and panegyrist to Sultan Sanjar (r. 1097-1118) who continued in service to the Seljuq Empire until his death in 1157.—Trans.]

In the intellectual impoverishment and the social welter of the final years of Savafid rule and the following centuries, that audacious soul who clawed at the lion's paws had decamped.

A people living in a fractured society are disjointed one from another. Each looks out for the here and now without neglecting the end of the affair, and secretly tries to dig a "tunnel" to God from within to secure the best of both worlds. Thus, decay gnawed at the four pillars of thought like termites, and it pulverized. The grand mysticism of Rumi whose human is God and whose God is human gave way to various lineages of "Dervish so-and-so Alishah," and the heroic martyr turned into a different kind of martyr.

The Hossein that the people of the land of Khorasan knew, the Hossein of a thousand years ago, dismissed the advice of his relatives and acquaintances and headed for Kufeh to fight, and on the day of the battle said to his enemies,

> Those among you know who I am, know, and those
> who do not, I am the son of the daughter of the Prophet
> and the son of his cousin . . . You have resolved to kill
> me in this desert and have no fear of God nor of the
> Day of Resurrection, nor feel any shame before the
> Prophet's soul. As I presently stand among you, I have
> not shed anyone's blood and I have not taken another's
> effects. What is your cause for shedding my blood?[95]

And six hundred years later, the Hossein of *Rawzat ul-Shuhadā* ("The Garden of Martyrs")—like the Hossein of our days—is a wretched and whining outlander:

> O people of Iraq, I swear to you that, as you know, I am the
> great-great-grandson of Mostafa of the tribe of the Prophet of
> God and the beloved child of Fatemeh Zahra and the apple

---

95. Yaqmaie, ed., *Tafsīr-e Tabari*, vol. 5, 1389.

of the eye of Ali Mortezā. My brother is Hasan Mojtabā . . .
My uncle, Jaʿfar Tayyār . . . How could you consider it licit
(*halāl*) to shed my blood and deny me water that is sanctioned
for animals wild and tame, and Jews and Christians?" . . .
Meanwhile, the cries of his female kinsfolk and children
weeping and wailing in the camp reached the blessed ears
of Imam Hossein. The venerable one was pained at hearing
them . . . so he dispatched Abbas and Ali-Akbar to "Go and
tell them that you shall have to cry excessively tomorrow;
don't be hurried to cry now." They quietened down, but the
Imam resumed speaking again and said, "People, know that
Almighty God has forbidden mendacity . . . Now that I have
come here based on your promises, you use covert schemes
to conduct shock assaults, and with the rock of treachery
and torture shatter the brittle glass of our hearts who are
outlanders. If I whispered a word of the fire of your ruse
that has scorched my patience and reserve to the mountain,
forthwith the maxim 'the mountains are broken down,
crumbling,'[96] shall manifest upon it. And if I should bring to
light the shadow of the thunderbolt of your tyranny that has
shattered the abode of my companions' forbearance at its
core, at once layers of darkness shall cover it 'one on top of
the other.'[97] And now because of you, I behold the province of
tranquility shattered from the rapacity of the army of agitation,
and the ship of hope capsizing in the maelstrom of melancholy.

The end of the ocean of sorrow is not in sight,
Contentment in the tidings of life is not in sight.
A hundred thousand shafts are caged in my heart,
Alas, imperceivable, an arrowhead is not in sight.[98]

---

96. *Wa bussat'il-jibālu bassā.* Quran, Sūra *al-Wāqiʿah* 5.—Trans.

97. *Baʿzuhā fawqa baʿz.* Quran, Sūra *al-Noor* 40.—Trans.

98. Kashefi, *Rawzat ul-Shuhadā*, ed. Ramezani, 274.

Centuries of tyranny delivered the goods. The feeling of helplessness and victimhood is the blood that keeps the heart of society beating. Hossein's bravery does not lodge in the mind of abject, dire-futured people. But they do sense injustice, which drubs like a deluge and runs under the skin like a worm; they reflect on it and, unable to counter it, wait for the end of time.

The ideal man of such a people is the oppressed soul who was led away as a captive along with his kinsfolk and killed, throat parched. The martyr of Karbela is a hero whose corpse is still prostrate on the dirt, as it were. With every injustice that strikes the populace body and soul, the hero dies again and fresh blood drips from his corpse. Martyrdom is a wound in the heart. May the murderer lay his hands on it.[99]

Until the Shi'a stay as they are, Hossein is a felled man exposed to torrents of calamities! And the faithful who worship his aloneness and thirsty lips nurse their own frustrations. The leader, *imam*, of the affrighted is a hapless man resigned to his fate. Such a man is what they present in a *ta'ziyeh* with his kin, and each presentation ends in weeping—evidently for a martyr whose only act in this world was to weep and nothing else.

Martyrdom is a sort of negative epic, whether in the case of Siavash or Hossein. When the wish or the potential will of the devotees is stunted and does not materialize, it is transferred as a perfect aspiration to an ideal man. In a world where humans lose, one way or another, death is the finale of the hero's act, especially if he embodies the devotees' arrested will. And the more unfair and painful the loss, the more thoroughly the devotees' needy psyche is satisfied.

In this existence of gains and losses where one must sacrifice a day of life for every day one lives and, to live mindfully, likely be obliged

---

99. Guerber, *Myths and Legends*, 80: In Germanic traditions, when the invincible Siegfried was dishonorably killed on a hunt, his body lay in a church where his companions laid their hand on him one by one. When the murderer's hand touched him, the wounds opened, and fresh blood gushed from the corpse.

to waive life's common bounties, martyrdom is the price one pays to be as devotees aspire to be, and the martyr is the one who delivers this aspiration.

God descended to earth in the body of Christ to redeem the Eden-banished human's "original sin." The Nazarene Christ was crucified to deliver the soul of Judas Iscariot and the body of Mary Magdalene whom Satan had possessed, and provide the possibility of redemption to those who aspired to salvation. And Mansur Hallaj hanging from the gallows delivered the God that resided in himself and his self that resided in God: "O people, deliver me from God! . . . for He has severed me from myself and will not restore me to myself and I cannot witness His presence and dread the severance for I shall be deserted and deprived. Woe betide him who is deserted after that presence and is severed after the union."[100]

The God of a mystic like Mansur, while united with him, is a wholly distinct infinity and inaccessible to that infinitely limited soul. Mansur is a wandering soul at once severed and united, a sober drunk and a dual singular "half from Turkestan, half from Ferghana, half a shore shell and half a whole pearl."[101]

By being freed from his earthly body, that man freed God, and himself became all God. "O You are I and I, You! There is no difference between my selfhood and Your Thou-hood, save between the originated and the eternal."[102] The martyrdom of Hallaj is the deliverance of the cosmic and the microcosmic universe.

So today, should a godless man's soul be possessed by the abhorrence of injustice and free him from commonplace obsessions, and should his sense of union with the world exhort him to rise like a dagger against the world, and should he be finally killed in some remote place,

---

100. Massignon, trans., *Akhbar al-Hallaj*, 10. [See also Herbert Mason's translation of Massignon, *The Passion of Hallaj*, 142.—Trans.]

101. Ibid., 7, quoting Rumi: #2309. The full verse describes the dual nature of his body and soul: "I am half soil and water, half spirit and heart, / Half a shore shell, and half a whole pearl."—Trans.

102. Massignon, trans., *Akhbar al-Hallaj*, 7.

his martyrdom is deliverance. The thought that is a captive in me turns into action in his hands and is freed. Although his martyrdom does not deliver me who am a prisoner and my own jailor, it liberates the quest for salvation from the cage of my heart. It drains me from my constrained nature and drives it toward a quest for liberation; what had been in my prison and died is now alive and cannot be seized.

The martyrdom of Siavash and Hossein and Jesus and Hallaj, or of that ordinary man who has renounced God, is a form of transcendence. Something greater than and beyond death ascends, and death becomes the source of life.

> When Afrasiyab captured Iranshahr and besieged Manuchehr in Tabaristan, he was asked a favor. Manuchehr agreed and in return asked Afrasiyab to withdraw from Iranshahr as far as the flight of an arrow. Then an angel named Spandārmaz appeared and ordered Manuchehr to lift the bow and arrow presented to the archer (as related in the Avesta). They summoned Ārash, who was highborn and devout and cultivated, and ordered him to lift the bow and shoot an arrow. Ārash stood up and stripped off his clothes and said, "O King, and O people! Look at my body that is free of injuries and affliction. I know well that once I shoot an arrow with this bow, I shall be torn to pieces and my body shall be destroyed. Verily, I shall sacrifice myself for you." Then he stepped to the side and with the strength that God had granted him drew the bowstring and shot an arrow and was torn to pieces on the spot. God commanded the wind to catch the arrow from Mount Rūyān and carry it far away to Khorasan between Ferghana and Tabaristan. The arrow struck a giant oak—which was unique among all the trees in the world ... and people were saved from Afrasiyab.[103]

Although Ārash is said by Ferdowsi to have declared, "In truth, I shall sacrifice myself for you," such a concept of martyrdom is an

---

103. The Persian translation of this passage was provided by Reza Saghafi based on Edward Zachau's edition of Biruni's *Āthār ul-Bāghiya*, 222.

interpolation and is not based on our ancient myths. Siavash does not "sacrifice" himself for anyone; he rescues his "inner-cosmic" self— namely, truth and existence. In fact, he not only does not covet death, but he covets his killer's death. As he was about to die,

> *Siavash said to the Lord, "Hear my appeal,*
> *Thou who art greater than the turning wheel!*
> *From my seed I beg you to branch a line*
> *That like the sun he may rise and shine.*
> *In avenging my death on my foes may he lead,*
> *And in the country entire establish his creed."*

(M3: 151–2)

Now that night is pulling Siavash to the depths, avenging him is on Kay Khosrow—to rise like the shining sun and implement his Siavashesque creed. That ending has closed, a beginning has opened. Siavash's end is the beginning of Siavash.

NIGHT

Mythological cosmology is the association between divine and super-natural forces and their origin and hierophany, or manifestation, in nature, and the cognizance of a nature whose every aspect is associated with the world beyond. In such a paradigm, humanity is defined by a sacred "Heaven–Earth" marriage, a hierogamy, whose twofold nature is a reiteration and recreation of the archetypes, the divinities.[1]

Humanity is not central to myth, though it is the main subject, meaning human beings think about and reconstitute the cosmos and set themselves within its totality; they are not the main subject, but they are, *unconsciously,* central to the thought. Here, an individual is a thought that is not aware that they are thinking and reconstituting their other externality—the cosmos and its order. In myth, individuals are not defined by their humanity but like all other phenomena in the world are measured and understood in union with *the existence beyond* and the nature of that transcendent existence. Their true reality transcends their body and behavior and lies in the essence of that union. It is owing

---

1. Eliade, *Le sacré et le profane*, ch. 4, "Sanctification de la vie," 142 ff.; idem, *L'éternel retour*, 52; and idem, *Traité d'histoire des religions*, 344.

to that symbiosis that we encounter *god-men* and *demon-men,* beings beyond the visible natural order, for in myth, the true order of existence is not the tangible natural order. Kiumars, Jamshid, and Zahhāk, or Zoroaster and Afrasiyab, are thus more real than other beings who do not reflect the cosmos as closely and to the extent they do.

But in epic, humans face other humans, the world, and God. The cosmos is an object of reflection not on its own account but because it encompasses humankind and is the landscape of their life and death. Here, individuals are defined by their humanity. Even in heroic poems such as the Mahabharata and the Iliad where gods engage and navigate wars through humans, they are essentially the epitome of humanity's spirited existence.

In epic, the main subject is no longer the cosmos; it is an individual who actualizes their will, gives form to their aspirations, and in the process struggles with a reality other than their own. The main subject here is the individual, not the larger, social being. For although an individual is cognizant of their social life, they do not consider themselves a social entity and are in pursuit not only of their personal reality but also of the source of societal relations outside of society: God and the cosmos. Thus, the individual is the main subject, but the individual in the macrocosm, and *unconsciously,* for they seek the source elsewhere. As such, the individual is a thought that does not know it is thinking of itself but knows that it is thinking and what it is thinking about.

Epic protagonists perceive and understand themselves in relation to the cosmos. To engage with a destiny mined and minded by the world, and to forge their own fate, they come face-to-face with the existence of the "other"—an engagement in accord and discord, in harmony and disharmony.

In living in accordance with their will and behaviors, worldly and otherworldly forces are either with or against them, and sometimes within them. Such individuals possess many supernatural—mythic— attributes. Arjuna is an archer with divine powers, and Achilles and Esfandiyar are invincible, one sanctified, the other sacred. Yet in death, all these "immortals" are like everyone else; thus, also in life, for being transitory, they come and go. As such, the epic individual is more "human" than mythic heroes.

Human beings grasp the concept of history through their own history, which itself derives from a perception of the past, or "historic time." "Spiritual time" flows from the other world. It is always present; it is not linear and has no past or future but is cyclical and when it returns to itself, it repeats—eternally so—allowing objects and events to be reborn. But historic time is of this world; it flows in one irreversible direction and because it is not repeated, passes on, annihilating things that live within it as it ends. The first is an earlier and mythic, and the second a later and historic perception of time.

Given such a perception of time, humanity's perception of itself also mutates over time. The individual—transitory and powerless—loses many of their mythical and supernatural traits and finds a different relationship with the other world.

A religious individual, though cognizant of their life in history, is also aware that historic time will at some point end, and that resurrection is a different existence of a different dimension and scale and of a lasting and continuous time, a timeless time.

In earlier times, "history" was an account of the world and humanity, which began with myth and moved through epic to arrive at history. "In the beginning God created the heaven and the earth"[2] and Kiumars was the first "Mortal Life";[3] we begin with the biblical Book of Kings or the story of the Kianids, until we reach history. It is only after the Renaissance that Western empirical and rational thought separated history from mythology and regarded only "facts" and the law of causality as valid.

Humanity's understanding of the world evolved at a slow pace. At times, varied and contradictory takes on a single subject from different

---

2. Genesis 1:1.

3. Av. Gayō.maretan, MP Gayōmard, the progenitor of humankind.

eras and sources coalesced in the human mind. Thus, no stringent demarcation separated history, epic, and myth, and many ancient concepts and their symbolic legacies found their way into history. In any event, the dominant concept and central subject of *history*—the events and personalities—is humanity's social experience at a *specific time and place*. Here, humanity is both central and the main subject. It knows that it is thinking about its personal as well as social self.

The historical individual is within the bounded framework of society, not in the boundless cosmos. Even from the viewpoint of the faithful, the impact of the supernatural on history is indirect and through human agency. The historical individual is thus severed from otherworldly forces and fields and is restricted to itself.

The nature of Afrasiyab's persona in myth, epic, and history is an example of such a development. The mythological Afrasiyab is a preternatural figure who

> erected an iron fortress to the height of a thousand men
> under the earth where he installed stars, a moon, and a
> sun for illumination, and amassed all that he desired,
> and aspired to immortality in that sanctuary. There,
> he sacrificed one hundred horses and a thousand oxen
> and ten thousand sheep to Aredvīsūr Nāhīd so he may
> seize the *farr*, which is a divine blessing that afloat in
> the Farākhkart Sea belongs solely to Aryan lands and to
> Zoroaster. Three times he plunged into the Farākhkart
> Sea in pursuit of the *farr*; thereafter they seized him.[4]

In passing from myth to history, Afrasiyab's supernatural character becomes natural and social. The demon turns into a sorcerer and then into a destructive king. On entering history, he is inevitably cast within the bounds of a "historical figure."

---

4. Yaqmaie, ed., *Tabari*, 616. In the Avesta (*Yt* 19), Xvarenah (NP Farr) is
protected by Mithra after it leaves Yima and by Fire when it flees from Aži
Dahāka and takes refuge in the Vourukaša Sea (MP Farākhkart) where
Frangrasyan (MP Frāsiyāv; NP Afrasiyab), attempts to grab it.

Nor is the Kāvus of epic what he was in myth. In earlier traditions, he was king over humans and fiends and ruled the seven climes; he chained the destructive demons of Mazandaran and protected the world from affliction. He built seven palaces of gold and silver and lead and crystal at the summit of Mount Alborz. Any decrepit person on the verge of death who reached and circumambulated his palace would turn into a fifteen-year-old youth.

Then the demons resolved to destroy him. Thus, the demon of wrath took possession of him and diminished the value of being sovereign over the seven climes in his eyes. He became obsessed with ruling over sky and earth and confronted the gods and along with demons was thrust into boundless darkness and the royal glory abandoned him.[5]

Thus, the Solomon of that era was entangled by those who tangled with him. When the demon of wrath penetrated him, it dragged the demon of greed inside as well, so that for Kāvus lording over the seven realms sufficed no more and he yearned to become God. With that, the tie between him and the upper world snapped, and he was severed from God. A god-man became a demon-man.

There is no sign of Kāvus' unmatched powers and lofty aerial abodes in the *Shahnameh*, or of bestowing eternal life where he is a powerless king who for a time is imprisoned by demons. In the passage from myth to epic, Kāvus sustains a twofold change of character. One, a turnaround like others: a cosmic god-man with smaller dimensions and power turns into a hero with cosmic connections. The other, a turnaround within. He is not the god-man become a demon-man; from the start, he is "the sickly branch from a sturdy root"[6] who defaces his father's legacy and deviates from his path. What befalls Iran and Iranians during his rule is not only due to Afrasiyab but also to his losing the *farr*. The moment he ascended the throne, a minstrel fiend enticed him to march on Mazandaran and battle the demons; then *Eblīs*, the Devil, derailed

---

5. *Dēnkart*, in Pourdavoud, trans., *Yašthā*, vol. 2, 230.

6. See Ferdowsi/Ganjoor, *Kingship of Kāvus* 1:5.—Trans.

his heart and urged him to aim heavenward. "Every one of his actions is worse than the other";[7] he does not merit kingship. In short, as the Iranian dignitaries proclaim, "the king is mad" (M2: 76, 77, 79, 151, 200, 202; and M3: 76, 199), and he promptly loses the royal glory.

The moment news of Siavash's death reach Iran, Kāvus is powerless and Tahamtan has full power. Following Gudarz' order and Gīv's efforts, they find Kay Khosrow. And when the retrieved prince reaches Iran, he takes over military command and governance and war and peace, for the "*farr*-and fame-deprived" Kāvus who did not uphold the tenets of kingship (M3: 199) was not equal to avenging Siavash. That braggart who had thought himself superior to Jam and Zahhāk and Fereidun and Manuchehr and Qobād (M2: 78, 82) finds himself alone in the fenced-off confines of his thoughts. The mirage of superiority taints his trust in everyone and, leaving no room for parley, allows the counsel of friends to fall on deaf ears. He ignores the advice of Zāl, and Sudabeh's warnings (M2: 81, 135), and is thence taken captive in Mazandaran and Hāmāvarān. Although Tahamtan helps free him from both prisons, his is so self-deluded as to order Tūs to hang Rostam (M2: 200). All the while, the demon of wrath that had possessed him has become his habit, making him explode in rage at the slightest excuse, controlling his mind and dictating his actions. In the words of Gudarz:

> *He has no wisdom nor learning nor care,*
> *Neither his heart nor his sick mind is fair.*

(M2: 154)

It is because of such a father that Siavash throws caution to the wind and goes away.

The Kāvus of myth is a remote and ghostlike ruler, a formless figure of blurred dimensions, while the Kāvus of epic is the familiar afflicted

---

7. See Ferdowsi/Ganjoor, *Sohrab* 10:13, Rostam berating Kāvus for injudiciously ordering Tūs to capture and hang him and Gīv.—Trans.

sort who "upon learning of Siavash's death grieves much, that [he was] the one who killed Siavash, not Afrasiyab."[8]

The king of Turan never wished for Siavash's death. The Afrasiyab of the *Shahnameh* loves the Iranian prince; awed by his face, figure, and *farreh*, and considering such traits to be superhuman, he says a father who repels such a son must be a fool. Afrasiyab cannot find repose without Siavash nor lie down to sleep without thinking of him. The prince is his "joyous spring, darling, and consoler" (M3: 82–4, 91). Like a father, he adores the son who has emerged from the earthly Iranian paradise as an image of perfection and beauty. Afrasiyab's life and riches now belong to Siavash, and he is tied to the prince body and soul (M3: 83).

At times, Afrasiyab seems like a father peerless in fatherly love. When his son Shīdeh is killed and he hears about the death of that "moonlike horseman, that streamside cypress,"

> *Afrasiyab spoke words all while weeping,*
> *"Peace I shan't know of, neither of sleeping.*
> *Give me ye succor now as I mourn,*
> *Each with me grieve and suffer forlorn."*
> *Tears full of blood he went on to shed,*
> *A pain that no healer was able to bed.*
>
> (M5: 277)

Afrasiyab cannot suffer the loss of a son alone. His grief is a curse as long as nighttime and as deep as death upon a soul weak as a human. The king of Turan who is matchless in fighting and feasting crumbles and tumbles and cries out from the depths: 'Save me!' Like a speared headstrong stallion, he roars under the vault of heaven and his plaintive rage pours upon the earth. His royal pomp is pulverized. 'Help me! I need each and every one of you—but not like a hazy crowd of

---

8. Nicholson and Le Strange, eds., *Fārs-nāmeh*, 41.

sympathizers; just as you stand by me bodily in battle, stand by me in this bereavement that is driving my soul insane, and each take a share of it into your body to lessen mine. Inasmuch as you produce the warrior spirit and heroism bodily, so, too, reenact my mourning in your form and figure even though the pain may not subside and no cure for it may materialize.' He declares the pain is substantial; it has weight and volume and is as real as a dagger that shreds the body.[9]

Kāvus' grief over Siavash's killing is not as grinding as Afrasiyab's over the loss of Shīdeh. On hearing what had befallen his son, Kāvus' "exalted head dropped" and he

> Cleaved his clothes and clawed his face,
> Fell to the ground from the towering dais.
>
> (M3: 170)

His pain exhibits no characteristics unique to a singularly wretched soul; it is vague and abstract and general and is not materially palpable. It is as if Kāvus' lamentation is a formality; ergo the poet expresses his lifeless pain in formulaic and familiar language and moves on.

Well, let us move on.

Afrasiyab, who was lying in wait for Kay Khosrow is shamefaced when he sees him and blanches, his heart moved by love (M3: 165–6). And in the case of Farangis—tormenting her notwithstanding—he never forfeits fatherly love. He is delighted that his daughter is with child and revered by Siavash (M3: 116–17). Similarly, despite his fatherly heart aching for his daughter, he persists in his decision and disingenuously says, "Perchance some good might lie in this adversity," yet he is unable to enact his aversion upon Siavash until she is dragged out of sight.

Afrasiyab is touched by the kindness of his kinsfolk and companions. When he learns of the death of his loyal general Piran,

---

9. See also Afrasiyab's lamentation for his other son, Sorkheh (M3: 181).

Afrasiyab writhing in sorrow did weep,
Strummed his locks and tears let seep.
"Alas, my world-wise one, alas!
My singular towering rider, alas!"

    (M5: 249)

It was this same Piran who had saved and reared Kay Khosrow, the enemy. Piran, now heading a defeated army, pleads for help and asks Afrasiyab to join the battle in person; and feeling guilty about Kay Khosrow, expresses remorse. Afrasiyab shows him gratitude, however, and responds: 'You have offered up your body and soul to me and endured much distress; the heavens have not produced your equal and no hero is as dear to me as you.' As for Piran's role in the saga of Kay Khosrow, he says:

That does not trouble me, I who am king,
At heart I have never begrudged you a thing.
Do not be anguished by any past fare,
The rust in your heart can be polished with care.

    (M5: 166)

He then cheers on Piran so he may not fear defeat.

In his approach to his people, Afrasiyab is not an "expedient" man with the profit-and-loss mindset of politicians and tradesmen—not if they are close and supportive or are believed to be so; he respects fellowship.

That trait is absent in Kāvus. He respects nothing—including himself. Short on wisdom, he lacks any insight into people and human behavior to be able to appreciate their value. Withholding the antidote from Rostam and neglecting the poisoned Sohrab to the point of death is his typical response to others' kindness.

At any rate, the kind-hearted Afrasiyab is on good terms with the world for a time. Once he meets Siavash, he expects the world to fall in line with him, certain that the two countries will now be relieved from the scourge of war (M3: 83). That is why the poet labels him "the sanguine lord" (M3: 96). When Siavash first marched against the Turanians, Afrasiyab had a dream and asked the learned to explain it. The dream exegetes said that if the king were to fight Siavash, multitudes of Turanians would be killed but also that should Siavash be killed, the world would fall into ruin and turmoil by vengeance. The king of Turan is vexed by the predicament and reasons to himself:

> Rather than covet the world and fight,
> Peace is the target I'll keep in my sight.

>   (M3: 52)

Before meeting Afrasiyab, Siavash was apprehensive and told Piran, 'If staying in Turan might bring misfortune, show me the way to a different land,' and Piran replied, 'Rest assured that although Afrasiyab is reputed to be evil, he is a man of God' (M3: 81). But Piran was speaking out of friendship and credulity for Afrasiyab's character is not so simple as to be described as thus and such. His personality is tortuous and complex, a concoction brimming with good and evil where the Devil in him drowns out the God.

The first time Afrasiyab is mentioned in the *Shahnameh*, he is a prince at war with Nozar. He appears restive and exalted and claims that his sword can sunder any knot (M2: 11). Afrasiyab conducts a manly war and then commits an unmanly murder. He slays the Iranian king Nozar who is his captive in retaliation for the death of the Turanian warriors on the battlefield (M2: 35). He kills his brother Aqrīras for failing to massacre the Iranian prisoners and releasing them instead.

That said, he does not wield his sword solely upon captives. In confronting the Iranian army, he ignores the risk and orders his troops:

> Ambush their fighters from far and near,
> Cut down the sun at the point of your spear.

>   (M3: 187)

When Rostam sees and recognizes him, Afrasiyab

> *Reared like a panther ready to rattle,*
> *Strained his legs and charged into battle.*
>
> (M3: 188)

This is one of the rare skirmishes from which Rostam returns just as he had started, empty-handed. No harm befalls Afrasiyab except that his horse is felled. Nor does he bend when fighting Kay Khosrow. Dismissing Garsivaz' advice, he refuses to abandon the frenzied combat until Jahn and Garsivaz grab his horse's bridle and pull him out of the fray (M5: 283).

Zāl knows the truculent Afrasiyab well when he tells Rostam, "Shield yourself from him" (M2: 64), for he is a spirited fighter who does not stand still. He attacks in a flash and flees instantly; this nonpareil fugitive is the wind and cannot be caught. Once he decides to decamp,

> *He vanishes boldly out of one's sight,*
> *'Tis as if a bird has just taken flight.*
>
> (M5: 316)

Afrasiyab himself boasts that if a burden becomes taxing, "I shall rise skyward like a star" (M5: 306), as if Vayu, the god of wind and death and war had blown his spirit into his body—which at times is in the clouds, and at times in the dragon's breath (M3: 195).

But despite such bravado, Afrasiyab is fear-conscious, which is why he repeatedly takes flight above and below. Fear darkens his spirit like a shadow when he feels vulnerable. He is a stranger to the ethos of the hero who confronts death out of manliness. When danger looms, he "mounts a safer steed, and along with the elect" escapes from the scene (M5: 80); he is likely reluctant to engage to begin with, but the grandees or the rank and file encourage and urge him into battle:

You hold Rostam in such fear, why?
Thereby gladdening the enemy, why?
Even if his body were of metal whole,
The warrior while brave is a single soul.

(M4: 270, 277)

He runs and flees. Underground, overland, and underwater, he is always in flight. In the end, too, Kay Khosrow is only able to capture him—alone and abject—with tremendous difficulty.

Kāvus is the exact opposite. If he goes to war, he is captured. He neither knows the mores nor heeds the advice of those who know better. When he loses his sight in Mazandaran and the White Demon captures him, he sends a message to Zāl saying, 'I rejected your guidance due to ignorance, and regret it. Come now and save me.' And when he is imprisoned by the king of Hāmāvaran, he offers a wise and valorous response to Rostam's messenger, but when instead of flying across the heavens he falls to earth, he is deeply indignant and glum. He who had aspired to be God now repents piously and begs forgiveness.

Every now and then, defeat and dejection restore that king's fleeting wisdom. But such "wisdom" is not gained from weighing things and actions and grasping their real import, and as a result is not followed up with appropriate behavior; it is superficial and evanescent, imposed by the outside world. Reality as an actual state, like blindness and captivity and plunging to earth, is a revelation to Kāvus who accepts it only when it is inescapable, as when he "accepted" being imprisoned. But once liberated and no longer obliged to adopt a "wise" course of action, his wisdom dissolves and he is once again as he was. That is because such wisdom is not the outcome of a clear and self-directed thought process; it is contingent upon a negative predicament—on vulnerability; like a shadow, it has a co-dependent exigency. Wisdom of that sort is the consequence of a forced action. When it becomes possible to act freely again, the "wise" person is not obliged to remain "wise" and reverts to their true self. That is why Kāvus is wise in captivity and unwise in liberty.

There are times when life brings Afrasiyab to his senses, but with a variant meaning and function. When he deliberates and finds himself vulnerable, he looks to reason for a solution. He has a problem-solving mind. One time in his youth, we find Afrasiyab partial to truce, but only after he beholds Rostam and realizes that truce is the only option. The enemy's might has opened his eyes. He tells his combative father Pashang:

> *Your only recourse is to sue for peace,*
> *Your army is not a match for this man.*
>
>   (M2: 68)

We do not see any signs of sound thinking by Afrasiyab again except in his old age. By then his tyranny is ebbing and the wheel of time is turning in Kay Khosrow's favor. Sensing his own decrepitude, he endeavors to undo the knot not by the sword but by scheming. And in that, he is devious in the extreme. He sends a message to Kay Khosrow awash in such apologies and threats and hopes and enticing promises (M5: 259) that except for the king and Rostam, all other Iranian grandees second him (M5: 266). In that message, he claims that while the entire army is ready at his command, he is loath to spill so much innocent blood—in fear of God, not of anyone else:

> *I speak to you thus not out of fear,*
> *It's my old age that's making me veer.*
>
>   (M5: 261)

Both he and the times have changed. The times disfavor him; he is fearful owing to the disfavor and even more because of his old age. And how he thrashes about in an attempt to emerge from the vortex with the least number of bruises! But Kay Khosrow realizes that Afrasiyab regrets attacking Iran and is seeking a devious solution (M5: 264), most deviously by telling Kay Khosrow: 'Come to me and do whatever you please and leave Siavash's vengeance to Kāvus and Gudarz; that will be between them and me.' (M5: 261).

Early in his kingship, he had once tested the tactic of setting one enemy against another while covering his own back. When Sohrab journeyed to Iran to face his father Rostam, neither of whom knew the other, Afrasiyab placed a garrison at the disposal of Hūmān and Bārmān to watch him. 'Do not let father and son recognize each other, and once the son finishes off his father,'

> Forthwith Sohrab you must fetter and tie,
> For one night sleepless, let him there lie.
>
> (M2: 181)

Sohrab was to finish Tahamtan and they were to finish Sohrab, stealing sleep from him for one night and depriving him of wakefulness and rest.

Greed, Āz, is the Ahriman-created demon that in the end devours the creator's creature. Being greedy, Afrasiyab is an Ahrimanic creature.

> The Turkish king's heart seldom did heed,
> For it endlessly strove to indulge his greed.
>
> (M5: 87)

And like Ahriman, he is the victim of his own greed. He wants to remain a king no matter what; but that supremacy is threatened from without and within, by the dream he dreamed, by Kāvus, Rostam and Gudarz, by Siavash[10] and Kay Khosrow. Fear surfaces and, like night gliding across the sky, gradually saturates his spirit. Sometimes that fear

---

10. Toward the end, Afrasiyab believes that Siavash covets his kingship. Pashang relates that belief back to him: "You embraced Siavash like a son / With a father's love and caring. / An ill wind blew over from Harā, / You turned against him in displeasure. / You were all spent once you felt / He coveted your crown, throne, and army" (M5: 257).

prevents him from facing the world and turns the hero into a trickster. When danger weighs hardest, he flies as hard as he can. He does not throw himself into fire like Siavash, though when in a predicament, he risks fire and water to save himself.

Although Afrasiyab is fear-conscious, he does not remain sunk in fear and transcends it. Ahriman holds sway within him; thus, wrath and revenge stamp out fear and take over Afrasiyab, and the immensity of that demon and dragon resurfaces in the sorcerer. As such, he is a king who even when his entire army deserts him in old age does not withdraw from battle, his heart so filled with "rage and roil" that he cannot heed any warnings. The fleeing fugitive stays on and fights hard—he who maintains

> *The mind of a warrior is mindless of wisdom;*
> *War and reason do not mix in that kingdom.*
>
> (M2: 41)

Afrasiyab considers folly a prerequisite of courage and himself partakes of a foolhardy courage, for such bravery can only surface by overcoming wrath and revenge. When Afrasiyab cedes self-control, fear disappears, and he is courageous. Thus, despite all that aplomb and exertion, the king of Turan is passive, not active. His courage is audacity.

If in epic the enemy must ultimately be destroyed, then the chief enemy's courage and fortitude must be such that he is necessarily unable to achieve complete victories. For such inability and defeat to be consonant with the cosmic order and the will of God,[11] which is Afrasiyab's ultimate destruction, his character forms relative to his "purpose" on earth.

In the matter of governance, too, it is fear that guides Afrasiyab's behavior. Greed consistently drives him toward the valley of fear.

---

11. "Such did God on high ordain / That the tyrant king be slain" (M5: 251).

Siavash asks Afrasiyab to grant him safe passage through Turan. Piran advises the king: 'Do something so he does not pass through but stays.' The king hesitates: 'Once a lion cub can strike, it will crush its keeper' (M3: 73). But in the end, he relents. Grim thoughts fade but they do not die. Siavash stays in Turan, grows to be everyone's favorite, and life is agreeable. Piran arranges for him to marry Afrasiyab's daughter. But despite such a joyous spring of good fortune, Afrasiyab tells him, 'I told you before and you disagreed that a lion cub will one day be his keeper's nemesis. Furthermore, I have heard that the child of Siavash and Farangis will conquer the world and attack Turan and topple me.'

> *Whyever tend a tree and act as its sitter,*
> *When its fruit is acrid, and its leaf is bitter?*
>
> (M3: 97)

Even at his most serene, fear does not let him be—fear of the country's ruin and the loss of crown and kingdom.

And Garsivaz will soon press upon that tender spot. The dream that had made Afrasiyab lose consciousness—the image of the country in ruin and himself, the captive king, cut in two—had never abandoned him. That dream itself is the troubled vision of a mortified man who would not have had such a dream had his wakefulness not been mortifying. That fear is the undoing of the king of Turan.

He wants the two countries to be friendly, and to save Siavash and to instill peace and prosperity. But in Afrasiyab this bias for benevolence is contingent on the security of his realm and rule. Benevolence is not the essence of his existence; it lies in the expediency of his existence.

Siavash knew in his heart that leaving for Turan meant falling into the arms of death. But because honoring his oath left him no other choice, he took his chances and left. Once the spiteful Garsivaz turned against Siavash, he determined to ruin him by whatever means. At first, he begrudged Siavash for defeating him in battle (M3: 146). Then the fear of a foreign king ruling over Turanians and making him lose everything (M3: 119, 124) justified and sanctioned that rancor and took possession of his entire being such that Siavash's death became his motive to live, to the point where he dissuaded Afrasiyab from returning the prince to Iran though that would have quashed the source of Garsivaz' fear. Now, it is hatred and rancor that rule supreme, not fear. Garsivaz no longer ponders a sound solution and a happy ending.

Good and evil are intrinsic to Siavash and Garsivaz respectively. Each chases their own "aspiration," which in one is alignment with God and the world, and in the other the annihilation of a rival who will inevitably rise like the sun, effacing his shadow. These two men are not driven by profit and loss. Their actions are a function of their nature.

Afrasiyab, however, is a man of profit and loss. This "thoughtful" king who knows no good or evil outside of the closed circuit of his self-interest continually considers the interests of his country and kingship and validates only such good and evil as may prove useful to him. As if he is neither king nor hero but a dealer who guards his throne so he may not lose his balance at a mere jab. He lacks the temerity to state, "I am not drab dirt that a gust may blow away."[12]

Afrasiyab passes his days in fear. The king is scared and suspicious, and readily assumes others to be enemies. That is why Garsivaz' murmurings affect him. Until Piran is in charge, life is to Afrasiyab's liking and he is as he wishes to be. But once Garsivaz' breath blows on him, that dormant fear awakens, his mind scatters and that calculating man gains only losses.

There is always a chance for such a canny man to fall into the trap of one "cannier" and, with his wits in dread, become entangled in the warp and weft of another's fabrication. The thoughts and sentiments of such a person are prone to corruption. Rostam says this of Garsivaz and Goruy:

---

12. Forouzanfar, ed., *Dīvān-e Shams*, vol. 2, 1376. [*Man khāk-e tīreh nīstam tā bād bar bādam dahad.*—Trans.]

Upon Siavash damnation they brought.
One man the key to the evil heart sought,
The other man Afrasiyab's mind distilled,
And draining life, blood as water spilled.

(M4: 215)

That "well-wishing leader" becomes what he never wished to be, an "evil-minded, disoriented and confounded" monarch (M5: 342). Afrasiyab is not free. Fear has stifled his freedom of thought and action. The fear that lines his mind inhales every thought and exhales it tagged and tinted. The obsession with holding on to his power and freedom has rendered him powerless and ensnared him. Now he runs into dead ends and does not have the courage to risk danger.

Garsivaz returns from visiting Siavash and muddles Afrasiyab's mind with lies, saying, 'Your efforts to ally Iran and Turan is blowing in the wind. Siavash is not the same old Siavash; he receives dispatches from Iran and China and Rūm, and masses of troops are assembling around him.'

To which Afrasiyab replies: 'Who can I confide in other than you who are a knower and the keeper of my secrets? I did not battle Siavash despite my dream; nor was I disadvantaged thereby, for he befriended me and was of one mind with me. I granted him a province and riches and gave him my daughter in marriage and shed my animus toward Iran. What excuse is there that I should turn on him now after all my kindness? I shall be disgraced and exposed before all, which God and men consider abhorrent. It is best if I send him back to Iran to do as he pleases and leave us to our own devices.'

'But this is not a game,' counters Garsivaz. 'An outlander came among us and saw and learned all our secrets. If he is now freed from us, he will be the enemy's guide to our domain and people and lives.'

Garsivaz' words sound right and Afrasiyab is aghast: 'I regret my thoughts and actions for I am ruined. This is a calamity without end and remedy. It is best that I wait and see what God wills and whom the universe favors. Perchance the wheel of time shall undo this deadlock.'

Confusion and hesitation propel Afrasiyab toward futile efforts. He who wanted to wait and see what might happen leaps to another thought before he has finished the first. 'Perhaps I'd better invite him to come so I can learn his inner thoughts and wait. Should he then commit ill and receive ill in return, I shall not be blamed.'

'But Siavash and Farangis are not as you knew them,' exhorts Garsivaz. 'They now think nothing of you. Should he march up with armed troops your men will join him. Show me troops that on sighting that king would remain under your command?!'

> *Oppressed by that reckoning, Afrasiyab*
> *Agonized and fretted under its weight.*
>
> (M3: 128)

Afrasiyab thus remains trapped and sees no other option but to wait. Time passes, Garsivaz' poison drips into Afrasiyab's heart drop by drop and hatred sinks in and settles there to the point where the king devises a scheme to draw Siavash to the slaughterhouse (M3: 129). But in killing Siavash, he is at a dead end again: killing will unleash Iranian vengeance, while not killing him will unseat the Turanian king.

> *To set him free is worse than slaying,*
> *To slay him will wreak havoc on me.*
>
> (M3: 149)

Afrasiyab "squirms in Siavash's blood" (M3: 149) and does not know what to do with him. In the end, he caves in and assuages his shamed conscience by resorting to the astrologers' pronouncements. They had said Afrasiyab was destined to be harmed by Siavash. At the critical moment when the fate of two countries, and his own, hangs in the balance, hesitant and mired in doubt until the very end, he lets events unfold and drag everyone along with them. Afrasiyab's wish and will play no part in the process of the events that lead to Siavash's death, only their absence plays a part. Finally, everything veers toward the moment of Siavash's death. To steal away from the terrifying stakes that encase him, Afrasiyab throws caution to the wind and orders his men to carry off Siavash and kill him.

Siavash's existence becomes an incurable pain for Afrasiyab but rather than seek a remedy, he, as always, runs from the pain. In this instance, too, he essentially behaves as he would on the battlefield: let us survive today and see "what game the world shall play" tomorrow.

But the world's game is such that

> To spill Kian blood should anyone crave,
> The world will fashion him only a grave.
>
> (M5: 66)

> Should a king in tyranny plant a tree,
> His crown and country will be doomed.
>
> (M5: 90)

He who kills Siavash has killed himself. A human being's body is a sacred cloak for their spirit; violating it is to attack God and His creed. If good is to ultimately vanquish evil, then such a violation will not go unpunished. That is what Farangis tells her father when imploring him to forgo killing Siavash.

> Your very own body is what you will harm
> As you remember words I raised in alarm.
>
> (M3: 150)

Afrasiyab remembers those words when his life is about to end, telling his captor:

Forgive me for I am helpless and naught,
Upon myself this affliction I've brought.

(M5: 36)

Whoever kills Siavash has given refuge to a parasite that muliplies and spreads inside him; he has spawned his own death. Even before killing Siavash, Afrasiyab is anxious about its outcome, warning the executioners, 'Do not let Siavash's blood spill on the earth lest a plant sprout from it.' He tries to elude retribution for the sin but in vain, for from the first time he saw Siavash and heard him speak, he bears responsibility for his death and is a "fratricidal and foul-bodied king-slayer" (M5: 342).

Yet this same man puts his own life on the line for a brother's love. The sorcerer Afrasiyab flees and plunges into Lake Chīchast and is out of reach. To enjoin him to emerge from the depths, they torture his brother Garsivaz on the shore. The tormented brother's cries pull him to the surface and cause the death of this fratricidal brother-lover. He had slain one brother who was a friend to his enemies, but now they are slaying a brother who is his friend. He had once told Piran:

If one's heart by a brother is broken,
Balms and cures are merely a token.

(M5: 166)

Garsivaz who had muddled Afrasiyab's mind and robbed him of wisdom and bloodied his hands also caused his death. In the end, Afrasiyab violated not only his own body but the whole earth.

With Afrasiyab perched on the throne,
The pith of the world to ruin is prone.

(M5: 266)

But the world is not ruined by Afrasiyab alone. The calamity started with Kāvus' kingship. When he asked Siavash to break the oath with Afrasiyab, Rostam told him:

> The thought that the king weighs in here
> Will cloud his luster and cost him dear.

(M3: 63)

And Afrasiyab's own luster was already clouded when Siavash left Iran to fight him so as to escape "Sudabeh's and his father's babble" (M3: 40), and what followed, followed. Even though Kāvus knows the truth, he cannot act on it and cannot keep his house in order. When he learns of his wife's abuse of Siavash, he resolves to kill her instantly. Strange, how this easily riled, assertive man pauses instead to reflect on the brutality of the king of Hāmāvaran, on his own captivity, on Sudabeh tending to him during that time, and on their children's misery should she be killed. He is not in a rush, for he is in love. He cannot bring himself to kill the beloved and forgives her every sin (M3: 28). The poet's words notwithstanding, Kāvus' hesitation cannot be explained by his recollections of the king of Hāmāvaran or Sudabeh's past kindness or concerns about their children. With Rostam and Gudarz and the Iranian warriors at hand, who is the king of Hāmāvaran to have held back Kāvus—who pranced on Mazandaran with such audacity? When they later kill Sudabeh, the king does not move a muscle; how could her past kindness have stopped him from acting? Nor, when angered, could he be tempered by concerns for children.

No, Kāvus is enamored of and afflicted by Sudabeh and besotted by her. How could he kill her?! Although he knows Sudabeh should be killed, he convinces himself that she should not. Perhaps he does not know what to convince himself of and those recollections are mere excuses for the only way he can behave.

Faced with Sudabeh's ruse and despairing of himself, he turns to the heavens in whose turning lies the secret of all secrets. First, he tells the astrologers about the kindnesses Sudabeh had shown him in Hāmāvaran, then he asks them to unearth the truth about her and tell him. The verdict stigmatizes her (M3: 30). But Sudabeh says: 'It is out of fear of Rostam that the astrologers have brought a verdict in favor of Siavash' as she weeps.

> *The leader of men, his grief could not hide,*
> *And wept along with her, close by her side.*
>
> (M3: 32)

That ruinous internecine love blighted Kāvus in ways that no shackles or enemy prison had done. Such boasts, and now such bitter tears! Kāvus cannot bear the burden of Sudabeh's transgression. He agonizes that the light of his life may darken. Love for Sudabeh is the only grace in the life of this insanely enamored king.

But then if Sudabeh is innocent, Siavash must be held culpable, and giving up such a son is no child's play.

> *On either one now should this blemish cling,*
> *No man shall evermore know me as king.*
>
> (M3: 34)

The dead end and despondency of Kāvus and Afrasiyab is each deadlier than the other.

Now the perturbed king turns from the heavens to God and assembles the priests to determine the *var*, the path forward, which turns out to be "hot": One of the two has to pass through fire. If guilty, they will be scorched by the flames; if not,

> *Such is the oath of the heavens on high,*
> *Injury to innocents shall never come nigh.*
>
> (M3: 33)

Siavash consents to the ordeal and as he emerges from the fire unscathed, the father, shamed and chastened by the son's innocence is hapless, for he cannot reclaim either wife or child without losing one or the other. The lustful queen who falsely accused the prince and forced him to risk his life by entering the fire should be killed.

As Kāvus threatens Sudabeh with death, she claims hopelessly that "this is all due to Zāl's sorcery" (M3: 37). Why and how, she does not know and does not say, but it does offer the king a narrow escape route: Stall, and delay. He who always ignored counsel now asks, 'What is the punishment for this wrong?' "Death," they reply. Every escape route is now blocked, and he must kill the one that his soul aches for. "Broken-hearted and sallow," he says, 'Take her away and kill her!'

Siavash is keenly aware of his father's heart-wrenching agony.

> He thought to himself that if Sudabeh
> Should lose her life at the king's hands,
> "He will regret it in time to come,
> And see me as the cause of his agony."
>
>   (M3: 38)

So, he begs his father to free Sudabeh so Kāvus himself may be freed; and the king concurs.

> Pretexts he did seek and pled with the king
> That upon her misdeed pardon he bring.
> "I shall grant reprieve to Sudabeh," he said,
> "For I did witness the blood tears she shed."
>
>   (M3: 38)

Time passes and Kāvus is once more the same besotted man who cannot take his eyes off the beloved (M3: 38). His love is barren, though; the beloved is not herself in love. Thus, the union that is the gift of love does not form. The love is also destructive for its incubator and nourisher are corrupt; it is a precocious seed that produces a stunted tree in an infertile soil.

Kāvus' love for Sudabeh is gainless, though only from the view-point of an impartial onlooker observing the roaring flood from atop a safe harbor, for from Kāvus' position whose being is consumed by a burning desire, what is gain, and what loss?

That love is thoughtless by nature; it does not discriminate between good and evil and is unwise in its essence. If "justice" lies in being mindful of and observing the law of the universe, then justice is contingent on the wisdom of the knowing actor. The unwise inevitably turn unjust. That is why Kāvus' love for Sudabeh is the fount of injustice. A king being foremost and first among men, his folly is the fount of the grossest injustice. Kāvus and Afrasiyab's indiscrimination in the case of Sudabeh and Garsivaz seeded the destruction of the world and humankind, saving neither the unjust nor those on whose behalf injustice was committed.

Wisdom is God's weapon and a virtue that emanates from his garment—from God's essence and ipseity and ammunition.[13] Folly is ungodly and Ahrimanic; like Kāvus, every unwise human has a hand in the destruction of the world.

Kāvus loves blindly. In the worldview of epic where free will and its enactment—the hero's quest and exploits—are woven into its fabric, folly, failing to distinguish between good and evil, corrupts free will. An injudicious hero pursues a quest that lies outside of their "self-purpose"; their will conflicts with the universe, and when such conflicted will is enacted, it carries the germ of corruption within. The universe subdues human beings unless they are aligned with it. Kāvus and Afrasiyab are not; their actions run counter to "self-purpose" and the world.

Both are unjust before God and the order of creation. Afrasiyab takes refuge in an iron fortress underground so death cannot reach him,[14] and Kāvus attempts to rule the heavens. The aspirations and

---

13. Zaehner, *Zurvan*, 120, 132, 377.

14. *Aogemadaēčā* 60–61, cited in Pourdavoud, trans., *Yašthā*, vol. 2, 211–12.

actions of both are at odds with the structure and organization of the world and disrupt the earth's order. That is injustice.

Centuries-old Iranian myths acquired their "final" form in conservative Sasanian society, where, influenced by the orthodox editors—the *mobeds*—who were intolerant of change and novelty, every heterodoxy and innovation was labeled Ahrimanic. Kāvus and Afrasiyab's rebellions were treated in the same way: the demon of greed was said to have driven both in search of the unattainable and toward conflict with God; they had sought divine glory, eternal life, and rule over sky and earth for selfish reasons alone. No one may rise against God and the cosmos armed with such trivial motives. Their revolt is Ahrimanic and impotent and destined to fail—quite the opposite of Prometheus' rebellion that sprang from his love of humanity, or Job's blasphemy that induced by extreme faith, had other motives and consequences.

Just as defiance and dissent were a "lie" and a sin in real life, so was rebellion a heresy in the realm of the imagination. Afrasiyab and Kāvus are, *in one sense*, the Mānis and Mazdaks of the world of imagination. In that belief system, rebels are unjust; therefore, they are sinful.

In that kingship of injustice, Sudabeh and Garsivaz are the king's accomplices—especially in the death of Siavash. Kāvus asks for Sudabeh's hand in marriage from her father when leading his army to Hāmāvaran. The father who "loved his daughter dearer than life" is heartbroken. But Sudabeh assures him that today, no one is a match for Kāvus who rules supreme; one must not feel chagrined by a union with him (M2: 133). The father is attached to the daughter and the daughter is seduced by the pomp of crown and kingship. She is not in love with the king; she is in love with kingship. Greed is the seed and stuff of her desire. She is shrewd, dauntless, and ambitious from the outset, and once she falls for the king, she rejects everyone else and bonds with the lover. Her love is the sort of mindless yearning that subjugates the self to satisfy an impulse. The conflict between love and reason climaxes in that tradesperson and the epic notion of injudicious love finds its paragon in that woman.

Thus, Sudabeh carries on for years alongside a barmy old man until a prince arrives "whose beauty had no equal in the world."[15] Suddenly, lightning strikes and, her heart suffused with love for Siavash, she declares:

> Whoever lays eyes on you from far away
> Will right away keel over and favor you.

> (M3: 21)

In fact, no favoring is at work here except on the part of love having swiftly caught its prey. It is now up to love's captive to catch the beloved, for that prey is itself a formidable hunter. It is only by capturing Siavash that Sudabeh can harness her wild heart and once she has saddled the beloved and is in control, calm down. There is no surrender in this love, solely a demand to surrender. The beloved is an object to be acquired by the lover.

That love is furthermore full of sundry calculations. She asks that Siavash maintain her status even after her husband dies and proposes in return to satisfy the prince's every desire (M3: 22). She who had thought it expedient to marry Kāvus now wants to both satisfy her thirsty body and be expedient. Her love is corrupt to its core, for though apparently smitten, she is hedging her bets and preoccupied with profit and loss.

There is not a moment, not even at the height of bliss, when Sudabeh is able to subdue her ego and the fear of being exposed and finger pointed. It is out of fear that she preemptively accuses Siavash. The raison d'être of her rapacious desire is upended by Siavash's rejection; she falls apart and, in that fall, upends her position. Anger, and then a ruinous hatred, replaces passion and unrequited longing, but the character and quiddity of those yearnings remain unchanged: Sudabeh is a captive of Ahrimanic greed.

---

15. Yaqmaie, ed., *Tabari*, vol. 2, 596.

Previously, she desperately coveted both Siavash, and upon his kingship, personal "esteem." She coveted both these for herself. Now those objectives are doomed but her ego, fallen apart and rumpled, is not and must be redeemed so it may endure. Redemption lies in destroying the idol so her ego may live. Scandalizing the prince will keep the queen's reputation and present "esteem" intact. Thus, in a swift pivot, Sudabeh recovers her old self and from then on tries hard to ruin Siavash through lies and schemes, and in the end succeeds.

> *The words of a woman took Siavash's life,*
> *Lucky the woman never born of a mother.*
>
> (M3: 171)

In destroying Siavash, Garsivaz is Sudabeh's Turanian alternate and double; he is Afrasiyab's brother and was closest to the king among all others. When Siavash first went to war, it was Garsivaz who led the Turanian army, and while he was forced to flee from the Iranian prince, he praised Siavash:

> *Gallant horseman of ardent words,*
> *The realm of wisdom he overlords.*
>
> (M3: 60)

And he would go on to say that in "comportment and demeanor" he is unrivalled. Afrasiyab who was captivated by Siavash gave him his daughter in marriage and a realm to rule as king. Building cities, palaces, and gardens, Siavash became the greater lord in Garsivaz' homeland. On visiting him a while later, Garsivaz thinks to himself:

> *Should Siavash last thus, in one year*
> *He shall count none as his equal here.*
> *Kingship, crown, and throne are his,*
> *Riches, learning, and troops are his.*
>
> (M3: 119)

Garsivaz who fears being dislodged by another will do anything to protect what he has. Greed is the sovereign of his soul, otherwise he would not bloody his hands. In the poet's words,

> *If one's heart is freed of greed,*
> *Land and crown one will not heed.*

> (M3: 97)

Envy is the first child of greed. Salm and Tūr were displeased with their father's decision due to greed and became envious of their brother Iraj. Greed is what seeded sowed envy in them, which finally drove them to kill their brother (M1: 91 and 97). Envy inevitably caught up with the greedy Garsivaz as well.

A canny hatred is the blood that runs in the veins of such burgeoning envy. Thus, Garsivaz feigns friendship for Siavash and lies in ambush for him. Sharp and shrewd, he fractures the bond between Siavash and Afrasiyab. In doing that, deceit is his greatest weapon, his sole weapon.

Siavash and Afrasiyab are friends. Garsivaz breaks up that friendship. He distorts the mutual relationship that holds between the Turanian king and the Iranian prince. They misinterpret one another and though neither has reason to feel hostile, each takes the other to be his enemy. Garsivaz does not assault reality with lies but with lies subverts a friendly reality into a real enmity. He sets up the friends in a hostile situation and that situation draws them into mutual antagonism. Garsivaz drives them into a closed circle where they believe they are free actors. In the end, unawares and unwittingly, one's dagger is at the other's throat.

In the kingship of Afrasiyab and Kāvus, Sudabeh and Garsivaz are successful survivors and Siavash is a goner. That is the infernal depth of depths, the heart of the night. And the world is as Afrasiyab had once predicted:

> *The reign of injustice by the king*
> *Shall wipe all goodness off the earth.*
> *The onager won't birth foal on the plain,*

The eyas of the falcon will be born blind.
Lioness will have no milk for her cub,
Water in its spring shall turn into tar.
Right shall fade and wrong shall reign,
Scarceness shall appear near and far.

   (M3: 52)

Afrasiyab's Ahrimanic age girds Siavash's twilight and Kay Khosrow's dawn like a scopious circle. *And here we are in this night of tyranny and this ungracious darkness that has eclipsed the light of my heart and found its way into the sunshine of my day and my desire. Who is it that not walking in the land of iniquity, whose grazing ground is not the tyranny that penetrates deep and sprouts out of the earth, who is not lost in this wilderness of injustice? I sip the bitter water of the wells of lies out of fear; silence has crept into the depths that engulf my spirit. In these times that Ahriman has an inroad into everyone and everything, we are a cluster as if woven out of oppression, disarrayed: comatose, oppressed oppressors beset with greed whose mores we follow, false victors and free slaves. I walk hand in hand with people I do not love. Thus, I do not love these hands of mine. What clumsy hands! They are as if not my own. Yet they are. Something has died in the dream, it seems: a horse and a meadow, or the euphoria of galloping equinely across the endlessness of the meadow. This ailing conscience of mine, I who creep along stealthily and ruminate my morsel in secret. It is ugly, the world that robs me of my human and turns me against it. It lets my breath out in silence and does not let my spirit transcend the prison of my body. The roots of my veins are drained. Will my soul find deliverance?* Lucky the fabulists of such wishful thoughts! Indeed, Iranian myths are sunny, and in the heart of such darkness lies the fountain of life.[16]

In contrast to Indian thought—where time kills the germ of every hope in its endless repetition and only the hopeless wish to be released

---

16. I have taken the liberty to italicize the author's personal/Siavashaic reflections in this passage.—Trans.

from this eternally grinding cycle survives—in Iranian mythology, the whole ensemble of existence is engaged in ending a span of time that will reach its finale at a fixed moment. Even the actions of Ahrimanic entities and demons, unaware and unavoidably, share the same fate. In such a worldview, darkness, though it takes its time, does not last. Long-lasting Time has an end.

Farangis is now carrying the epoch-making Kay Khosrow within her. When they kill Siavash, his wife is heavy with his child.

In patriarchal societies where women are men's "farmland" and "one may plough them at will"[17]— especially in epic, which is the locus of wars and manhood—women are ranked in terms of men, the greatest of them being the most manlike.

When Kay Khosrow and Gīv reach Iran, Farangis is no longer mentioned in the story except once when she is given in marriage to Fariborz. The death of such a woman goes unrecorded; it is only when the king is taking leave of the handmaidens that, behold, we learn she has died (M5: 409).

On the other hand, Rudabeh and Tahmineh play an active role in love; they want, they declare, and they achieve what they want. When handmaidens reproach Rudabeh for loving Zāl, she yells at them in anger and demands that they facilitate her meeting with the hero. Tahmineh goes to Rostam's bed chamber, tells him what she knows about him and that she wants him, adding, "I am now yours if you want me" (M2: 175).

The behavior of these women is woven of the same cloth as the daring deeds of heroes. Both Gordāfarid and Gordiyeh don chain mail and enter the battlefield where they cannot be distinguished from men. Gordiyeh plants the tip of her spear in the ground and leaps upon the saddle in a flash, and in her capacity for wine astounds the men (M9: 188, 189). The warriors tell her:

---

17. See Quran, *Al-Baqarah* ("The Cow") 2:223.—Trans.

Mounts of metal do not rattle your stance,
In manliness you are the leader of men.

   (M9: 173)

Manliness is a virtue that noble women partake of and the person
who partakes of it, whether man or woman, is eminent. Even Katāyun
and Farangis—both feminine women in the *Shahnameh*—are not
denied the praxis of riding and raiding. One gallops from Balkh to
Sistan as a messenger to alert the king to enemy attack; the other
crosses a whole country fighting and fleeing alongside a prince and a
paladin. Manliness is the standard. "My father is the principal for my
mother is a passerby."[18]

But a mother "under whose feet lies paradise"[19] is not a "passerby";
she is the spawning source and the enduring earth from whom springs
every hero's spirit. Her reality was indeed more profound than any
conscious understanding of her, so, rising above his society's and his
own views of women, the poet creates female protagonists beyond the
"male-centric" bounds of heroic epic.

Siavash's spouse and proxy Farangis is an ideal woman. She tries in
earnest to stop her father from killing Siavash and articulates the clear
risk of doing so. Her foresight is the paradigm of ethical conduct and
pragmatism. 'Killing the person who sought refuge with you is a sin,
especially as he is a king and guiltless. The universe and the Creator
do not approve and hence will not let that pass and will kill the killer.
Just as other killers could not escape the grips of that fleeting striker,
you, too, shall be struck down. Killing is to plant the seed of hatred
and to throw Turan to the wind; it will ultimately ruin yourself. This
act is unjust and injurious.'

---

18. "*Asl-e kār pedaré, ke mādar rahgozaré*," a popular Bakhtiari maxim.—Trans.

19. A *mursal* ('unreliable') hadith popular among the Shi'a and commonly
    attributed to the Prophet Mohammad.—Trans.

Farangis' words are not some wise but hollow counsel; they are the cries of a woman that start with her own agony: "Do not abuse my body who am innocent." Killing Siavash is an assault upon the body of Farangis, the body of Afrasiyab, and the body of that mournful water, meaning the Earth (M3: 150). Farangis' grief imbues the world. Wise to the future resurrection of that abused being, she exhorts that "spilling blood is not like hunting game." Starting from her own agony she ends at a grievous world that brims with the blood and ardor of her grief.

The effect of these words on Afrasiyab is his order to kill her, which, owing to Piran's intercession, is not discharged. Loyalty to her spouse brings her to the brink of death and soon she abandons her homeland and kin. She is the only one who knows the secret to reaching Iran. She has kept Siavash's armor hidden and knows the whereabouts of Shabrang-e Behzād and how to locate him. Without that armor and that steed, it would have been impossible to flee Turan. Not only by giving birth to Kay Khosrow but by dint of knowing the mystery of the heavens, Farangis, the knower of mysteries, nurtures the destiny of the world. Gīv tells her:

> *The earth will regenerate as paradise through you,*
> *Through you the heavens will breed good and vice.*
>
> (M3: 212)

She contains the seed of paradise within her and knows how to save it from hell. Farangis is the garden of paradise in Afrasiyab's wasteland of famine.

In Iranian myth and epic, paradise is formed in hell and light grows in the heart of darkness. The world is never wholly Ahriman's.

Siavash built the paradise of Kang during Afrasiyab's rule and in the land of Turan—in that time and place.

In mythology, the cosmic and symbolic—not geographic— mountain at the center of the world is the anchor of the sky and the earth, the axis and meeting point of the world above and below, and the most befitting locus for divine epiphany and for human crossings to the supernal sphere.

Such a mountain is the highest point on earth and sometimes a passageway between heaven and hell, the source of all waters, the protector of plants, and the symbol of fertility and prosperity.[20]

According to Avestan mythology, Ahriman's attack triggered an earthquake, and pandemonium and panic engulfed the Earth. The Earth erected the mountains as a rampart and refuge against Ahriman. Harā Berezaiti (Alborz) was the first mountain to rise and extend along the eastern and western lands. The stars, moon, and sun revolved around it. At the "lofty and luminous" summit of the multi-ranged Harā Berezaiti there is neither night nor darkness, neither cold wind nor heat, no deadly diseases or impurities. *Īzad* Mehr surveys and guards the world from the crest of that mountain[21] and *īzad* Nāhīd who is as wide and plenteous as all the rivers in the world streams from its peak Hukar (Hukairya) that reaches the stars.[22] *Īzad* Hōm offers a sacrifice at the summit of Harā and prays for victory in chaining the sinful Turanian Afrasiyab.[23] The hundred-columned abode of *īzad* Sorūsh lies atop the highest peak of Alborz.[24]

The "Hymn to the Earth," *Zāmyād Yašt*, begins with praising and naming innumerable mountains, then continues in venerating the Kianid glory, *farr-e Kiāni*, and those endowed with it.[25] There is a connection

---

20. Eliade, *L'éternel retour*, 30, and idem, *Le sacré et le profane*, 34.

21. Corbin, *Corps spirituel*, 49, and see *Zāmyād Yt* 1, in Pourdavoud, trans., *Yašthā*, vol. 2, and *Rašn Yt* 25 and *Mehr Yt* 50 and 51, in idem, *Yašthā*, vol. 1.

22. Darmesteter, *Le Zend-Avesta*, vol. 2, 374, and Corbin, ibid., 50.

23. *Gēuš (Goš)/Drvāspā Yt* 17, in Pourdavoud, trans., *Yašthā*, vol. 1, 383. In Hedayat, trans., *Zand-e Vohuman Yasn*, 61, Čagād i dāidīg, the "Judgment Peak," is a Pahlavi name for the summit of Harā Berezaiti that is as high as one hundred men. One end of the Chinvat Bridge rests on it.

24. *Sorūsh Yt* 20, in Pourdavoud, trans., *Yašthā*, vol. 1, 547.

25. *Zāmyād Yt* 9–96, in Pourdavoud, trans., *Yašthā*, vol. 2, 323–51.

between the guardian of the earth and *farreh*; when that divine grace descends from the heavens to earth, it manifests upon the mountains.

In the Avesta, Siavash also builds Kangdež, an earthly paradise on the impassable distant peak of a sacred mountain[26] from where those who are fated to renovate the world may one day initiate resurrection. Beyond the China Sea and Āb Zareh that take seven months to sail across and on the farther side of an arid desert lies a mountain that rises higher than all else and touches the stars; it is as high as one and a half or two leagues, *parasangs,* and its perimeter measures a hundred leagues. Other than a single door there is no access to it; a few vigilant guards can block its path against one hundred thousand men. There are hunting grounds on the mountain and deer in the meadows, and pheasants and peacocks and partridges everywhere. On that mountain, Siavash builds a city that reaches to the station of the moon, and he erects ramparts around it two hundred cubits high and thirty-five wide made of stone, lime, alabaster, and some other unnamed substance. There is no scorching heat in that city and no chilling cold. No one is infirm. Everywhere there are creeks and streams with clear sweet water. It is perpetually springlike in the city, and "in every corner, fountains and flower gardens." In brief, "it is the garden of paradise, nothing less" (M3: 105–107 and M5: 352 and 354).

The Avestan "soaring and sacred" Kang is not meant for daily life and work in the *Shahnameh* either. Once Siavash has built it, Afrasiyab invites him to come to Turan, there to assume kingship, which he does (M3: 111). In Khotan, he builds Siavashgerd, a city like other cities, two leagues in length and breadth, with a public square and a pavilion and a palace and gardens and spacious mansions, but without any mysterious or otherworldly attributes. With scenes of royal and heroic hunting and feasting adorning the buildings, Piran extols Siavash's work when he visits. This is where Siavash will rule and where he will

---

26. In *GBd*, Kangdež lies a few *parasangs* from the sacred Farākhkart Sea, and in *Mēnōg i Xrad* 62:13–14, close to the star Satavēs/Sadvēs in the east. (See Pourdavoud, trans, *Yaštā,* vol 2, 219–20).

be killed (M3: 112–13 and 167–8). It is an earthly city that is open to other people; everyone can learn and talk about it.

But the paradise of Kang is a spiritual realm from the start, east of resurrection so that one day another sun may rise from it. A prince in peril built a stronger fort in the most outlying space, but not for himself. Astrologers had declared the founding of the city inauspicious (M3: 104) and he himself, like the prophets, was cognizant of God's intent and the fate of the world. When the work was done, he told Piran, 'My life will be short. I shall not last in this place long. The time will soon come when I am killed by Afrasiyab, and battles and bedlam shall beset the earth.'

> *I speak of God's glory and how 'twill flow,*
> *Likewise, the high heavens' secret I know.*

> (M3: 109)

Kangdež is the seat of the kingship of Pashūtan, son of Goshtāsp. In Mazdean belief, Kang continues to exist, with the immortal Pashūtan as king. According to one tradition, he will arise from it following Zoroaster's millennium.[27]

> Nēryōsang and the righteous Sorūsh will journey from the
> rightful Čagād to Kangdež that the luminous Siavash built
> and will call on him, saying, "Arise, O Pashūtan of radiant face
> and form, son of Goshtāsp, and righteous restorer of the Kian
> *farreh* creed. Arise in these hamlets in Iran that I and Ohrmazd
> created and restore the foundation of faith and godliness."[28]

---

27. Hedayat, trans., "Yādgār i Jāmāspi," 3.

28. Hedayat, trans., *Zand-e Vohuman Yasn*, 61.

Pashūtan then emerges, and with the help of the deities and one hundred and fifty followers expels the demons, Liars, and sorcerers to the infernal depths of hell.[29]

In the *Shahnameh*, there is no sign of Pashūtan or of his resurrection from Kangdež; lost is any memory of the spiritual "function" of that paradise-fort.[30] We find only a hint of it in the conflicts between Kay Khosrow and Afrasiyab where the king of Iran conquers Kangdež and decides to reside there for a year and is not keen to leave (M5: 354).

In Iranian mythology, the king of Turan has an iron fortress deep under the earth called the *Hang* of Afrasiyab that in epic survives in name only. The Afrasiyab of the *Shahnameh* has a Kangdež of his own close to Golzarriun. Built by Indian and Roman experts (M5: 297), it is of enormous height with paradisal fountains and pools, a replica of Siavash's Kang but without any spiritual form or function. It is a palace-fortress for assemblies and receptions and routs and refuge that the son of Siavash conquers using Sasanian methods for breaching forts (M5: 291, 297, 311). He writes to Kāvus:

> *Afrasiyab's Kang has at present been breached,*
> *The end of good fortune he has verily reached.*

> (M5: 323)

The Iranians' contrasting reaction to these fortresses (M5: 311, 353) illustrates their opposing nature and function, one spiritual and sacred, the other material and profane.

While in epic the spiritual "function" of Kangdež was lost to memory, Siavashgerd—absent in myth—was fashioned. From the moment Siavash's blood was spilled there and the soil would not

---

29. Ibid., 62–3, and Bahar and Gonabadi, eds., *Tārikh-e Balʿami*, 93.

30. In *GBd*, Kay Khosrow slays Afrasiyab in the third millennium, then withdraws from the world to Kangdež. (See Darmesteter, *Le Zend-Avesta*, vol. 2, 402).

absorb it, the city assumed paradise's spiritual function. Now that soil will keep Siavash's blood alive and wakeful.

> *From the blood of Siavash spilled on the soil*
> *The hero bloomed into a cloud-high tree.*
> *Every leaf on it was etched with his guise,*
> *His love whirled whiffs of musk in the air.*
> *Greening in fall as though 'twere spring,*
> *Hallowed temple for people in mourning.*
>
> (M3: 168)

Because his blood spilled on the soil, that ground is sacred, and death's ground is the nurturer of immortality. On Siavash's spot a tree sprang with multiple Siavashes.

In the *Shahnameh*, Zoroaster is depicted as a tree as well, bearing leaves and fruits of wisdom. Then there is the newly converted Goshtāsp who plants a cypress before the material–spiritual fire temple Mehr-Barzin. He erects a monument of gold, silver, and amber over it adorned with the likenesses of Jamshid and Fereidun (M6: 68, 70) and proclaims throughout the country that 'This cypress

> *Was sent me by God from yonder heavens,*
> *Saying from here you can turn heavenward.*
>
> (M6: 70)

And great men make the pilgrimage to the "Sapling of Paradise" that is the means of reaching God. Now that a tree of such a nature has sprouted in Siavashgerd, that ground is a sacred shrine.

Thus, like time, place is not only the stage but the shaper of human and world destiny and consequently the author of its own resurrection. "The elements, divinities, and stars, each have their "self-purpose" and the "function" of Ahrimanic creatures is to prevent the world from attaining Renovation."[31]

In such a system, all objects come into being for a purpose and serve either an angelic or demonic function. The raison d'être of objects lies beyond them. They are not merely things but have a transcendent essence; their reality surpasses their visible form. Nature is real, not illusory, and human beings are the worthiest of all creatures, which means other created things are also worthy. Humans and objects travel a shared path toward a desired destination.

Unlike the lyric poet, the epic poet is interested in the external world with an inner meaning—encompassing human society, social institutions, tangible and visible entities—and views protagonists in connection with it. From that point of view, for an individual to turn from a thought into an action and enact their desires, objects—natural and social—are not merely a means and a stage for exerting their will but are themselves creators of a space where thought can turn into action and will be actualized.

Although the world is made for humanity to benefit, among other things, from God's blessings, humanity has not applied all its potential mental and physical powers and talents in seeking to benefit from it. Nature is not for consumption to the utmost exploitable level but is the birthplace and nurturer of the mission-bound individual who coexists with it.

Nature and objects are sacred. Creed, *Daēna*, manifested in the waters of Lake Chīchast[32] and Ahura Mazda's "all-knowing wisdom" poured like water into Zoroaster's hands; he drank it, and became a seer of existence.[33] Like Kay Khosrow and Rostam, one may swear an oath by the sun and the day and night, by love and by the sword, by the king and by the battlefield (M4: 14; M6: 285).

---

31. Paraphrasing Molé, *Culte, mythe et cosmologie*, 426.

32. Hedayat, trans., *Zand-e Vohuman Yasn*, 55.

33. Ibid., 34.

Sacred objects play a significant role in humanity's destiny. The defeated Gudarz sends Bižan to Fariborz so that

> *The standard that Fariborz shall bear,*
> *May turn the foe's countenance purple.*[34]
>
>   (M4: 97)

And when Bižan carried the star-blazoned banner to the Turanians,

> *Hūmān declared that it is that star*
> **That is the cradle of Iran's might.**
> *Were we to capture that purple banner,*
> *The king would lose the power to fight.*
>
>   (M4: 98)

These days not only have objects lost their higher-order value and assumed different realities and meanings, even a human being, "prized" as a utility in production and consumption by the state, the economic system, laws, and other institutions—themselves born of numbers and formulas that gauge physical and mental utility—has lost their humanity and is considered an object among other objects in the social system, even though they are not an "object."

But from the vantage point of myth and epic, objects and human beings share the same essence. Objects are humanized, and objects unique to gods help contrive the destiny of the world.

---

34. A reference to *Derafsh-e Kāviāni*, "The Kianid standard"—and later the Sasanian royal flag—a purple cloth with a star (lotus) at its center originally crafted by Kaveh the blacksmith who hoisted his leather apron on a wooden spear and led an uprising against the tyrant Zahhāk. His revolt heralded the reign of Fereidun who then adorned the banner with gold and jewels and colorful tassels.—Trans.

In the cosmic battle between Hormozd and Ahriman, each dons a robe that is their essence and selfhood, their weapon, and the means by which goodness vanquishes evil.[35]

Ahura's robe is holy, luminous, and white and connected to the zodiac in the sky and to holy men on earth; wisdom is a blessing that emanates from it. Only that robe can expel Ahriman from Ahura Mazda's creation and defeat him. Ahriman's robe is grey.[36] "Ahura Mazda chooses wisdom as his weapon, and Ahriman the weapon of greed. Both choices are equally instrumental in overthrowing Ahriman."[37]

In that cosmic war, human beings also wear a robe that serves as their weapon: "The essence of humans is spiritual; the earth is like a robe that they don to fight the *Druj* with the help of God."[38]

In earthly wars, too, weapons are among the principal elements and agents of fate. The mace—the wind god Vayu's weapon—is the weapon of many protagonists in myth and epic.[39] Tahamtan's tiger skin is a garment superior to a caftan and cuirass; it does not burn in fire and does not become wet in water and, upon sporting it, Rostam takes wing, as it were[40] (M4: 200).

Some adversaries also wield effective, though demon-made, weapons. Using sorcery, Afrasiyab fashions his son's armature and helmet such that no one's weapon could crush them—unless the wielder was endowed with divine glory (M5: 267–8).

In the *Shahnameh*, no weapon is as otherworldly as Siavash's chain mail. Fire and water, spear and sword and arrows have no effect on it

---

35. *Dēnkart*, in Zaehner, *Zurvan*, 377.

36. Ibid., 120, and see 118 ff. on divine garments/weapons and their relationship to Zurvanite beliefs.

37. Ibid., 132.

38. *Dēnkart*, quoted in Duchesne-Guillemin, *La religion de l'Iran ancien*, 352.

39. Fereidun, Afrasiyab, Kay Khosrow, Kay Goshtāsp, Rostam, and Garshāsp, in *Zāmyād Yt* 92 and 93.

40. In the *Mahabharata*, Karna, the invincible hero who is the son of the sun god is born clad in armor. Dumézil, *Mythe et Epopée*, vol. 2, 128, 133.

(M5: 125; M3: 227; M4: 56, 60). When Farangis shows Gīv to Siavash's treasure chamber, he chooses that numinous armor before departing so that "he may not be daunted by the sting of arrows" (M4: 56). That is how he single-handedly overcomes a whole army and forces it to retreat as he flees Turan (M3: 214). In another battle, clad in the same armor, he takes Piran captive and trounces his troops. Siavash's chain mail is a haven; shooting arrows at it has no effect (M4: 60) and whoever dons it is rendered invincible. After suffering defeat, Piran tells Afrasiyab:

> As many drops as may fall from a cloud,
> Even more arrows showered on his head.
> Yet he rode his steed as if pacing a garden,
> Looming hermetic matching a mountain.

(M3: 225)

But in the Battle of Kāsseh-rūd,[41] the same hero without that armor fails in his efforts though backed by all the Gudarzians and is forced to flee, while his son Bīžan donning Siavash's chain mail averts the blows of a mighty rival's weapons (M4: 59, 62; M5: 125). Without that celestial armor, Gīv could not have later escorted Kay Khosrow to Iran unharmed. Once he has brought him to Iran safe and sound, the armor's mission is accomplished.

Siavash's horse, too, has a parallel mission in transporting the prince to Iran. In war, among everything else, a horse is the hero's best friend and his double. In life and death, Rostam's horse Rakhsh, the image of equine perfection, is without his rider only once. When the hero strikes at the heart of the enemy's army, he benefits from God's help and the stunts of Rakhsh who is like a mountain and the wind, deer-like, water-friendly, word-wise, and lion-hearted.

---

41. An Iran-Turan frontier river and the site of fierce battles with a deadly toll on the Iranian army.—Trans.

Choosing a horse is a rite of passage to the heroic order. It is only after searching for and finding their war-mate that Rostam or Sohrab and Kay Khosrow are, as fighting men, ready to enter the fray. Without such a mate, the hero is incomplete.

Like an individual, a living weapon might have a God-given name of its own.

In the *Shahnameh*'s opening verses, God is not only the creator of the body, mind, earth, and time, but also of *nām*, "name" or speech (M1: 12).

If our forebears believed that names were issued from above and that a spiritual connection held between a name and the named,[42] then the names of Raksh or Shabrang-e Behzad not only served to identify them among their ilk but also signaled their purposeful and self-purposed existence. In the mourning ceremonies for Sohrab and Esfandiyar, their horses' mane and tail were cut (M2: 216; M6: 313). A horse without its rider is not the "iron-hooved steed that ... standing on four legs cried out nine hundred and ninety-nine laments";[43] it is a wanting and barren quadruped.

The horse, which had played a major role in the tribal life of nomads and the livelihood of shepherds, persisted as a vital survival mechanism in times of war and peace even after they had settled on the Iranian

---

42. When Bahrām, son of Gudarz, realizes that he has lost his whip in battle, he tells his father that if the Turks were to find it, the world would darken before his eyes, and adds: 'My name is inscribed on that hide. / Should it fall into Piran's hands, / I know by the stars my luck will turn / And my name shall turn to dust' (M4: 101).

43. The lamentation of Zarēr's black horse whose rider is slain by the sorcerer Wīdrafsh (Bīdrafsh) when the Xionite Arjāsp battles Wīshtasp (Goshtāsp) for having accepted the Mazdayasna faith; Zarēr's 7-year-old son Bastwar (Bastvar/Bastūr) then joins the fray and avenges his father, in MP *Ayādgār ī Zarērān*, "Testimonial of Zarēr" (NP *Yādegār-e Zarēr*), which is the only extant epic in Pahlavi and derives from the Parthian *Gōsān* minstrel traditions.— Trans.

plateau. Illustrious figures whose compound names are formed with the word "horse" are a testament to the status of this animal in real life and in the imagination.[44]

Siavash, meaning "having black stallions," is one such case as indicated by the name of his horse, Shabrang.[45] When he races through fire, he is on that black horse, which, like its rider, emerges on the other side unscathed.

> A black Arab stallion readied to ride,
> Hooves raising dust, high as the moon.
> Siavash apace spurred the black sire,
> Tranquil at heart, raced through fire.
>
> (M3: 35–6)

Once death approached, Siavash released all his horses except Shabrang-e Behzād. He drew close and whispered a secret into his ear, then let him go (M3: 143). Behzād whiled away the time by a creek in a meadow on a high mountain awaiting Kay Khosrow (B: 721; M3: 209). When, guided by Farangis, Gīv and Kay Khosrow found him on the promised site, Gīv showed him the saddle and reins that Siavash used to place on him, but the stallion did not lift its foreleg in greeting.

---

44. Pourdavoud, trans., *Yaštā*, vol. 1, 195, and vol. 2, 266, 269; idem, trans., *Yasnā*, vol. 1, 163. In Widengren, *Les religions de l'Iran*, 151, "According to extant records, they sacrificed horses to the Sun God. In ancient times, these horses were highly celebrated . . . Cyrus the Great owned several sacred white horses . . . The close tie between the sun and the horse is again attested when electing Darius. His horse being the first to neigh at dawn, he attained kingship."

45. Pourdavoud, trans., *Yaštā*, vol. 2, 234. [*Shabrang*, "the color of night," from *shab* ("night") and *rang* ("color"). Siavash is the NP form of Av. *Siiāuuaršan*, MP *Siyāwaxš*, "Having a black stallion," from *siyāh* ("black") and *asb/(aršan)* ("horse"). The horse's moniker, Behzād, means "high born, pedigreed."—Trans.]

The saddle of Siavash the tiger eyed,
His quiver and long reins of hide.
His forelegs firmly set in the creek,
To offer a greeting, he did not seek.

(M3: 210)

Then Gīv showed him his face. Shabrang recognized him and wept (M3: 209). After that, Siavash's steed became Kay Khosrow's.

Of course, the cosmic role of horses is mediated and passive by comparison with that of humans; it is enacted through humans and because of them. Though a horse must merit its rider, it is the rider that rides it. Kay Khosrow is the raison d'être of Shabrang-e Behzād.

While Farangis and Siavash's armor and horse are helpers along Kay Khosrow's transformative journey, there is yet another being without whom Kay Khosrow's "purpose" would have been unfulfilled and his journey not traveled.

In the Avesta, Hōm, the "plant god," is Ahura Mazda's son and has a "radiant and immortal spirit." His earthly incarnation is a plant that grows on mountain tops, notably at the summit of Alborz.[46] Its juice is healing, a source of health and an averter of death; whoever carries this "bodyguard" in battle shall escape captivity by the foe.[47] The person who presses it as ordained and drinks it will be rewarded in both worlds. Vayu was the first to do so and was rewarded by siring Jamshid, "who during his kingship rendered animals and people immortal, water and plants eternally moist, and food an undiminishing nourishment."[48] Then Ābtin and Sām pressed and drank it. Their rewards were Fereidun and Garshāsp, one of whom slew Zahhāk and the other a dragon.[49] The

---

46. Bahar, "Joqrāfiyā-ye Asātiri," 37.

47. *Bahram Yt* 57.

48. Pourdavoud, trans., *Yasnā*, vol. 1, 160.

49. Ibid., 162: By the grace of Haoma, Sām had another son, called Urvāxšaya, who was a "judge and a lawgiver."

fourth virtuous man was the father of Zoroaster who then acquired such a son. Haoma appeared as a man most pleasing to the eye and told the prophet, "You drove all the demons below the earth who in former times roamed upon the earth in the guise of men."[50]

Hōm is on the one hand connected to immortality; on another, he is expressly an enemy of demons. His personal quest is to capture Afrasiyab and deliver him to Kay Khosrow.[51] His worshipers are rewarded with sons who destroy demons and despots. One of these sons, Urvāxšaya, is himself the image of justice and its execution.

In later Zoroastrian literature, that divine plant is the icon of immortality, "the White Hōm, patron of health, the pure, sprouted in the spring of Aredvisūr. Whoever drinks it shall become immortal."[52] It is Hōm who does not let the human soul perish like the body and protects it from death.

But in the *Shahnameh*, Hōm is a holy man who, aided by the divine Sorūsh (M5: 371), finds and captures Afrasiyab who was concealed and could in no way be located. The king and the warriors are also on the scene, but it is Hōm who captures the king of Turan.

Here, the divinity's heavenly nature morphs into the holiness of a man with an esoteric relationship with the world. In the passage from myth to epic, a god becomes a man but his hostility toward demons remains unchanged. It is with his help that Afrasiyab's life is extinguished.

From the point of view of weaving and concluding the story, Hōm's persona is not essential. The tale could have equally closed without him. He makes a brief appearance and then disappears; he does not play a formative and integrated role here, though it is a decisive one. He arrives as an outsider, facilitates the capture of Afrasiyab, and departs; he is a foreign element in this story. But if we insert that figure of fable into historical times while keeping his journey from myth to epic in

---

50. Ibid., 159–64.

51. Pourdavoud, trans., *Yaštā*, vol. 1, 383.

52. *GBd*, quoted in Zaehner, *Zurvan*, 215.

mind, we can grasp his reality: On this longest night of winter, Hōm is a lightning bolt that strikes and exposes Ahriman hiding in the darkness before all who seek him. Here! Grasp what you have been searching for.

In the kingship of Afrasiyab and Kāvūs, "cloud and wind and fog and sun and sky are at work"[53] in a collective quest for Renovation, which is the destiny of all destinies. In the hustle and bustle, death is unable to deter humans from fulfilling their "self-purpose," for militancy is the *faravahars'* most distinctive feature. After the human body dies, the "work" of the immortal *faravahars* continues. The spirit is continually at work from creation until Renovation.

> And the righteous whose material body dies in *druj* and doom
> shall be freed from these miseries and fly to far off Lie-lessness and
> the paradise that is the sturdiest stronghold, and fight fearlessly.
> That is how Jamshid's *faravahar* dispels plague and pestilence
> and Fereidun's *faravahar* wards off the sting of serpents, and the
> *faravahars* of other deceased persons slay numerous *druj*.[54]

That is how Siavash's *faravahar* routs Afrasiyab's tyranny.

Siavash's death does not extinguish his "self-purpose." His active and militant life begins only after death. In Afrasiyab's night, Siavash propels the era to its end through a dream. And he achieves that thanks to the aid and interpolation of *īzad* Sorūsh who is the lord of the night and of the sleep people fall into and the dreams they have.

The ever-vigilant Sorūsh is allied and linked with *īzad* Mehr, the one-thousand-eyed, one-thousand-eared sleepless watchman. The chariot of each is drawn by four shining, shadowless, golden-hooved steeds, and both reside at the summit of Mount Alborz.[55] Sorūsh is the

---

53. Saʿdi/Ganjoor, *Golestan Prelude* 11; the second hemistich reads: "So you may have bread and not eat it irreverently."—Trans.

54. *Dātestan i Dēnīg*, quoted in Molé, *Culte, mythe et cosmologie*, 107.

55. Pourdavoud, trans., *Yaštha*, vol. 1, 519.

lord of "Iran-vēj,"[56] the "guardian spirit" and patron of well-being, and after sunset, the guardian of the earth and Ahuric creatures.

As Mehr is the lord of light and the day and the guardian of covenants among the good and the evil, so Sorūsh is lord of the night and sleep and a witness and enforcer of those same covenants. The "embodiment of the sacred word,"[57] he is the first to offer sacrifice and the last judge, the guardian of souls on the first three nights after death and their guide to the place of judgment. Sorūsh is a formidable warrior, and his victorious weapon is prayer, not arms.[58]

In later Zoroastrian writings, Sorūsh is the messenger of the gods and "lord of the earth as Ohrmazd is lord of the heavens. And just as Ohrmazd is the protector of the soul, so Sorūsh is the protector of the body, and since demons and other maleficent beings are more active at night, he descends upon the earth after sundown"[59] and seeps into the lives of the good and the evil[60] by creeping into their dreams.

Kay Khosrow seeks release from this world when his time has come. He utters a solemn prayer. Five weeks later, with his eyes asleep and "his soul awake" he encounters Sorūsh who tells him to 'move thus and so toward your fate for you have released your earthly body and dwell near God' (M5: 388).

---

56. Av. *Airyanem Vaējah*, MP *Ērān-wēz/vēz*, "expanse/land of the Aryans."— Trans.

57. Av. *tanumathra*, *Tan-farman* in Pahlavi commentaries on the Avesta, is a somewhat cryptic epithet of Sorūsh (Av. *Sraoša*), meaning "wholly obedient to" or "embodying" the holy word *manthra* that is also applied to Mithra and human beings.—Trans.

58. *Sorūsh Yt*, in Pourdavoud, trans., *Yašthā*, vol. 1, 516–55; Darmesteter, *Le Zend-Avesta*, vol. 2, 402; and Dumézil, *L'idéologie tripartite*, 70–71.

59. *GBd* 26:46–8, and *Rivāyāt-e Pahlavi*, quoted in Zaehner, *Dawn and Twilight*, 95.

60. In the *Shahnameh*, he enters the dreams of Sām, who is in search of Zāl (M1: 141–2); and those of Jarireh, prior to the death of her son Forūd (M4: 62); and of Bābak, the governor of Pars (M7: 117), heralding the rise of the Sasanians.

Siavash, too, sees his final moments in a dreamscape:

Fire and water raged one on each side,
Elephants and Afrasiyab in the forefront.
  (M3: 139)

Men wielding spears stand on the shore. Flames flare up from Siavashgerd—Siavash's deathbed. Afrasiyab is in rage and Garsivaz is fanning the fire. The finale is clear. Siavash sets up his unborn son's task, then prepares to take his leave.

Afrasiyab learns of his destiny in a dream as well:

I dreamed of a desert ridden with serpents,
The air full of dust, the sky full of eagles.
The ground so parched it seemed the heavens
Had never looked down since the world began.
A wind then eddied, swarming with sand,
And brought my banner down headlong.
On every side was a stream of blood,
Upturned was my tent and camp.

"They killed multitudes," continued Afrasiyab," and took me to the son of Kāvus; when he saw me,"

He blasted a cry like thunder and roared,
At once my body he split with a sword.
  (M3: 49–50)

Thus, Sorūsh descended upon Afrasiyab as well, but like a calamity. The dream turned him delirious, feverish, trembling, and he collapsed, mindless and senseless (M3: 48). His dreamscape is a symbol of his kingship. It is all darkness and Ahrimanic serpents, and eagles—eagles (*oghāb*) used by the poet as a proxy for vultures (*karkas*) to fit the rhyme—a parched and arid soil, streams of blood, crestfallen heads and worthless bodies, isolated from kin and allies, a torment that wipes out wakefulness and wisdom (M3: 49–50).

Of course, Siavash is also distraught and shaken by the unsavory reality of death. But he starts out of sleep like "a drunken elephant." In the dream, the two sacred elements of fire and water enfold him. Afrasiyab merely blocks his path as his troops face him on the shore but do not attack. It is evident that the prince will have a supernal end and be absorbed in the two purificatory elements that bear life and death. The aura of each one's dream is consonant with the quality of their wakefulness and existence.

In wakefulness and sleep, Siavash is the image and incarnation of the divine Sorūsh. Like "Sorūsh, the pious, well-built, victorious, world-adorner, sacred, lord of truth,"[61] he is associated with *īzad* Mehr. Siavash fled Iran and went to his death to avoid being a "*druj*-Mehr," an oath breaker; he is an "embodiment of the sacred word." Sorūsh is the sovereign of Iran-vēj; Siavash is the prince of the same land with attributes that echo that deity's traits. Siavash is a "Sorūshaic" man, a victim and martyr who partakes of the idiosyncrasies of the "first to offer sacrifice" and wields his weapon, prayer, and its alternate, curse.

Thus, by abusing Siavash's body, you, Afrasiyab, aroused the ire of the deity who is the protector of the human body and became "an abuser of your own body." Know that when Siavash's sun sets and darkness permeates all, he will sweep down upon you. Because body and soul are of the same essence, the protector of that abused body is the guide of his soul as well, and will ever lead him against the king and demon that you are.

Now his dream is pervaded by Sorūsh.

> And *sorūsh* means hearing or listening. Those who hear also
> listen to the word of God . . . For Iranians as for ancient Hebrews,
> to hear/listen means obedience. Thus, *sorūsh*—the aptitude
> to hear the word of God—means accepting God's command,

---

61. *Sorūsh Yt* 1:1, quoted in Pourdavoud, trans., *Yaštā*, vol. 1, 525.

which is the prerequisite discipline for obedience. Sorūsh is also God's all-hearing ear and hears the cries of people who suffer abuse at the hands of demons—the evil-minded . . . and descends upon earth to confront and punish them. So, Sorūsh . . . is also the mediator of God's word and the punisher of abusers who do not hear and do not obey commands.[62]

He who is favored by that deity is the wakeful sleeper, the word of God and His herald among the people; he is an enemy of demons. For a divine dream—a truthful vision—is a manifestation of true wisdom. Ahura Mazda revealed "all-knowing wisdom" to Zoroaster in a dream and the prophet's heart and mind was awakened to mysteries in the dreamworld.[63]

> *Be wary thou of doubting a dream;*
> *Know that prophetic it may stream.*[64]

The night is Sorūsh's realm, and the prophecy of dreams belongs to him. On occasion, Siavash, too, as a symbol of that deity, enters dreams in a Sorūshaic mode and offers guidance prophetically. A deity and a human are allied and work alike in doing the "work" of the two worlds. When Kay Khosrow came into the world,

> *The Turanian general saw in a dream*
> *A candle lighted from the glowing sun.*
> *Siavash stood there, sword in hand,*
> *"Heed now," he said, "do not rest!*

---

62. Zaehner, *Dawn and Twilight*, 44, 95.

63. Hedayat, trans., *Zand-e Vohuman Yasn*, 29, 35. In the MP book *Ardāvirāf-nameh* (Afīfī, trans.), the holiest among holy men Ardāvirāf fell into sleep for seven days and nights. Guided by *īzad* Sorūsh and *īzad* Ātash [Fire] he beheld hell and purgatory and paradise, and on returning from his inward journey told the devout to entertain no doubts whatsoever as to the veracity and propriety of religion.

64. *The Tale of Būzarjomehr* 3, *Shahnameh*/Ganjoor: 1.—Trans.

Shake this sweet dream off your head,
Set your mind on the fate of the earth.
For this is a new day and a new way,
This is the eve of Kay Khosrow's fete."

(M3: 158)

Siavash the sun lights a candle through himself and sword in hand protects it from harm. He tells Piran—who is Kay Khosrow's defender and guardian amid the enemy—that this is not the time to rest, but to reflect on the end time. Here the ender, here the beginning of the end! A night like this when Afrasiyab's death is born of a mother is a unique day unlike other, forgettable, passing times. It bears a new creed. Because of the passerby who streams through it, this moment in time is not of a sense and essence of the passing kind. It is a tangled intersection wherein the future is already present; Afrasiyab's extinction is Kay Khosrow's dawning.

At another crucial moment, it is Sorūsh himself who appears and transfigures the spirit of the times. Afrasiyab was ravaging Iran; plants and the earth were scorched; no rain showered from the sky and there was a drought that lasted for seven years (M3: 198). It was during such times that

On a long night as Gudarz dreamed on,
A water-logged cloud rose over Iran.
Out of the raincloud Sorūsh spoke clear,
"Hear me, Gudarz," he said, "lend me your ear.
If you want to be rescued from this plight,
From this Turk dragon of ample might.
In Turan lies a babe worthy of fame,
Kay Khosrow the King, known by name.
Should ever Iran embrace his good core,
The heavens will grant him all he asks for."

(M3: 198)

The dragon's rule means drought and famine. The messenger of the gods appears in a raincloud, which signals a wet season and plenitude and brings good tidings of deliverance. The sky champions Kay Khosrow. Once Gīv brings him to Iran, famine and Afrasiyab will depart.

From here on, the saga takes a new turn: Search and rescue.

Kay Khosrow reaches Iran. During the great wars between him and Afrasiyab, the Iranians are at one time so devastated they are almost at the point of no return; the troops have been decimated at Hamāvan and the Turanians are on the cusp of victory. The Iranians have lost all hope when the "clear-sighted" Tūs—the commander in chief—sees Siavash in a dream; there is water and a candle. In dreams, water signifies brightness, so here is light upon light. Siavash's throne rises out of the water—the eradicator of Afrasiyab's drought. Siavash approaches Tūs in that anguished state and tells him to stop grieving the dead. 'We are all wine feasters in this rose garden. Stay strong and persevere, for you shall be victorious.' The Iranians wait until Rostam arrives, then everything changes (M4: 160).

Finally, it is with Sorūsh's help that Afrasiyab meets his end. He moans in his sleep, feeling unsafe in Sorūsh's realm. Thanks to Sorūsh, Hōm hears Afrasiyab and captures him (M5: 371, 376).

So, at every critical point of Afrasiyab's journey, the Sorūshaic Siavash or the Siavash-like Sorūsh is present and drives his life until his death. Much harm befalls the Turanians from the harmless head of Siavash (M5: 269). Siavash's wakefulness is in sleeping. Death brings his body to life. He assembles the tools for his son's escape while alive, and in death paves his path to escape until Kay Khosrow reaches the Iranian frontier.

If fleeing to Turan was night, reaching Iran is dawn. At this halfway point, the star of one individual's fortune begins to dip and that of another to rise. Piran knows that if Kay Khosrow reaches Iran, the land and life of Turan will know no peace (M3: 216). In Afrasiyab's words:

> *Once Gīv and Kay Khosrow cross the Oxus River,*
> *All of our labors will be blowing in the wind.*
>
> (M3: 226)

DAWN

Here is dawn and here the germination of *parsiavashān*.[1] Kay Khosrow is a young lad, a shepherd. Afrasiyab who lives in dread of the vengeance for Siavash tells Piran, 'Bring the boy over here.'

Piran, who fears for Kay Khosrow's life, teaches him how to speak to Afrasiyab to save his skin:

> *"Erase your mind," he said, "clear it of reason.*
> *If he talks of war, talk of feasting season.*
> *Pretend you're a stranger, act unawares,*
> *Only say words that a madman dares.*
> *Should you circumvent all reason this way,*
> *He might let you live yet one more day."*
> *The lad was brought close to the mighty king,*
> *As Piran the general had been guided to bring.*
> *To Afrasiyab he crept up, and stood nearby,*
> *The grandsire looked rueful, a tear in his eye.*

---

1. See "Twilight," n. 61.

Gazing in earnest as he surveyed the mate,
Love filled his heart and chased away hate.
Eyeing his royal mane, his stately arms,
His stride and stature, his seemly charms.
The sire passed a while, his face in a smile,
The love in his innards his heart did beguile.
"O fledgling shepherd," he ventured to say,
"What do you know of the night and day?
What do you do as you stand by the sheep?
Of goats and ewes' count how do you keep?"
In reply he said, "I've no traps in my place,
No bow nor a string, no arrow nor chase."
He queried again about what he'd learned
Of goodness and evil, how the times turned.
In reply he said, "When a tiger pounds dirt,
The sharp-clawed men no doubt 'twill hurt."
Thrice Afrasiyab asked, and asked another,
Of Iran, of his city, of his father and mother.
In reply he said, "A lion, ferocious,
Can't heel a war dog for it's precocious."
"Would you leave here, with Iran in mind
A seat by the lord of all heroes to find?"
In reply he said, "In the meadow and hill,
A rider went past me, it's two nights still."
At that the king laughed and bloomed like a flower,
On Kay Khosrow poured words kind as rain shower.
"You have no desire to hold to account,
Never on a foe revenge will you mount."
In reply he said, "From milk no oil's got,
I desire to chase that shepherd off the lot."
The king laughed again at his words and loops,
Then turned to eye his leader of troops.

"The mind of this lad isn't set on its seat,
I ask him of head, he talks about feet.
No evil or good will from his side issue,
Men who are vengeful are not of his tissue."

    (B: 676–8)

Kay Khosrow's replies are "idiotic," just as Piran wished. But like the shaded light at the cusp of dawn, the mind's eye can detect an intelligent mind behind that idiocy.

Afrasiyab talks of sheep and goats and ewes, but the shepherd who is drawn to the beasts that roam mountains and meadows, rather than to tame animals, says there is no chase and he has no weapons—an archer's arms are idle. And when Afrasiyab asks about the good and bad of life, the "idiot" sees an evil age: a tiger tears out men's hearts and is king over them. Then the "tiger" asks of his land and lineage, and Kay Khosrow, thinking of Siavash and Kāvus—the "lord of all heroes"—says a ferocious lion is unable to maul a combative dog. And as the "war dog" wants to know whether the young man is headed for Iran and Kāvus' court, the prince offers a more cryptic answer: 'I saw a rider at night.' Who is that night rider who brings good tidings? The Siavashaic Sorūsh and Gudarz' truthful vision? The lone seeker Gīv, or Kay Khosrow who will race toward Iran night and day, riding Siavash's steed? Who, indeed, is that night rider? Afrasiyab's eyes cannot see clearly to recognize him at his side, otherwise he would not ask plainly whether he wants to know right from wrong and take revenge upon the foe; he is thinking about himself and the calamity that has not yet come but which shall. Speaking in a shepherd's idiom, the idiot savant is saying that today things are bereft of blessings (thanks to an evil king)—milk is diluted with water, as it were—and that 'I shall chase that corrupt shepherd from the lot, from where he tends the flock, from my country and my land.' The end of the exchange heralds Afrasiyab's end and the birth of a new creed.

Kay Khosrow's winsome manner and stealthy awareness beguile Afrasiyab, who is distracted by the lad's appearance, just as the poet's wit escapes our grasp. Once we catch that fugitive, we will grasp, through the witticisms of that "idiot," a different awareness of how the world operates. Every truthful poem evinces a new awareness of humanity and the world, which serves both the wise and the ignorant; the former learns, and the latter becomes more aware. The eye's field of vision expands, revealing an unfamiliar, or a familiar but wider, horizon. Increased awareness requires an understanding of history and how it changes our mental and emotional state and our understanding of the creator and the created and being and non-being and the nature of human life. Without history, humanity is rootless and uprooted; without that soil, it withers and does not thrive.

Though many have come and gone under the sun, "There is a time for everything, and a season for every activity under the heavens."[2] Everything that occurs in time has a life and a death; that is its history. As such, all realities decay and new realities are born so they may live and die gratingly.

Every myth and epic that does not die young has a history that is the story of its times; it is prone to alteration and does not stay fixed—except in the mind of someone who when thinking about a myth or epic is closed within and inflexible, dead, a lifeless thinker and a thing that has been thought without a chance to connect, meaning a void! For time flows through death, too, and does not precipitate merely one immutable grasp of it. The living in different historical periods have varying concepts of the thing that has died. That there is any understanding of it at all, though, testifies to its having had some form of life in the past. So, the living think again about a "dead" life or a "dead" that is alive.

---

2. Ecclesiastes 3:1 ff.: "a time to be born and a time to die, a time to plant and a time to uproot, a time to kill and a time to heal, a time to tear down and a time to build, a time to weep and a time to laugh, a time to mourn and a time to dance . . ."—Trans.

Sometimes, however, a concept loses its history and becomes moribund. A man who today views the Persian Quran through the eyes of Nezami-e Arūzi[3]—who was sharp-eyed—both kills the book with deadened eyes and crawls through history on dead hands that are not his. A man is someone who is a man of his times.

The writer of the Four Discourses was unaware of how we reflect on good and evil and God and the world today, as was the learned master Ferdowsi. Once someone reflects on a subject, though it may have been described by others before, it can acquire a different color and meaning and cease to be as it was.

To catch the drift of the *Shahnameh* today, a book that is a thousand years old, one must take a step back, consign it to its proper history and context, and oneself to one's personal history and times. Starting a thousand years back, informed by culture and tradition, before proceeding to oneself and the present time, the reader becomes a part of the book, absorbed into the past like a historical relic. Then, returning to the present, imbued with the poem's core concepts—which, further enriched, continue to inform our lives today—the reader is, thanks to the poem, a thousand years old and the book in turn is a thousand-year-old poem that takes on a new life and is refreshed like nature in spring. Even as the reader grasps a new meaning from the book, they also give it a new meaning. At that point, the *Shahnameh* is embedded in the reader's mind, and they can roam its hills and dales at will.

The *Shahnameh*'s concept of humanity has ancient roots. The understanding of people and of the world and myths and beliefs that had accumulated over several hundred years was reproduced as an epic by a poet *at a time when for a variety of reasons people aspired to reclaim their noble spirit*—their *āzādegi*. But the poet was not interested in relating that history. Today, we approach history from a different perspective.

---

3. Nezami-e Arūzi-e Samarqandi, twelfth-century Persian writer and poet at the Ghurid court. He extolled ancient Iranian kingship in language conducive to Islamic thought. His *Chahar Maghaleh* ("Four Discourses"), the four disciplines that merit court sponsorship, was composed around 1156.—Trans.

The heroic age of the *Shahnameh* is on the one hand the war between Iran and Turan in vengeance for the blood of Iraj and Siavash. But feuds were always motivated by varieties of social and personal issues; blood revenge may have been one of them. Indeed, in the *Shahnameh*, vengeance is merely an excuse for combat and conflict, not its true motive, which is a separate reality and discourse.

Today, humanity is conscious of its conflict with nature from where it issues and wherein it lies, and is a witness to ethnic, national, and social feuds, all of which it finds to be reflected in its own conflicted self. As such, the battle between Piran and Gudarz—which in the epic is general and generic and not particular and personal—resonates not only as a war between Turan and Iran in the past but also as a reflection of the present age and the weighty burden of the tensions and conflicts within the individual. As war has come to acquire a different meaning, peace is therefore not what it was either.

In view of the writings of those who succeeded Ferdowsi, such as Rumi, the Master of Illumination Suhravardi, Hafez . . . one can now examine the notion of time in the *Shahnameh*, and the life and death that flow through it, from a different perspective. Much of the epic has of course dated with the passage of time: where the poet wants to talk history, and in fact does, the book has more of a "historical" value and is readable as an account from the past about the past. But where the poet consciously or otherwise writes as an artist and not as a historian, his accounts of the protagonists' lives, the world that bred and nourished those life stories, and the heroes' actions in a fleeting existence still have the power to make us pause and reflect on life and death—a different type of reflection.

The above truisms are based on our understanding of reality, which is at variance with Ferdowsi's perception. But as our guide to these facts, the tome is not merely a passive and lifeless object of study but, seeping into our mind, is instrumental in reshaping our thoughts and actions. Once it influences us, we are the thing thought, and it, the object, the thinker. In so far as the poem has crept in and taken root in our thoughts, we are now one, a union of the thinker and the thing thought. As such, a writing from that age, like an individual in this age, is current and *indirectly* lives in the present.

Ferdowsi has his sight on the heart and his hand on the pulse of this life, though he may not know about the nature of blood circulation. People have always been aware of their heartbeat but have discovered blood circulation only in recent times. That is the domain of science. The poet consciously and unconsciously observes the general facts of human nature or else expresses what he believes to be factual from a general point of view. And that general point of view is itself a fact; the poet is not concerned with psychology and the mechanics of the human mind.

Ptolemy told us once how the stars revolve around the Earth and another time Copernicus made us aware of different facts about planetary revolutions. Regardless of Ptolemy and Copernicus, people have always observed this "soaring, simple, and stippled ceiling"[4] and turned their thoughts from the revolving planets to the wheel of life, and likely felt much closer to and in unison with the universe in antiquity than they do today.

Not knowing about blood circulation or astronomy does not impede thinking or observation; for the most part, people think without knowing how thought works. They have ideas about good and evil and heaven and hell and being and nonbeing and everything else without knowing—or knowing "for a fact"—why and how these thoughts have occurred to them, where they originated and how and where they might lead.

A poet like Ferdowsi thinks about the world and human beings and erects a "towering castle" out of the building blocks of thought and "plants tulips in a rock" (MS: 239). His protagonist confronts himself and God, and at times others and the world. The story places him in that spot and as it unfolds concretizes his thoughts and actions—thoughts and actions that themselves are the building blocks of the story. The

---

4. Hafez/Ganjoor, *Qazal* #71:4: "What is this soaring, simple, stippled ceiling? / No sage in the world has solved this puzzle."—Trans.

poet's worldview runs through the entire story as through the veins of a living body and is thereby mediated to the reader. The poet relates the life of others but by the same token tells us about himself.

A poet is neither a philosopher nor a historian. He recounts neither thinking nor the history of thought. Even when Ferdowsi believes he is relating history, history is mostly a means for telling and embellishing a story. He presents the history of his own times believing he is retelling the history of the past. He regularly reminds us that he has not omitted any part of it[5] but he does not divulge that he has added the spirit of the times and his own—the book's lifeblood—to it, and that nothing has been left out.

That is his inverted awareness, being steeped in his own time while presenting the past. But given his social objective, Ferdowsi does not stay in the past. "A towering castle was erected over long years with much grief so that Iran may come to life by this Persian."[6] The most helpful assets for achieving that objective lie in history, the nation's raison d'être and the terrain for cultivating its life story, which he harvested to "grow a shade tree so it may serve the people"—national assets for a national goal! Thus, Ferdowsi was not recounting history. Retelling the past was a means of staying alive to live in the present and in the future. That objective kept pulling him out from under the rubble of time and it suffuses the epic with the spirit of the raconteur's times.

Such is the poet's unawares awareness of his work, which is not to be dismissed! For ours is a contemporary discourse; Ferdowsi was indeed well aware of history and his self-awareness a thousand years ago was consummate and flawless.

---

5. "Were the story to miss a single line / I'd be in mourning at this time" (M4: 86).

6. The statement paraphrases the verse "*Basi ranj bordam dar in sāl-e si / 'Ajam zendeh kardam bé in Pārsi,*" which is a late interpolation attributed to Ferdowsi and, though not original, is exceptionally popular among Iranians. It appears toward the end of the *Shahnameh*'s account of the reign of the last Sasanian king, Yazdgerd III (r. 632–651 CE), and the Arab conquest of Iran.—Trans.

There is a consistent order to Ferdowsi's thinking that is the product of his intertwined thoughts and their guide, like stars whose positions relative to one another form astral spheres where they are no longer stars but constellations with their own shape and position in space, observing which one can ascertain the position of the Earth in time and space and in relation to other orbs. Similarly, the harmony and unity across the spectrum of thoughts in the *Shahnameh* can be detected in the poet's consistent vision—with occasional inescapable inconsistencies.

To him, an orderly world and a mindful humanity presume a creator that is the First Intellect, a pure mind, wise, and just.[7] Yet the world is replete with inanity and injustice.[8] So, what is to be done? The poet cannot attach injustice to God and cannot say humans deserve the injustices they suffer the way prophets can. He therefore looks for an inane tyrant beyond God and humankind—the world, the age, the firmament, the heavenly sphere, "that drunken tumbler who plays his hand seventy different ways."[9] He thus separates the Creator from the wheel of time (M3: 151). Then again, is it not He who created all this? The poet's harmonious and ordered vision becomes stuck in its inconsistencies.

> *I cannot unravel the heavenly sphere,*
> *Nor the workings of the God of the stars.*
>
> (M4: 240)

---

7. Though one person's lot may be kingship and greatness and another's "misfortune, frailties, sorrow, pain, and hardship," there is no injustice: "In the bright sun and the dark earth / All I see is God's justice" (M4: 88).

8. "Someone raised in plenitude / In time may suffer destitute. / A sudden attack may ruin his joy, / Bring him anguish and torment. / Coming from naught to naught we go. / Equity we seek, iniquity we find" (M5: 200). "If death is justice, what is injustice? / What's all the clamor concerning justice?" (M2: 169).

9. Citing *Borzu-nāmeh*/Ganjoor 15:197—a late eighteenth-century epic in the style of the *Shahnameh* by Ata'ie Rāzi (Nākūk) about the conflict between Rostam and Sohrab's son Borzu and their mutual recognition and reconciliation at the eleventh hour.—Trans.

"All our knowledge is for naught"; the world is full of wonders, and no one knows its secrets (M4: 301–2).

That means one should avoid questioning and judgment, advice Ferdowsi himself cannot follow. Of course, this questioner with no answers thinks about his own work and judges it. He is in search of the truth of myths and legends and grasps their hypertime truths. He is bewildered by the form and framework of such tales and does not know why they have taken shape that way but says that, where they do not make sense, they subsume mystery and symbolism; one must crack open the shell to discover their truth and significance. In the introduction to the epic, he says:

> Don't think of this as if a fable and tale,
> Don't think it holds mere fibs in its trail.
> Whatever it ferries that baffles the mind,
> A mystery it holds and a meaning to find.
>
>   (M1: 21)

At times, he elucidates that "mystery and meaning," as when Kāvus and Kay Khosrow stand before "the brazier of fire" (*mehrāb*) at the Āzar-Goshasp temple and, overcome with tears, importune God to reveal Afrasiyab's whereabouts to them:

> They stood before God seven days long,
> Their eyes in worship swelled with tears.
> Do not think of them as worshiping fire,
> Fire was the altar in the bygone years.
>
>   (M5: 365)

And at times, as in the story of Kāvus' eagles rising to the sky, he merely hints at the "secret" and passes on.

This story as known, in whatever guise,
None know its secret, but the most wise.

   (M2: 153)

And with reasoned insight, he tries to unravel the secret and the mystery.

The god of the Avesta is not a god of power, or of love, as in the Torah or the Bible; it is a warrior god of goodness. Humanity's essence is godly, so it is good by nature and has been born to eradicate evil. Its earthly mission is ethical, as is Iranian mythology and epic. The territorial war between Iran and Turan is also an ethical war between good and evil. The heroes' attributes and fate are not dissociated from ethics. By the same token, a tyrant is never safe:

Should you ever thirst for blood,
And dip the dagger in that flood,
For your blood, the times will thirst,
Hairs like knives will stab your chest.

   (M2: 237)

Ferdowsi has an ethical view of life. He holds that when you quash an ethical principle, you will have quashed yourself, for then not only another strongman but a stronger and more potent force—vengeful times—will thirst for your blood. The poet's "aesthetics" are based on that ethical vision.

That is not to say that the heroic portion of the *Shahnameh* is didactic poetry or "wisdom literature" like the *Golestan* and *Bustan* where the author, waxing lyrical on the "wisdom of contentment" and the "virtues of silence" or of "kindness" and "modesty" imparts practical wisdom and his own ethical values in the guise of an anecdote or a story to indoctrinate the reader. In that category, the end is preconceived and, to achieve it, a piece of prose or poetry is composed. Ethics slips into speech indirectly; the writer or poet is a preacher.

But the stories of the *Shahnameh* are about a world full of "lessons and learning, top to bottom" (MS: 202). Here, "ethics" is part of the function and germ of a world that the poet learns from as he observes it. In such a "lesson" no one assumes the mantle of a preacher; the poet and the reader are partners.

Sudabeh and Garsivaz are duly condemned, but when a Sohrab or a Siavash is killed—besides Rostam, Afrasiyab, and others—the world that kills good souls is called "mean and evil-spirited," "tyrannical and querulous." The poet is aghast and upset, and refusing to accept the injustices of the world curses it, for whether openly or silently, he is always passing judgment in his heart. He judges good and evil through the lens of ethical principles and measures everyone by the same standard, even the enemy.[10] To acknowledge an enemy's greatness is to recognize the truth, and a sign of one's own integrity. And yet, a specific principle holds when fighting such an enemy: loyalty to one's home and country, to one's king and kin.

Ethics, like water in a sponge, has saturated the poet's mind. On occasion when his personal views about certain subjects collide with them, ethics rules the development and final form of the protagonists. For example, despite the poet's own [unfavorable] perception of women, his Farangis is the paragon of human perfection and emerges from the underbrush of the story impeccable and intact, for she cradles a plethora of ethical values.

---

10. Bahar and Gonabadi, eds., *Tārīkh-e Balʿami*, 610–12: "Kay Khosrow came into the battleground . . . He saw Piran . . . lying there, dead, under Gudarz' standard. Kay Khosrow was heartbroken and recalled how he [Piran] had reared him, and the goodness he had showered on him. He pulled the rein and kissed his forehead and wept, saying, 'O generous man, the high mountain that none could scale, the wieldy tree that profited all . . . I offered you my land and myself and you did not choose right; in the end you were snared by lies and fooled by Afrasiyab's ruse and in loyalty to him rose against my army and now lie dead . . . Alas, your good temper and sincere heart; alas, your honesty and trust and fealty.' And he lamented thus and wept."

Of course, epic poetry is not a manual on heroic morality and conduct as found in wisdom literature, which is why one should not look for the *Shahnameh*'s perfect man in such writings. For in the *Shahnameh* the perfect man must be endowed with something superior to heroism and its ethics: the divine glory of Siavash and Kay Khosrow. Although these two are not the most heroic men in the book, in the poet's mind they are the greatest and, in a sense, "most beautiful" of heroes. There are several other stars in addition to these two divinely blessed figures, Sohrab and Bižan among them. They do not have a divine mission, nor are they depicted as perfect men, but their nature and conduct epitomize pure heroic beauty; they are the immortals of this short-lived life, the "perfect" in this imperfect existence, and the free in this mandated enslavement.

Compared to Siavash, who is heavenly even on earth, Sohrab is earthly even in the heavens and falls owing to the flight of his aspirational will.

The mixing of Parthian "heroic–historical" figures and legends with Sasanian "religio-philosophical" concepts in the cauldron of earlier myths might have contributed to the formation and development of these two types of "earthly–heavenly" individuals, ultimately unifying in Kay Khosrow, who is the unqualified ideal.

Iranian and other nomadic tribes of Central Asia had migrated to the Iranian plateau since prehistoric times and continued to do so even after the *Shahnameh*'s completion in 1010 CE. The settled people's resistance to the invaders provided the ingredients for tales of wars between Iran and Turan. Random battles aside, the heroic age of the *Shahnameh* is the account of these wars, which were instigated by the killing of Iraj and brought Kay Khosrow into the fray.

Siavash's son accomplishes his twofold mission in this and the other world through war. A large portion of the *Shahnameh*'s heroic cycle is devoted to his battles with Afrasiyab, or to battles between Iranian and Turanian heroes during his kingship. War is the only means of ending Afrasiyab's era.

Before transitioning to epic poetry, war had its own roster of gods in mythology. One such god is Vayu, who cries out:

> My name is He who Roars; my name is He who
> Rushes Forth, He who Rushes Back, He who Sets
> on Fire, He who Shatters, and Scatters.
>
> My name is the Swiftest among the Swift, the Bravest
> among the Brave, the First among Strongmen, the
> Sharp Spear, the Stout Spear, the Naked Spear.
>
> My name is He who Foments, He who Propels, He who
> Flares, who Fells with a Blow and Vanquishes.
>
> My name is The Receiver; He who Receives Glory is my name.[11]

In ancient Indian and Iranian traditions,

> Vayu, "wind," was a divinity of the atmosphere and supremely
> powerful. With a major cult in eastern Iran, Vayu continued
> to be worshipped through the Parthian and Sasanian eras.
> He is a god of warriors and of the dead, and conversely,
> a god of plenitude. He is also a god of fate and rules over
> life and death ... He is the idol of the Aryan warrior.[12]

In Pahlavi texts, Vayu has two halves, the "good" Vāy and the "evil" Vāy. The Avesta adulates his good half that is the enemy of fiends.

In ancient Indo-European societies—Indian and Roman, Germanic, and Iranian—there were bands of warriors who, worshipping that divinity, constituted a distinct social stratum with rites and rituals and customs exclusive to their group. Such "fraternities of warriors"

---

11. *Rām Yt* 11: 43–48, Darmesteter, trans., *Le Zend-Avesta*, vol. 2, and Pourdavoud, trans., *Yaŝhtā*, vol. 2, 153–4. [*Yt* 15 is named after *Rāman Xvāŝtra/ Rama Hvastra*, a divinity of "peace and pasture [i.e. plenitude]," but is in fact a hymn to the (good) "Vayu of the Bounteous Spirit."—Trans.]

12. Widengren, *Les religions de l'Iran*, 24, 33.

or *Männerbünde* and their war gods and warring praxis influenced the development of myth and epic in their respective societies.[13]

Iranian "brotherhoods" in the Aryan age were composed of young (Av. *mairyō*) warriors. These "societies" extolled manifest fervor. Their ethos was licentious frenzy, hence their motto "fury" or "wrath" (Av. *aešma*, NP *xašm*), and they self-identified as "wolves"; their adversaries referred to them as "two-legged wolves" more dangerous that the quadruped kind.

In their rituals, the men eulogized dragon-slayers such as Fereidun or Garshāsp . . . Their banner was black and if not shaped like a dragon, at least displayed the likeness of one.[14]

Traces of both the *yazata* Vayu, who was forgotten in epic, and of those "frenzied" men can be found in Afrasiyab. Hoisting the same black banner,[15] he is a warrior of immense fury, swift as the wind, and a wrecking sorcerer.

Other heroes besides him also exhibit "berserk," out-of-control behavior, including Rostam, who can slaughter and scorch the land unsparingly, at times "without cause." His banner is purple and lion-shaped; it is not black but is stamped with the image of a dragon (M2: 214; M5: 314). Tahamtan replaced the mythical dragon-slayer Garshāsp in the national epic. The instant he led his army to avenge Siavash and broached Chin and Māchin, he brazenly indulged in fetes and feasts, and once he marched out his army, he pillaged and massacred from Turan to Rūm and left no land or territory intact. He beheaded young and old alike and enslaved women and children. There was death and destruction for six long years (M3: 194–5).

---

13. Widengren, *Hochgottglaube im alten Iran*, 39, citing Wikander, *Der arische Männerbund*, ch. 6.

14. Wikander, *Der arische Männerbund*, 40, 41.

15. The banner of Afrisayab's son Shideh (M5: 314) and of the Turanian heroes (M4: 255; M5: 132, 264, 314) is also black.

A hero of such stripe swamps the enemy through terror and tyranny, night raids and ruses and whatever other stealthy tricks may be handy. He is a panther, a tiger; he waits in ambush, he blindsides; he attacks from every corner; he uses his wit and agility; and when he is upon an enemy, he roars savagely and tears him to pieces.

The victorious hero lives and the defeated one dies, his name all but forgotten; once defeated, it is as if Kāmūs and Ashkbūs had never existed. The triumphant warrior is "willful"; a visceral rage and an unrestrained urge dictate his behavior toward others. He does not restrain his mania, for he is not interested in exercising self-control. Exerting power is his principle and conquest, his goal. Here, willfulness is considered the "ethic" and measure of good and evil. Whoever is more willful is more ethical. But only the victor is willful; as such, the one who achieves his goal achieves ethics, which is then voided, for the function of ethics is to justify the means to an end, and once it becomes one with the end, everything is permissible. Thus, the victorious hero is in a sense "unethical"; reason does not rule his mind and the fiery current of life storms his body.

In such a paradigm, war exhibits its terrifying and destructive features; it has a primitive and "uncivilized" character; it is the most decisive solution to rivalries among social groups or populations; the sword is the first and the last arbiter.

But war has another feature too: it brings peace and security for the inhabitants. The tool of death is itself a preserver of life.[16]

"In the Indo-Iranian world, war was by all evidence the domain of two gods, one who represented strategic thought and the other

16. Dumézil, *L'idéologie tripartite*, 62, and idem, *Les dieux souverains*, 11: In the tripartite system of Indo-European mythology, each of the three functions of sovereignty, war, and farming-labor and associated social classes have gods (heavenly, atmospheric, and earthly) with contradictory and complementary features.

vindictive rage. Based on Indian mythology, Vayu is the personification of the first protocol and Bahrām (Av. *Verethragna*) of the second."[17]

"We worship the Ahura-created Bahrām, the one who bestows virility, who brings death, who resurrects; he who bestows benevolent peace and accomplishes the good."[18] He appeared to Zoroaster "in the shape of the graceful, swift Ahura-created wind"—the good Vayu—and in other shapes, and granted him healing power and strength and divine glory—the mark of warriorhood and victory. He is "the best armed" of all *yazata*s, stronger, more triumphant, and more glorious, more benevolent, more beneficial, and the most healing. He vanquishes the enemy, humans, demons, and fiends. If people venerate and worship him as decreed, the hostile army and their chariots and hoisted banners shall not reach Iran; if they do not, "the hostile army shall suddenly be upon Iran . . . hundreds, thousands, thousands of ten thousand, ten thousand one hundred thousand."[19]

"Bahrām who shatters the enemy lines outright, who smashes the enemy lines outright, who drives the enemy lines into a stranglehold, who unhinges the enemy lines outright,"[20] this "militant victory"[21] goes to the battlefield to find out who has lied to Mehr and turned their back on the righteous Rašn—the divinity of justice. He binds the hands of oath-breakers, the *Mehr-druj*, behind their back and robs their ears of hearing"[22] and batters them with disease and death.[23]

The concepts of oaths and justice (truth) are the warp and weft of this vision of war. Mehr contributes to wars in collaboration with

---

17. Widengren, *Les religions de l'Iran*, 34.

18. Hedayat, trans., *Zand-e Vohuman Yasn*, 11:28.

19. Ibid., 48:53.

20. *Bahrām Yt* 21:62, Pourdavoud, trans., *Yaštā*, vol. 2, 132-33.

21. Dumézil, *Mitra-Varuna*, 138.

22. Mehr treats his enemies the same way (*Mehr Yt* 11:48); here as elsewhere, Bahrām and Mehr share similar traits.

23. *Bahrām Yt* 22:63.

Bahrām and like him is a patron of warriors and the agency of their victory. "For long, the military in Iran and parts of western Asia and Rome worshipped him as their personal god"[24] and propitiated him to grant them victory. The cavalry exalted that giver of strength and success; Mehr protected his devotees from enemy missiles and, assisted by the god of wind (the warring Vāy), swiftly rushed to their aid.

"Thou art both good and wicked to nations, O Mehr. Thou art both good and wicked to people, O Mehr. O Mehr, thou art the agent of peace and of war among nations."[25]

Although Mehr—the peerless warrior who drives a swift chariot, the stout-armed one of tremendous fury—takes on some of the war god's dual nature, his "function" over and above anything else is to safeguard covenants.[26]

Whoever defies Mazda and "justice," whoever lies and breaks an oath will be struck down by the arrows and the spear and the mace,

---

24. Widengren, *Les religions de l'Iran*, 253.

25. *Mehr Yt* 8:29, Pourdavoud, trans., *Yašhtā*, vol. 1, 439.

26. The Avestan *yazata* Mithra (Vedic Mitra; MP and NP Mehr) is covenant personified; the common noun *mithra/mitrá* means "pact" or "promise"; hence, Av. *mithram kar* (Vedic *mitram dhā*), "to conclude a pact," and MP *mehr-druj*, "oath-breaker." The etymology of the term is uncertain but has been suggested to derive from an Indo-European root **mei*, "exchange," or **mē*, "measure." In later Sanskrit, *mitra* means "friend," a term close to the still later New Persian *mehr*, "friendship, love." The exact relationship between "friend" and "contract" remains an open question, but I believe it may be explained by the still current Iranian institution of *mehriyeh* ("dowry") that in a marriage contract determines the amount a man owes his wife while married or upon divorce. This is based on interpreting *Mehr Yt* 29:115–16 to specify the worth of an oath, *mithra/mehr*, the cost of breaking which depends on the relationship between the two parties: "Mithra is . . . 50-fold between spouses . . . 70 between pupil and master . . . 100 between father and son." Thus, *mehriyeh* appears to be the legacy of an ancient Iranian institution that quantifies a formal pact of friendship between spouses, which explains the later development of the NP *mehr*, "love," and of the female proper name Mitra, the association with the male god Mithra having been forgotten.—Trans.

the chief weapon, of this strongest of the strong.[27] He fights against all demons and liars who defy the order that underlies the world, the "covenant" between Ahura and Ahriman.

Bahrām looks for oath-breakers and the unjust to destroy them, and Mehr pursues the unjust and the oath-breaker. In this process, the divinity of justice, Rašn, like Sorūsh, is one of Mehr's constant companions.[28] Oaths and justice are thus correlated concepts. For to uphold oaths is to preserve the law, or the order that leads the earth to its ideal end—it is justice; and oath-breaking is to disrupt the world—to lie in the broadest sense of the term—and is injustice. Thus, upholding an oath is to be just and breaking it is to be unjust. In other words, injustice is oath-breaking, and one must wage war against it.

Bahrām and Mehr are gods of such a war. This war is in essence ethical for it is conducted to keep the world harmonious and life and death orderly, as sanctioned. Siavash refused to fight "on account of the oath he had sworn," and Kay Khosrow fought on account of the oath he had sworn, for like all the good creation, he has a covenant with the world that his "self-purpose" must execute: wage a war against every oath-breaker and unjust being, fight every Afrasiyab.

By killing Iraj, Salm and Tūr rejected Fereidun's social justice[29]—the division of his realm among his three sons—disobeyed their father and shed innocent blood. They thus broke their oath with the world and disrupted its order; they committed injustice, whereby dissent and rebellion, considered a "lie" in the aristocratic worldview of Iranian mythology, gained dominance.

In Iranian thought, lying was considered the greatest sin. Nor was a worse transgression named in the Achaemenid empire. Kingship was considered a divine blessing: the king's command is by Ahura Mazda's

---

27. *Mehr Yt* 24:96, 477: "A mace with a hundred knots and spikes, golden, the most powerful and victorious weapon," and see Dumézil, *Mitra-Varuna*, 138.

28. *Mehr Yt* 25:100 and 126.

29. Dumézil, *L'idéologie tripartite*, 27.

grace and in harmony with world order, meaning with *justice and truth*; hostility towards it is injustice and a lie.

When Darius importuned Ahura Mazda to protect his land from the foe, famine, and the lie, by "lie" he meant disloyalty to the king, dissent, and rebellion.[30] In the Bīsotūn inscription, he declares: "When Cambyses[31] went to Egypt, the army revolted; then the lie gathered strength in the country, both in Pars and in other provinces."[32]

In temporal and spiritual rule, order and stability and law are truth and justice and integrity; their opposite is injustice and the lie.[33] In such a worldview, the prevailing cosmic and social order is just, and violence against the social "status quo" is tantamount to violating the order of creation.

This static and reactionary vision of history grew more humanized in epic and through a particular interpretation of ethics was synchronized with human expectations: If kings turn to wickedness, they must not be obeyed. Jamshid's sin destroyed a paradisical era; the overlord of the "status quo" betrayed his incorporeal and corporeal mission. No one harbors admiration for the kingship of Kāvus and Goshtāsp.[34]

---

30. Zaehner, *Dawn and Twilight*, 156–7; Dumézil, *L'idéologie tripartite*, 20, and idem, *Mythe et Épopée*, 617.

31. OP *Kambūjiya* succeeded his father Cyrus the Great, founder of the Achaemenid Empire (r. 550-530 BCE), and died in 522 BCE from an infected wound on returning from Egypt to deal with turmoil at home. Cambyses' younger brother Bardiya, or the magus Gaumāta, an impersonator, briefly succeeded him but was overthrown by Darius the Great (r. 522-486 BCE).—Trans.

32. Widengren, *Les religions de l'Iran*, 163.

33. Ibid., 128: In the Avesta, the personification of order is Sūšiyans, a symbolic name meaning "savior," the embodiment of *aša*, truth. In the beginning, incorporeal existence lay still. Ahriman's assault introduced movement and change into it. At the end of time, Sūšiyans will restore it to stillness.

34. In the Avesta, Goshtāsp is Zoroaster's celebrated patron. In the Sistan heroic cycle, he is a disgraceful figure who plans the death of his son Esfandiyār.—Trans.

Kingship is held to be sacred in epic as well but given the reality of foreign or deviant Iranian kings and of Ahrimanic eras, epic "history" was structured such that the actions of noble kings and heroes and their battles against the prevailing order justified the end.

The enacted will of these noble spirits demonstrated a restless thirst for life as opposed to the calm and stasis sought by the state and the authorities. Those who rose in vengeance for Iraj and Siavash ended up restoring the trampled laws of the world order. Where the status quo has the nature of Zahhāk and Afrasiyab, he who fights it is not a liar and unjust; he is Fereidun and Kay Khosrow.

Darius' admonition against the "lie" turned into a demand for justice in heroic literature; the concept of justice and injustice infused the landscape of war and God inevitably entered the fray.

Thus, in a turbulence whose end was not obvious, Kay Khosrow turned to God and pleaded with Him for victory if his war was just, and he won (M5: 293). Another time, a divine power came to the aid of his army during a night raid (M5: 332). Rostam clasped his girdle "by the power of God" (M4: 202) and rode onto the battlefield and after defeating the enemy said his victory was a boon from God. And Bižan facing a mightier but unjust rival implored God to reinforce his strength and body and slew his opponent (M5: 130). In the Battle of the Twelve Rokh[35] when the Turanians face their rivals,

> *All their strength and arms were drained;*
> *God their stake in power had strained.*
> *There they tangled, wretchedly trapped,*
> *For all the blood they'd unjustly sapped.*

(M5: 190)

---

35. *Rokh*, "face" in NP, refers to the twelve warriors who fought each other in single combat.

The unjust also know that

> *Whoever unjust shall a combat seek*
> *Will end enfeebled and bodily meek.*
>
>   (M4: 290)

Piran addresses Khaqan in remorse, saying, "From injustice springs justice" (M4: 227). In the poet's view, when injustice obtains, God destroys one thousand men at the hands of one (M3: 175). On delegating the army command to Gudarz before a great battle, Kay Khosrow says: "Mind you do not act unjustly" and not be wreckful and not kill those who stay out of the battle; that is not pleasing to God (M5: 93).

But Kay Khosrow's war against Afrasiyab has a more palpable motive and does not stop at the remote realm of religion and ethics. For Kay Khosrow is Siavash's son. A doctrinal and general matter also becomes deeply emotional and personal and comes home, for that "personal emotion" is itself a general doctrine. Here, the father–son relationship is not only an emotional but also a religious matter. A son is considered the legacy and guarantor of the continuity of the father's name, where a name does not merely name a man but is a symbol of his roots and identity. As such, a son perpetuates, *in this world,* the temporal existence of the father who gave him life, endowing him with a kind of virtual existence after death. But only a son can perpetuate a father's name; it was common to say, "So and so, the son of so and so." Therefore, having a son is a sacred blessing; the father not only endures longer but is a fruit-bearing tree. He is blessed so he may not be fruitless and not waste the godly and natural favors he enjoys and be able to return them manifold to the world. So, he who is without a son is barren and more impermanent than other mortals.

Meanwhile, the father passes procreation on to his son, or opens him to the world of possibilities, and will in time relegate his sacerdotal or military position to him, or his land or profession and trade—his social station. A son is the father's heir.

This type of relationship applies to societies with classes and guilds and stable and established social and family relations. It presumes the heavens to be as orderly as the earth, with productive gods who grant believers plenitude and blessings, herds of cattle and horses and strong, fighting sons.

Humans protect their lives and livelihood more readily with the help of their relatives and associates than delimited social institutions such as the state, laws . . . that are not operative in every corner of society. Given that, family and tribal relations are guarantors of life and its unconditional validity. God is the Lord of existence, and a father is the "lord" of the family. He who slays this "lord" has injured that unassailable Lord. It falls upon the son, followed by the family, clan, tribe, and all other relations, to seek justice for the slain and the injured.

> *A father slain leaves vengeance behind,*
> *A son will act with that burden in mind.*
>
> (M5: 302)

The Turanians likewise begrudge life until their dead are avenged. To ignore blood that has been shed is a sin that God will not forgive (M5: 160, 250, 156).

Under the Sasanians, the socio-historical causes of tribal wars were represented in epic literature as if motivated by religion and ethics. Having forgotten the "actual" events of history, a reconstructed narrative framed by a new ideology settled in memory. Epic battles were not elucidated as a religious and ethical conflicts per se, however, and were not said to be driven by the nitty gritty of creed and morality. Iranians fight the invading Turanians to avenge their dead; they fight for the land they inhabit so they may remain alive and endure. Rostam is anguished that should Afrasiyab win nothing will remain of Iran:

> *Neither farmer nor worker shall hereto abide,*
> *Neither country, land, nor the countryside.*
>
> (M4: 291)

Therefore, the only option is to risk it all.

> *For land and country and all that is near,*
> *Wife and child and the young we hold dear.*
> *We must let everyone be brought down low;*
> *Better than to give up the land to the foe.*
>
>   (M4: 278)

We should note that an ethic also holds here: Embracing death for the sake of something other than oneself. But this is not an abstract morality, nor is it born of doctrine and creed; it is emotional and practical. The Turanians started the war, just as Ahriman initiated the cosmic assault, and by protecting the earthly Iran—this world and material life—the Iranian heroes are saving their other world as well. In this great battlefield of light and darkness that is the world, they are performing their martial "purpose," but their purpose is necessarily also "ethical."

By grace of his divine glory, Siavash is an axis between heaven and earth who paves the way for humanity to reach God. Thus, not only Kay Khosrow but all noble beings are his relatives and kin. "Siavash is my refuge and my conscience" (M3: 42), whoever sheds his blood has slain people's souls and desiccated God's crystalline spring.

The kings and heroes who now rise to avenge Siavash execute "justice" in the world even as they protect the land from the enemy, drought, and the lie. Everyone is mourning Siavash and the quest to avenge him is the inexorable motive for war and the warriors' raison d'être. That is why when news of his death arrives, the enraged Rostam kills Sudabeh degradingly, then declares to the heroes:

> *"By God I swear that, until my last breath,*
> *My quest is vengeance for Siavash's death.*
> *Solely on battle shall I center my sight,*
> *In feasts and wining I shall no more delight."*

The heroes assembled before his presence,
Rostam's words hearing, grasping its essence.
Together in chorus they cried and roared,
As if the blood of the boards had boiled.
Vengeance for Siavash pervaded the land,
As if seawater boiling had swept over sand.
The star-blazoned banner was hoisted high,
In blood to be drenched, come the war nigh.
Iranian heroes dressed in war manner,
And leading the army, the Kāvian banner.

> (M3: 173)

The heroes, the Gudarzians and Rostam, not the king, launch the vengeance for Siavash. Rostam sits in mourning in lieu of Siavash's father, and "all of Ērānshahr" turns to him (M3: 172). It is under his military command and leadership that they will attack Turan where Rostam will rule as king. At the time, Kay Khosrow is a captive child and Kāvus is a king preoccupied with himself. Rostam who has not previously played a significant role in the story, now

To battle he rushes like a father in pain,
The bounty of warlords he turns into bane.

> (M4: 219)

Upon Siavash's death, he who had nurtured him body and soul acted like a father and rose to avenge his "son." At a time when everyone hankered for truce with the murderers, only he and Kay Khosrow dissented (M5: 266).

The epic Rostam is king over the country of Nimrūz, as decreed by Kay Qobād and Kay Khosrow (M2: 72; M5: 403). The historical Rostam was a notable figure in the Parthian era. "This Rostam was powerful and there was none as powerful as he in the world, or more gallant, and he was the lord of Sakastān. The cities were prosperous, and overlordship of that region was his on behalf of the kings of 'Ajam."[36]

The Ashkāniān (Arsacid) dynasty, established by Parthian nomads who had populated the eastern Iranian steppes retained the ways and customs of tribal life in their political organization. Regional kingship was held by members of the Parthian nobility. The kings' level of authority and privilege was somewhat hedged by two groups. The first included members of the most prominent Parthian families plus select members of six other important clans and played a key role in state affairs, the most prominent among them being the houses of Suren, Qāren, and Espahbad. The second group comprised the priesthood and the Magi and was less influential than the first. Kings were evidently elected by the heads of the great clans, taking the previous king's will into account. The foundation of the feudal families' power rested on regional land ownership. Suren took ten thousand of his special forces into a battle against Crassus, then governor of Roman Syria, whom he defeated; the coronation of kings was an inherited right of his clan.

Provinces such as Pars, Ēlam, Media, Azarbaijan, Armenia, and Sistan were ruled either by Parthian princes or other autonomous kings, some of whom exerted wide political power, minted coins in their own name, owned land, an army, and *their own private* standards. The King of Kings was the head and, especially in war, commander in chief of these provincial rulers who were known by Arabs as tribal lords, *mulūk ul-tawāyif.*[37]

Economic and military independence favored autocracy and willfulness. Provincial kings were not nominally equal to the King of

---

36. Bahar and Gonabadi, eds., *Tārīkh-e Bal'ami*, 596. [Note:'Ajam, Arabic "mute," meant non-Arabic speakers and foreigners in general. Arabs referred to the Persian Empire both as Bilād-e Fārs and Bilād-e 'Ajam, the latter pejoratively during the earlier Umayyad period.—Trans.]

37. See D'yakonov, *Ashkanian*, trans. Keshavarz, 60–61, and Christensen, *Iran dar Zamān-e Sasanian*, trans. Yasami, 1–10.

Kings, but they acted as such where conditions sanctioned the type of behavior and ethics commensurate with epic traditions.

The historic Gudarzians who appear as the greatest heroic clan in the *Shahnameh* are also Parthian; by royal decree, their chief is appointed king of Qom and Esfahan (M3: 231; M5: 404). Men such as Tūs and Piran who belong to earlier traditions and have now been hauled into the Parthian era also partake of the story's idiosyncrasies. Tūs is king of the country of Khorasan (M5: 405) and Piran who is foremost among the Vīsehs, a clan that boasts heroes such as Hūmān and Lahāk and Farshidvard and Nastihan, is king of Khotan where he lives and where he moves Farangis and gives her refuge. After defeating the Iranians and visiting Afrasiyab, he returns to *his own country* (M3: 154, 158; M4: 144).

In the conduct of war, family members of the great king outrank provincial kings. Thus, in marching on Turan, Siavash is in command of the troops, and in the Battle of Hamāvan the Iranians are led by a prince, Fariborz, though they owe their victory to Rostam (M4: 178).

Tūs contests Kay Khosrow's kingship; he causes Forūd's death, and his leadership brings on defeat. Kay Khosrow says of Tūs:

> No brain in his skull, in body no vein,
> Tūs and a dog in my eyes are the same.
>
> (M4: 117)

By contrast, Gudarz and Gīv were deferential to Kay Khosrow and his kingship from the start; they were wise to the task and victorious warriors, and the king returned their friendship in gratitude. But on the battlefield, these notable men were under the command of Tūs who once commanded Rostam as well (M4: 195), for Tūs has the golden shoes and the bugle and the Kāvian banner; he is a descendant of Nozar and Manuchehr and Fereidun (M3: 236) and thus of the Kianid race, complete with dynastic privileges.

Kay Khosrow calls him "King of the Nozars" and conveys salutations to the troops on behalf of him and Kāvus (M5: 145). It is clear that his troops are on the battlefield alongside Kāvus' army. If on occasion a prince comes under the command of a hero, it is due to a special circumstance as, for instance, a battle that also calls for avenging the death of Gudarz' seventy sons (M5: 113–14).

The prominence of a clan not only points to the size of their territory, their legion of kin, and the plentitude of their herds and horses and armaments and the strength of their troops; it also underscores the self-sufficiency and autocratic power of a feudal king vis-à-vis the King of Kings. Thus, Tūs of the Nozar clan questions why, in his absence, the Gudarzian elected Kay Khosrow as king—who is related to Afrasiyab on his mother's side—instead of Fariborz, who is a son of King Kāvus.

> Without me you choose a creed and a way,
> A new lord you appoint to over all sway.
> I do not approve what from your lot hails,
> So, stop telling me of Khosrow such tales.

>   (M3: 237)

Tūs had a quarrel with Kāvus and the Gudarzians over who should be elected king, Fariborz or Kay Khosrow, and it escalated to where the choice became contingent on which candidate could breach Bahmandež.[38]

The King of Kings ranks higher than the provincial kings and heroes, but his rule is contingent on the alliance of these subordinate free agents. Assembling an army on behalf of Kay Khosrow for the war with

---

38. Bahmandež is an inaccessible, demon-infested fortress on Lake Chīchast. Fariborz fails to breach it after encircling it for a week and returns. Kay Khosrow then rides out with his army. He writes a note "in Pahlavi" and asks Gīv to shoot it at the fort, pinned on a spear. As soon as it hits the wall, there is thunder and lightning and snowfall and the walls crumble into a mass of black dust. The army pelts the demons with arrows; many of them perish while others are captured, and the sun comes up again. Kay Khosrow returns to the court and is elected king.—Trans.

Afrasiyab demonstrates how the king is king by dint of the powerful; the provincial kings are needed by his side. Letters were dispatched to all the notables and "autocrats," any chief who was "headmost in kingship." The kings of Khūzian, Kerman, Yemen, Kabul, and Sūrian, other men of royal lineage and dignitaries from various cities and countries came to Kay Khosrow's court, troops in tow (M5: 241–3). Each chief carried a standard (M5: 133, 248) signifying a level of military autonomy and clannish self-sufficiency. He who leads his own army channels his authority and freedom and can actuate his will.

Rostam's attitude toward Kāvus illustrates the autonomy of the hero who takes orders from none but himself. When news came of Siavash's death, a large army from Kashmir and Kabul assembled around Rostam. He headed for Kāvus' court and told him, 'Your temper has finally borne fruit; you are a light king and a weighty burden and an even heavier blow to us.' Then he killed Sudabeh (M3: 172).

Gudarz, too, calls Kāvus who had aspired to rule the heavens an unwise, unlearned, and irrational man who has lost both mind and heart and tells him, "You belong in an asylum not an orchard" (M2: 154).

Zāl (Dastān), upset by Kay Khosrow's decision to abdicate, addresses a man of such standing in these words:

> "If this, O King, be what you design,
> No one at your flanks will ever align.
> Regret you shall feel for what you just said;
> Repel now the demons, turn back your head.
> If you should pursue what's the fiend's line,
> The Lord will purge you of glory divine.
> Your heart full of sin, your mind full of sore,
> No one will call you a king ever more."
> The words of Dastān having come to an end,
> The gallants together their voice did lend.
> "All of us countenance what the old man said:
> The truth must never be turned on its head."

(M5: 394)

Enemy protagonists also display the same independent spirit. When Piran learns of the death of Siavash and the king's intent to kill his daughter, he journeys to Afrasiyab's court and tells him:

> How did the demon win over your heart,
> Excise all prudence from the king's mind?
> You killed Siavash, though he was blameless,
> Trampled underfoot your name and stature.
> The world lived in peace, guarded from evil;
> A sanctified order was in sight near and far.
> A guileful demon rose right out of hell,
> And nailed the heart of the king of the Turks.
> You'll regret your action at the end of the day,
> You'll writhe in pain when all's said and done.
> You assumed a posture like a man insane
> And stubbornly fostered all that is wrong.
> You shall be cursed for the rest of your days,
> And when you pass on, your lot will be hell.

(M3: 156–7)

The gallant Piran is unacquainted with the etiquette that guides slithery royals; his raw simplicity is the nakedness of the sun in a bare desert. But despite his eminence, the hero ranks below the king and can never abandon him. Loyalty is the prerequisite for being a hero.

In Indo-European tribal society, the king headed the warrior class. In time, the latter's power came to surpass that of the priesthood—itself a powerful class—and the king rose to lord it over priests as well. The military's fealty toward the king represented their conscious and unconscious fealty toward their class and societal privileges. Piran explained to Rostam:

> Deserting Afrasiyab is out of my bounds;
> There's no other place where I can find rest.

Wealth there is here and land and cattle,
I do not see how I can leave them behind.
Sons reside here and many young women,
Related each one with this or the other.

    (M4: 222)

But the hero does not fight only for his own life and riches and other miscellanies of livelihood. His lands, relatives, and wealth are not his per se; they are God's blessings. He is one of them and a part of them; if he does not fight for them, he has scoffed at divine blessings. To fight—and for everyone to be able to stand up—he must remain loyal to his king. Loyalty is a social expediency that is elevated to an ethical principle. The loyal hero dismisses personal profit and loss to the point where he risks his own life.

Pilsam is a Turanian hero and a fan of Siavash. When his efforts to rescue the prince fail, with "his cheeks blood red" and "his mind full of grief," he declares, "Hell is better than Afrasiyab's haunt," and leaves the king's court and territory. On the other hand, when Tahamtan attacks Turan, this same Pilsam is breathless; he asks for a horse and a weapon to behead Rostam and loses his own head (M3: 147, 154, 183).

A hero is his own master; he will join the king, feast, or fight, as he wishes. The alliance between the two, spoken or unspoken, is voluntary; it is a pact between free men. Unless people are against a would-be king and "refuse to join his pact," disloyalty amounts to oath-breaking. He who joins a pact must do so to perfection.[39]

Gudarz' troops tell him, 'You have sacrificed your "body and son and all"; we are with you as you are with the king' (M5: 182). Except for two or three men, the entire Gudarzian clan lose their lives in vengeance for Siavash and for the love of Kay Khosrow (M5: 417).

---

39. Hūmān spoke thus: "Whether right or wrong, / When the noble king issues an edict, / One should acquiesce obligingly / With a heart fully entrusted to him" (M4: 129).

Siavash was neither disloyal to his father nor to Afrasiyab. Piran, too, remained loyal to Afrasiyab.

If Siavash's loyalty to Afrasiyab was in synchrony with the world, Piran's loyalty to the king of the Turks was necessarily enmity with Kay Khosrow, the patron of world order. The general's loyalty to his king is disloyalty to the world, and ill-fated.

But this "religious–ethical" vision does not diminish the absolute value of loyalty. Piran's stance vis-à-vis Afrasiyab is like Gudarz' behavior toward Kay Khosrow. Both "good" and "evil" have a heroic character, for in confronting the world they enact their will in equal measure. In that struggle, he who sings to the godly tune survives, otherwise like Piran—though wise and good-hearted—he expires. Either way, he is a hero.

They kill Piran without wishing for his death. Kay Khosrow had told Tūs, 'Don't you ever kill him, for he is special to God and partial to me' (M4: 129). Though at times "his gentle heart was full of trouble and ached for a fight" and he had a "head full of doom, a heart full of hate" (M5: 99; M4: 107), Piran was not immoral or bloodthirsty; he was simply devoted to Afrasiyab and at his command (M5: 99)—thus, his fate was sealed.

Between the wise Piran and the unwise Tūs, final victory belongs to the one who acts in consonance with the world order; God helps him and endows him with his own force.

God, who is just, grants power and victory-wielding glory to everyone.

> Tahamtan told them that power and glory
> Is a favor granted us by the just God.
> Everyone here has a share of that favor,
> Leaving no reason to gripe against God.

(M4: 275)

But this "everyone" is only that select group that is privileged with power and accorded victory. The rest are extras who, armed with makeshift weaponry, follow the cavalry on foot.

There are countless references in the *Shahnameh* to large contingents of fighting armies who "raise so much dust as to eclipse the sun and darken the sky," and such. But "the extras do not count" where one man is a match for a battlefield full of men. A rank-and-file fighter is not accorded individual distinction and is never vividly painted. If he happens to be present at a spectacular event, he will repeat the hero's words, not singly but as part of a chorus, and does not share the hero's attributes. When Siavash is racing through fire,

> *A throng of people watched Kāvus in vain,*
> *Every mouth cursing and hearts full of pain.*
>
> (M3: 35)

They borrow the hero's rage, but that rage is muted and does not manifest except in cursing. When Siavash is being slain, the Turanian troops ask, "What is his crime?" and caution the king (M3: 146); counsel and watch—that's it. An ordinary person lacks a singular trait and persona, and a group is formless like smoke and dust. Their words, while true, are lifeless for they do not belong to anyone in particular. The presence of a collective that lives in the shadow of society remains colorless and nondescript.

By contrast, those who can strut about the front line are the pillars and anchors of society. Rostam is a perennial harbinger of victory. It is he who accomplishes the Seven Labors and rescues King Kāvus from the dungeon of the Mazandarani demons and Hāmāvaran. He overpowers paladins as mighty as Kāmūs and Ashkbūs, and the earth despairs at the pounding hooves of his horse. In the Battle of Hamāvan the devastated Iranian army's only hope is for Rostam to come and deliver them from their dire predicament (M4: 167). On the Turanian side, so long as Piran-e Viseh is around, Afrasiyab is safe, myriad highs and lows notwithstanding. As a country, Turan's hope is centered on this skillful warrior whose defeat would spell the end of Afrasiyab (M5: 172–4).

These men always retain their abilities; old age merely indicates added years, not decrepitude.

Time is peripheral and extrinsic to epic poetry where it is used to express an action that unfolds in it; it is not intrinsic to humans and does not propel them sequentially from childhood to youth and old age and death.

In epic, the thinking is action oriented. In such a perspective on life, a wish is actionable. Action is how a hero gives depth and form to his persona and thereby transforms the world—destroys or creates. Battle is the perfect destructive creator.

Such bona fide behavior is the spirit of the world as the epic poet envisions it, or the spirit of his vision of the world is that "active." The poet projects the passive and active nature of his vision onto natural phenomena—including the external manifestations of time—and constructs a mental image of it. For the day to begin, light *does something*, and *something is done* to darkness.

> *When the sun from its bowels drew a sword,*
> *The dark night disappeared from the world.*
>
>   (M4: 12)

The sun rises in the heavens like a golden shield, or emerges from Leo and subdues the night, or sickened by the tar-like tent tears it apart, and the cobalt night is tethered (M3: 99; M4: 118, 149, 242).

The sun is a hero, as it were, that gives life to itself in a battle at every dawn, whereby the latent light becomes the actual day.

In the *Shahnameh* when "the dark night marches an army across the sky" (M4: 61), a nocturnal behavior seethes—a night raid, a feast, love, or, as in the prelude to the story of Bižan and Manižeh, an occasion for reciting heroic exploits.

But wars and other important affairs belong to the day, which is why the book is preoccupied with daytime and speaks so often of the rising sun. If day and night are a motif for describing an action that occurs in that timeframe, then time is the cradle of action.

> *When radiant sun from the mountain rose,*
> *The day dawned bright and crowned the heights.*
> *The troops, ere scattered, converged as one,*
> *Recounting the myriad tales of their fights.*

> (M4: 112)

The day dawned so that the troops may do this and that.

Time is extrinsic to the hero's reality, too; it is not intrinsic to it. In *Yādegār-e Zarēr*,[40] Bastvar, though a child, rushes onto the battlefield and avenges his foully slain father. Siavash's sublimity and Kay Khosrow's wisdom are not "realistic" either given their age. Rostam as a child and Sohrab as a youth have superlative strength, while Esfandiyar and Afrasiyab are champions the moment they step into the tale. Nor does the passage of time affect Piran and Gudarz and the like; they bide, virile and spirited, while they live. The elderly Rostam pins a foe to a tree from the bottom of a pit. It is as if the grinding wheel of time has no effect on the body and soul of such figures. Because heroes and holy men are not nurtured and brought up in tandem with time, they do not share an eclipse in parallel with it either, and therefore do not die from natural causes or old age; they are killed in battle. A few, like Kay Khosrow and his companions, disappear, and there are others whose fate we never learn, lost in successive waves of the epic flux.

For that reason, heroes' biographies are not chronologically recounted but hinge on their major feats and battles and feasts. In their boastings, all that Rostam and Esfandiyar proclaim is their lineage and exploits, only a lineage whose notables have accomplished great feats being notable. Rostam's pedigree is of note for he descends from a man

---

40. See "Night," n. 43.

who slew a dragon and a demon (M6: 257). He says, "Our legacy is our feats" (M6: 261) and enumerates his exploits in different parts of the world. Esfandiyar replies: "Here is what I have done" (M6: 259): The Seven Labors, plus battles in Turan and China and religious crusades!

A hero's biography is their report card. But the poet does not organize their exploits in sequence. The story prompts the protagonist toward action and the hero's nature provides the connective tissue between acts. Because the hero's deeds are rooted in his nature, the system is self-organizing; the multiplicity of events is not random.

Time being incidental to the protagonist's being, it does not affect the crux of the story and remains external to it. We do not learn about the progression of time as the story unfolds; the poet informs us about its passage. For instance, speaking of Kay Khosrow's childhood and growth, we are told, "Thus turned the wheel of time," and "When he reached age seven . . ." and "In that vein the days went by" (M3: 161–2); or, after defeating the Turanians, Rostam ascends the throne and "Thence he hunted with panther and falcon. / A long time passed in that fashion" (M3: 193).

Here, Time, "the vault of heaven, the world, the turning wheel," and so on, meaning "cosmic time," drives the world toward its end. While time leads humanity toward its origins in step with the cosmic order, it is detached from human beings for it is inaccessible and unfathomable—like the stars in heaven—and has a preordained effect on them from the outside. It is a time that "builds and wrecks again" and no one is evidently immune to its capriciousness. Appearing to Tūs in a dream from the world beyond, Siavash says of himself:

> *In the rose garden, we while away with wine,*
> **Not knowing how long we shall be drinking.**
>
>   (M4: 160)

Nor does death solve the puzzle of the eternal spinner.

Because time is not part of the fabric of the hero's life, his life does not change gradually or by the day; the dimensions of such a time being cosmic and not worldly, the hero also lives much longer than the earthly human—a hundred years, or even several hundred years!

The hero is an immutable model and ideal. Gudarz is always an elderly sage who is wise to the arts of war, fighting with discernment and deliberation; and Bižan, always selfless when war erupts, can never contain his excitement; Gīv is the paragon of unconditional loyalty, and Piran the exemplar of a cognizance that does not tempt fate. By contrast, he who is not a hero does not endure and is caught in the carrion claws of the daily grind. Kāvus at sixty-five is old and running out of time (M3: 65), and although he does not die, his being or nonbeing is the same.

The hero's spirit, too, like his body, does not evolve gradually in time. He is the same from beginning to end; if he changes, he is in dissonance with the times. In the story of Rostam and Esfandiyar, Tahamtan stops running away and stays and accepts death, but this change is not due to reflection and a pause; it is the sudden reversal of a spirit that recovers its sense of pride, a fall and rise that the spirit can sustain only under special circumstances, like someone dispatching the dreadful fear of death in battle.

Tūs has a twofold character in the *Shahnameh*. First, he is as he always was, fractious. But after hearing Kay Khosrow's reprimands, he feels remorse. Saddened, he pleads forgiveness for the pain he has caused his army and hopes to be freed of shame by risking his life (M4: 120). From that moment on, he becomes a different man, valorous, loyal, and *wise* (M4: 139, 140, 147, 151). The Christlike murmuring of a sacred king has awakened his soul; he promises to be judicious and rational and remains true to his promise to the end.

In both these instances, Tūs' nature is "static" and inert. His character transformation is not the result of observation and experience over time or any internal decisions but a quick reversal due to external factors; if a hero attains a higher state, it is thanks to an active event—an external tug of war.

Just as a mystic attains a spiritual state through contemplation and completion of successive stages, the Seven Labors is Rostam's rite of initiation into the heroic state; Esfandiyar endures his own Seven Labors right before fighting Tahamtan. From the outset, though, both are endowed not only with physical force but with heroic qualities, otherwise they would not have been ready to throw themselves at such a perilous test.

Unlike novels where protagonists are created and tempered as the story and the events unfold, characters are introduced into heroic poetry fully formed. From that standpoint, epic is static and inert.

But these sweltering tales of life and death cannot be inert. The essence of heroism lies in the risk-taker's will that has the potential to be actualized. In Rostam's words, God has bestowed power and glory on "everyone," so there's no reason to complain. The source of the story's vibrancy and dynamism is a forceful will that does not let the hero rest for a moment, constantly propelling him toward a fresh exploit to turn the world upside down.

When Kay Khosrow decides to relinquish the throne, the Iranian grandees tell him:

> *If the sea be the cause, we'll turn it to dirt,*
> *We'll darken the sky that covers the earth.*
> *If the cause be a mountain, uproot it we will,*
> *Every foe's heart we will slash with our blades.*

(M5: 387)

Such a forceful will asserts itself and keeps the man afloat; it is greater and more powerful than him. Whenever Kay Khosrow needs someone to take on a perilous task, Bižan jumps in compulsively (M4: 19). He is defiant and rebellious; if they try to stop him from going to war, he rends the Kāvian banner in two with his sword and rushes to the battlefield with one half; he rebels against his father.

In the Battle of the Twelve Rokh Gudarz has been waiting for an auspicious omen and a propitious hour when Bižan loses patience. "He walked to his father, his clothes rent, / Hurling dirt on top of his head," saying , 'We have rested for five days; no swords drawn at sunrise, no dust in the air, no blood rushing in any vein' (M5: 106).

Piran's brother is yet another Bižan. The pause between the two armies lasts seven days and neither commander takes the initiative to start the battle. Hūmān grows impatient and on being denied permission to fight tells Piran:

> You are e'er inclined to settle,
> My inclination is to battle.
>
> (M5: 110)

He flouts orders and readies for battle and with much persistence calls for a challenger and is finally killed by his counterpart, Bižan.

A will to fight, brimming with a selfless courage, drives the two men to the battlefield, which is their playground. These two adversaries among the most sterling of epic heroes are drawn swords, for they are more valiant, and ready to die. Fear of death does not stifle being free in life. Without such courage, the hero's will does not move from potential to actual and the thought of action does not turn into execution. The hero's essence is an actionable will and a paramount valor such that the one freed of the fear of death may access the entirety of living. A mortal body and an immortal heart!

Afrasiyab's son, listening to the man showing him an escape route from the battle, says:

> But to me more pleasing than flight
> Is to stay put and in battle delight.
>
> (M5: 274)

One can engage in conflict and be relentlessly belligerent if to give up and yield is more unpleasant than dying. A risk-taker does not shy away from trials and tribulations no matter how unpalatable and does not look for an easy victory.

> *A hero is he who looks for trouble;*
> *A night raid is not a manly pursuit.*

>   (M4: 91)

Kay Khosrow says, 'Let life not be without a Rostam who pursues thirst and fatigue and hardship and has never chased happiness!' (M4: 158). And Gīv's sufferings on Kay Khosrow's behalf are such that they may not be left unmentioned' (M4: 121).

There is no limit to the risks a hero may take. The more dangerous the task the more meritorious. To fight Rostam means to face death. Nevertheless, when Kāmūs-e Kashani hears about Rostam's exceptional fighting skills from Piran,

> *He was pleased by the words he heard,*
> *That heightened his aura even further.*

>   (M4: 200)

Death, more enduring than lingering time, awaits. Time will come ashore someday, and the world will end. Death is the destiny of the world.[41] The earth's resurrection also lies in its death, for when its time comes, it will be freed of "mixture." Likewise, a hero is he who can turn to his own resurrection, to death.

---

41. "You and I have no choice but to die. / Nothing is stauncher than shrewish death" (M4: 96). In *Mēnōg Xrad*, quoted in Zaehner, *Zurvan*, 90, "Fate is lord over all beings and objects and the Ahrimanic Vāy (god of death) is that from which there is no escape. Zurvan (Time) never stays invisible and there is no remedy for it. When someone's time comes, there is nothing to be done."

He knocks on the door of death
Who mounts his horse and hastens.

(M2: 231)

In that context, "fortune" is not a blind web woven at random. The stars above, the cosmos, the revolving wheel, and the times design one's fate, or "fortune." In the contrivance of the twirling cosmic order, humanity is captive to an indifferent mandate. The secret of the universe's victory over humanity is that I am time-bound, while it is Time; I am "mortal life," while it is a remote and alien heavens and star endlessly fabricating my "time." It streams itself in me for a while, brings me forth and takes me away. And yet, should I rush toward death, I shall have reclaimed my "time" from it and not only come to own its weapon but become the lord of my own time.

*He is not dead who **by choice***
Perishes, meets his final fate.

(M5: 223)

He who has voluntarily chosen his own end and dies by his own will has gratified his wish. He is fulfilled and the times is unfulfilled, for the will of the times, or the age, no longer governs him. His wish has dictated the duration of the "time" that the times may stream in him. The hero does not leave this fate in the hands of the times. Even when he knows resistance to be futile, he faces off with the times (M5: 201) and tries to be killed at the hands of an equal:

When you're caught in a quagmire in life,
It's best they see your face than your back.

(M4: 96)

Since my death is all but certain,
Better my life should end in battle

> *At the hands of a warlike rider,*
> *A captain, a hero, a truculent man.*
>> (M4: 130)

A hero chooses when to die, how, and at whose hands.

In that context, a human being intermixes with the "birth-and-death" of the cosmic order and freed from the mandate of the times thanks to death, conquers it and rules over "fortune." Gostahm declares with his last breath: "I have not died but in honor and there is no higher reward in life" (M5: 221). A hero's wish is to live in honor and die honored, honor meaning pride and manliness, greatness, and distinction.

> *May one's name abide in honor,*
> *Even as one is roped in by death.*
>> (M5: 181)

A hero does not flee from death's noose so he may escape dishonor and the fear of being harmed.

> *To die in honor has more charm*
> *Than a life lived in fear of harm.*
>> (M4: 166)

Living wrongfully and in fear is to live not according to one's will but by another's standards. Such an existence is discordant with the hero's nature, which is why he snatches death as if it were a blessing. He wills death and thereby annihilates an unwilful existence. Death determines life, and by accepting it, the hero recovers the freedom to live. The hero is a free slave who, brimming with life, not only constantly lives with death but given its presence, always brims with life.

> *We are born of mother bound in death,*
> *In bondage we live though we live free.*
>> (M4: 16)

That kind of man is the floodplain of life and death and the strata-gems of the heavenly sphere no longer have ready access to him.

To begin a battle, Kay Khosrow and Afrasiyab each had an astrologer at their side to watch the heavens for signs and ciphers and learn which side the stars favored. Pashang objects, telling his father Afrasiyab:

> *Why take action by astrologers' words?*
> *'Tis by the sword men move into action.*
>
> (M5: 259)

Once the warriors give up hope in the star and watching turns into action, the operative star waits to see what the warriors will do. This time it is Afrasiyab who tells Pashang:

> *Two armies brimming with blistering heat,*
> *As the star watches from high in its seat.*
>
> (M5: 259)

The fate-shaping star is now anxious to see how the warriors will shape their fate.

By accepting death, the hero exits the orbit of "this old wolf's trap," the vault of heaven; he is no longer simply a part of it but its equal and of the same weight, its counterpart. Kay Khosrow tells Rostam:

> *You are the nurturer of crown and throne;*
> *The king acquires his splendor through you.*
> *The wheel of life is at the tip of your sword,*
> *Sky, time, and earth are under your thumb.*
> *You cut off the White Demon's heart and head,*
> *The source of our hopes is bound to your grace.*
> *Earth is subject to the dust of your Rakhsh,*
> *Time treats you as would a loving mother.*
> *It is by your sword that the sun embroils,*
> *It is by your mace that Venus sheds tears.*
>
> (M4: 157)

How can the cowed and fearful vault of heaven—which turns not by its own volition but as decreed and is a slave to its own fortune—tie the hands of such a free soul behind his back? Addressing Esfandiyar who has been sent on a fool's errand, Rostam says:

> He orders you to go fetter me, Rostam,
> Yet even the heavens cannot bind my hands.
> Should the sky order me to listen and yield,
> I shall strike it down with my mighty mace.

(M6: 262)

Not only is the vault of heaven petrified, it also bends to kiss his hands (M4: 197).

Gīv stands out among all these men. A champion like others, at one point in his life he is tasked with a holy mission, which is to find Kay Khosrow and rescue him from Turan. In that period, Kay Khosrow's divine glory is Gīv's guide and guardian, thanks to which he is endowed with both earthly and spiritual singularities.

In Sasanian religious literature, Gīv is one of the immortals, and in epic he is the sole figure who can locate Kay Khosrow far away in Turan (M3: 199). He is dispatched everywhere as a prophet at large (M5: 94, 377, 385): to Piran and Kāvus and Rostam. This messenger of good tidings is as if sanctified by Sorūsh, the divine messenger who proclaims it is Gīv who should be sent to look for Kay Khosrow. Gīv leaves and finds him and brings him in, and in the end disappears from the world alongside the king.

In a book where the span of some of the events and the descriptions and repetition of details can at times be tedious, the travels of a lone hero wandering in enemy territory—itself an apt subject for an epic like the *Odyssey*—is brief and rushed. A quest that lasts several years is narrated in a few lackluster verses, then suddenly Kay Khosrow is found.

But Gīv's return to Iran is packed with fights and flights. He single-handedly takes on the Turanian army chiefs and troops (M3:

214). To confront Piran, he dons Siavash's armor and rushes onto the battlefield alone where the Turanian general tells him:

> *Though a rider be an iron mountain,*
> *A thousand men will ring him like ants.*
> *Into small rubble his armor they'll shred;*
> *And like a carcass they'll drag him about.*
>
> (M3: 219)

But he takes Piran captive and attacks his troops and kills many. In response to Afrasiyab's retort as to how an entire army could have been thwarted by one man:

> *Replied Piran, "Not a fierce lion,*
> *Nor a raging wolf, nor a wild tiger*
> *Ravages battle lines, waging war,*
> *Like Gīv, my lord, alone by himself."*
>
> (M3: 224)

"Even when, like raindrops from a cloud, / A multitude more spears showered on his head," continues Piran, Gīv rode his horse as if in a rose garden. Everyone fled from him except for Piran, whom he knocked to the ground unconscious.

> *I do not know the heavens' secret,*
> *Why it withholds its grace from us.*
>
> (M3: 225)

The secret unknown to Piran is Kay Khosrow's divine glory (B: 762, 730; M3: 214 n., 218) and Siavash's armor, which when donned renders Gīv invincible and impervious to any weapon. Now this vehicle of Kay Khosrow's victory shall vanquish all.

The victory of one man over a contingent of army leaders and warriors does not jibe with reality and lacks fervor. Divorced from reality, the story would be a dull account of a prefigured end. That is not the case, however, for Gīv's opponents are not merely up against a single hero—that would render their collective defeat questionable; they are fighting a higher power, Kay Khosrow's divine glory. Thanks to Gīv, a supernatural power—the vault of heaven, which has a hand in this work—is leading nature toward a final deliverance. Here, Gīv has a spiritual "purpose," and until he achieves it, another force inhabits and protects him. But though Gīv knows that his status is supernal, and that God is his ally (M3: 218), he knows he is not immune to death. But dead or alive, God is his ally. That is why when Piran catches up with the fugitives, Gīv reconciles with death as he prepares to fight him. In battling Piran, his victory is not assured in advance and battle retains its character, which is risk-taking.

Once he accomplishes his mission, however, this same Gīv is like all the other captains in the great war with the Turks where numerous relations of Kāvus and Gudarz and his sons are killed. Gīv's prowess does not deliver, and the Iranians suffer a crushing defeat (M4: 96). He is now the same vulnerable hero as before his journey. That heavenly boon was extrinsic to him and mediated by Kay Khosrow for a specific time and task so that "he may save the low earth and the high heavens" (M3: 200).

Heroes are "world" saviors and "illuminators of the sun and moon" (M5: 206), but in the end they go to dust, their aspirations notwithstanding. Their work in avenging Siavash and ending the age of Afrasiyab culminates in the Battle of the Twelve Rokh where the Turanians are indeed demolished, Piran is slain, and Afrasiyab is crushed. But no age can come to its end except at the hands of the celestial human, the one who is the first, the guide and leader of the noble-spirited, endowed with divine glory, "free of disease and death,"[42] a memorial of Siavash

---

42. *Āfrin-e Payāmbar Zartušt* 23:7, quoted in Darmesteter, trans., *Le Zend-Avesta*, vol. 2, 661.

who bears the closest resemblance to him (M4: 11) and whose identity the astrologers had previously disclosed (M3: 97).

> We importune the *faravahar* of the holy Kay Khosrow . . .
> for the instant destruction of enemies . . . for a lucid
> knowledge of the future and of the best life (Paradise) . . .
> for a luminous kingship, for longevity, for all blessings,
> for all remedies, for withstanding sorcerers and evil
> spirits, for withstanding the evil done by oppressors.
> . . . Kay Khosrow, the victorious leader who fettered
> the oppressor Afrasiyab and his brother Garsivaz, the
> avenging son of the valiant Siavash who was killed by
> treachery, who avenged the brave Aqrīras."[43]

It is said in the *Shahnameh* that Kay Khosrow, the king of a "new creed," would cleanse the world of pain, of evil words and deeds, and forge a new foundation (M3: 151, 158; M4: 158; M5: 342). His life was intertwined with the history of the earth, and the world would not have achieved deliverance without him:

> The blessing from Kāvus was that Kay Siavash issued
> from him . . . The blessing from Siavash was that Kay
> Khosrow issued from him and built Kangdež.

> The benefit from Kay Khosrow was that he slew Afrasiyab and
> demolished the temple of the idols at Chīchast and restored
> Kangdež. It is with his help that the marshal of the dead, the
> victorious Sūshiyāns, can initiate resurrection at the end of time.[44]

> *Though blood issued from Kāvus' mind,*
> *One such as Siavash issued from his back.*

---

43. *Farvardin Yt* 29:132–5, quoted in Pourdavoud, trans., *Yaśthā*, vol. 2, 103–4 (and repeated in *Zāmyād Yt* 11:77).

44. *Mēnōg i Xrad*, cited in Molé, *Culte, mythe et cosmologie*, 432.

And from him the pure, just Kay Khosrow,
Who placed the crown on Lohrāsp's head.

(M6: 262)

"The age holds a secret in Kay Khosrow," so it safeguards his vital force and disrupts Afrasiyab's plans (M3: 160; M5: 308). He looks a year old at birth and merits nothing less than kingship (M3: 159). By grace of the divine glory and his dual-world mission, he is foremost in wisdom and valor.

On their flight across the Turanian frontier, Gīv tells Kay Khosrow: 'Should Farangis and I drown in the Oxus, rest at ease, no adversity shall befall you,' for

Your mother bore you as the hope of the world,
And now, the King of King's throne is waiting.
'Tis also for your sake I was born from a mother,
Thus, such adversity shouldn't trouble your heart.

(M3: 228)

Though humanly impossible, he crosses the river without a boat and his companions likewise reach the shore thanks to him. The goddess Nāhīd, the wellspring of the world's waters, answers Kay Khosrow's prayers and protects his life so he may become the greatest king of all lands, vanquish all evil, and ride his chariot ahead of all others.'[45]

"Since you're Kay Khosrow," said Gīv to the king,
"For you these waters good fortune will bring.
Why would the waterway contrive an ill norm
For one of great glory and a gracious form?"

(M3: 227–8)

---

45. *Āban Yt* 13:49–51, in Pourdavoud, trans., *Yašthā*, vol. 1, 253–4.

If that father was of the essence of fire, this son is "rainlike."[46] In the *Shahnameh*, the first time we meet Kay Khosrow he is standing by a bright creek, lofty like a cypress, handsome, wine cup in hand with a garland of flowers on his head (M3: 206)! Water, wine, and plants, symbols of the bounties of one whose kingship was "the downpour of clouds, the streaming of rivers, the lushness of nature, the solace of pained hearts, and the balm of the beleaguered, turning the earth into the Garden of Paradise" (M4: 9). When he stepped on the arid desert, "the firmament would become blanketed in clouds and the earth in grass and flowers and sweet basil" (M5: 310).

The aspiration of that "chief priest king of good thoughts" (M5: 311) was to destroy the idols and rid the world of them with the help of warriors and God (M5: 310). When he ascended the throne, with hunting as a pretext he crisscrossed his domain, rebuilt ruined settlements, distributed wealth, and feasted on wine.[47] He traveled to the fire temple in Azarbaijan to worship and pledged an oath to Kāvus to rout Afrasiyab (M4: 12).

Taking charge of coordinating the final battle with Afrasiyab, he assembled warriors from across the land and dispatched them against the enemy; ahead of the most crucial encounter with the Turanians, his strategic planning guaranteed success (M5: 92–3). There is no comparable preparation for war anywhere in the *Shahnameh*. He is a master of the art of war, and like Bahrām "brings death, and refreshes, and spreads peace, and achieves ends," as if the war between Afrasiyab and Kay Khosrow were between Vayu and Bahrām or two concepts of war compared.

---

46. In Pahlavi, *wārān-kirdār* is an epithet of Sasanian kings. See Widengren, *Les religions de l'Iran*, 75. [In New Persian and other modern Iranian languages, *bārān* is employed for beneficial rainfall and the Arabic terms *tūfān* ("typhoon"), *barq* ("lightning"), and *ra'd* ("thunder") for storms.—Trans.]

47. Even enemy land was the subject of his bounty. Upon conquest, he said to his troops, "Do not destroy, but build, for this is my domain" (M5: 322).

This founder of the Āzar Goshasp fire temple[48] and enhancer of Kangdež, the killer of Afrasiyab and destroyer of the temple of the idols, the giver of rain and eradicator of drought, is the perfect holy man, the perfect warrior, and the perfect producer. He is the symbol of the three Aryan social classes, the perfect implementer of each class's self-purpose, their lord and commander, and the embodiment of the ideal sovereign, "superior to all the kings" (M4: 13).

Ferdowsi begins the account of Kay Khosrow's rule by stipulating the four imperatives of kingship: proficiency, pedigree, essence, and wisdom.

> *Should these four conjoin in a man,*
> *He's freed from envy, pain, and grief.*
> *When a king becomes freed by the four,*
> *Fortune shall shower on all from on high.*

>   (M4: 9)

Kay Khosrow is not only a perfect king; he is a perfect man.

The closer a human resembles God the closer he is to perfection. Among human beings, a king who follows the Good Religion, a *behdīn*,[49] is the more perfect among the perfect. He partakes of God's "all-knowing wisdom" and can also apply it on earth. He is the most masterful, discerning enemy of Ahriman among humans, who are themselves the best of all creation.

Shahrivar (*Xšathra Vairya*), one of the Amesha Spentas, partakes of Ahura Mazda's essence. He is a hypostasis of ideal sovereignty, the bestower of kingship, and lord of the sky. His earthly representation is

---

48. Pourdavoud, trans., *Yasnā*, vol. 2, 150.

49. MP *Wehdēn*, literally, "Follower of the Good Religion," the Mazdayasnian faith. See *Yasnā* 44:10 and 53:1-4, where Zoroaster calls *daēna* the "good/best" creed.—Trans.

metals, which are the source of weapons, which are the tools of war. As leader of priests and commander of warriors, the king is the "Shahrivar" of the earth and the personification of the sky who can apply warrior power and priestly wisdom against Ahrimanic creatures.

If we take Siavash to represent the perfect Zurvanite man—whose fabric is woven out of fate—Kay Khosrow is the perfect Mazdayasnian man who weaves the fate of the world, the inevitable history of earth, into his own fabric.

Religion belongs to Ahura Mazda alone, but power belongs to both Ahura Mazda and Ahriman; both can fight and are at war. A misguided king is power absent religion and Ahriman absent Ahura Mazda; he is a serpent shouldered Zahhāk, which means a king may be the best or the worst among men, and Kay Khosrow is the best. He disdains bloodshed and, while formidable, is a patron of the frail and the needy (M4: 30, 34). Though he fights Piran, he cherishes him (M5: 226–7); and he forgives a damaging friend and a despondent foe.[50] He reflects the singular but twofold ethos of heroic chivalry and mystical mercy.

Moral perfection is the due corollary of the mystical spirit of a man who, after long years of ruling in fairness and justice, withdraws from the world.

> *In seeking vengeance for my father,*
> *I wandered far and enriched the world.*
> *I slew those who deserved to perish,*
> *The miscreants who contested God.*

---

50. The king of Turan flees the fortress (*kang*) of Afrasiyab; Kay Khosrow captures its demonic inhabitants, the "veiled ones," but releases them (M5: 317). In Hamza Esfahani, *Payāmbarān*, trans. Shoā'r, 36, he also slays a dragon on a mountain top between Fars and Esfahan. Cf. in Indian mythology, Widengren, *Les religions de l'Iran*, 59: "In the beginning a dragon was lord over life, and the earth was parched. A divine hero emerged, captured the dragon's fort and vanquished the beast. The waters, bound in the fort, were released and the enslavement of the females imprisoned in the dragon's harem was ended."

None equals me in rewards and renown,
In greatness, goodness, peace, and gnosis.[51]

    (M5: 380–81)

China and India and Turan and Rome are his. Afrasiyab is gone
and justice pervades the world. Kay Khosrow is now a king with no
other task than to rule. He holds earthly power without an otherworldly
mission, and because power can turn its holder Ahrimanic, he fears
falling into the ego's trap like Zahhāk or Jamshid and becoming an
ingrate like Afrasiyab or Kāvus (M5: 380).

The peak of earthly power is very slippery; the power holder is
liable to lose his bearing, and confusing his status with supremacy,
proclaim—like Jamshid—that "I am the world" (M1: 42). Furthermore,
Kay Khosrow has accomplished his self-purpose and has no other
cause to pursue.

I have now found all I sought,
And forfeited the earthly throne.

    (M5: 400)

Kay Khosrow lost his raison d'être, therefore, he shut himself away
and prayed to God to 'Grant me sapience and discrimination between
good and evil; protect me from the demon and show me the path to
the heavens' (M5: 381, 384) for "this kingship is not to my advantage"
(M5: 387).

Kay Khosrow's advantage lies in moving on from the "twilit"
earth to the absoluteness of light. In fighting against darkness, he was
enlightened and found God in himself just as God reclaimed Himself
in him. "The perfect man is called by multiple names with supplements

---

51. The Persian term translated here as "gnosis" is *jām*—as in *Jām-e Jam*, the
    truth-revealing "cup" of Jamshid. In Sufism, *jām* signifies the Perfect Man, the
    seeker and knower of Truth.—Trans.

and credentials . . . imam, caliph, axis (*qutb*), the Lord of Time (*sāheb-e zamān*), as well as the world-revealing cup (*Jām-e Jahan-namā*), the earth-revealing mirror (*āyeneh-ye guiti-namā*), the great cure (*taryāq-e bozorg*), and the supreme elixir (*eksīr-e aʿzam*)."[52]

"The perfect man absorbed that elixir to perfection and wholly separated light from darkness; whereas light had not found nor beheld any equal to itself anywhere, it found and beheld its equal in the perfect man."[53]

Thus, light enters an individual to see itself in them and recover itself, and the individual is enlightened by the grace of the light that is inside them. There is no path to anywhere without the light of God.

Kay Khosrow was a man of God, divinely favored and initiated in the mysteries. From the beginning, a divine consciousness had opened his mind's eye. The moment he saw Gīv, he recognized him and knew who he was searching for and what he would do (M3: 206). Thanks to his "enlightened soul," he read Gīv's mind and vocalized it; nor was the hero surprised.

> Gīv said to him, "O exalted king,
> That you be versed in secrets is apt.
> With divine glory and a Kianid line,
> There is no daylight here in between."
>
> (M3: 211)

Kay Khosrow foresees the future of Afrasiyab and Piran and how they will die (M5: 174, 178, 228). On seeing him when he first reaches Iran, Kāvus says:

> From Jamshid through Fereidun,
> None has seen a king so pure.

---

52. Nasafi, *Kitāb al-Insān ul-Kāmil*, ed. Molé, 4.

53. Ibid., 25.

No one's suffered in life as you,
Nor seen clearly what's obscure.

(M5: 363)

He possesses the world-revealing cup like Jamshid, and the omniscient eye of the sun and the vision of the prescient God. He is sight and insight with a heart that mirrors the world. Not only does the world reflect itself in it, but it thereby beholds itself and comes into being. An existence in chaos mutates into an orderly world. This world is in Kay Khosrow's thought; he thinks it. The same way that existence was in Ahura Mazda's thought before creation, the life of the world also exists in Kay Khosrow's thought. He is a man of the Good Religion before the advent of the Good Religion. The invisible and the yet inexistent are present in him, whence he is cognizant of the occult and the nascent; he circumscribes the world. Therefore, he not only appoints the unsung Lohrāsp to kingship "so he may predicate God's path" and for his son Goshtāsp to pave the way for Zoroaster (M5: 407), but he himself lives on till the end to bring the world's destiny to its conclusion.

> Then, the millennium of Sūshiyāns arrives. Sūshiyāns seeks
> Ohrmazd's counsel, embraces the religion, and administers it in
> the world. Then Nēryōsang and Sorūsh come forth. They resurrect
> Kay Khosrow, son of Siavash, and Tūs of the Nozarian and Gīv of
> the Gudarzian and others, along with a thousand treasure troves
> of army leaders and remove Ahriman from the midst [of creation].
> People on earth become of one thought, word, and deed.[54] Among
> the best good kings and religious leaders to come, the best is
> the Renovator Sōshāns and his collaborator, Kay Hōsrōy.[55]

At the end of time, six hallowed immortals shall rise from six countries, and aided by Sūshiyāns who has risen from Xwanīras, carry

---

54. Hedayat, "Yādgār i Jāmāspi," *Sokhan* 1: 4 and 5.

55. *Dēnkard* 334:2, quoted in Molé, *Culte, mythe et cosmologie*, 39.

out the Renovation.[56] The seven earthly climes shall be regenerated by seven holy men—which evokes the seven *Amešāspand*s—and become incorporeal.

That Renovator persona is not forgotten in epic; he merely withdraws from life. Kay Khosrow crosses a mountain pass and follows "a long, arid and harsh path without plants and trees and foliage" that not everyone can brave. This journey is itself a minor renovation. Seven gallants accompany the king; three return and the other four remain. At nightfall, they reach a creek. Kay Khosrow bathes in the "clear water"—which guards the seeds of the Renovators[57]—and recites Zand and Avesta (M5: 413). He is cleansed and purified body and soul. Then, come universal resurrection when humans "move through molten metal and turn brilliant as the sun," he says,

> *When the radiant sun hoists its banner,*
> *And earth turns purple as molten gold,*
> *That will be the day for my departure,*
> *And with Sorūsh, a close encounter.*

> (M5: 412)

At sunrise, the earth will be like molten gold; that is the time for separation and union, separation from the corporeal and union with the spiritual.

When Siavash went to Turan, he was a sun that set into the abyss of the night. Now, Kay Khosrow is a sun that unites with the sun; he does not set, he departs and, without dying, disappears so he may rise again. His "death" is rebirth. "Behold that in truth the body became soul,

---

56. Pourdavoud, trans., *Yaštha*, vol. 2, 100, n. 1.

57. Cf. Zoroaster's visionary journey to Ērānwēj in Pazhdo, *Zarātusht-nāmeh*, which dates from 1278 CE.

form became spirit, and occluded as vapor. How could elemental events affect him? Do you not see that when he died, Jesus rose to the sky?"[58]

Kay Khosrow's salvation eludes his companions. When he gave up the world and decided to join God, they all felt confounded and distraught. Now that the entire world is yours, when it is time to harvest and rejoice, how could you leave? They were at their wits' end and asked Zāl and Rostam for help. The seasoned Zāl was likewise baffled and thought Kay Khosrow deluded and entranced by demons:

> One said the king has gone insane,
> His mind is from reason estranged.

>   (M5: 400)

They remain mystified by his motive to the very end, and "roiling and boiling" yet helpless and powerless, submit to fate. They have a right not to know. Kay Khosrow is mad. His decision does not stand to reason. He owns a world that everyone envies; he gives it up voluntarily and hastens to the other side of life that everyone shuns.

The madness of this son in abandoning the world is like the madness of that father in "abandoning kin and country." If Siavash went to Turan in concert with the divine Mehr, Kay Khosrow goes to the heavens in concert with Sorūsh—a divinity closely attached to Mehr. The king is infused with the idiocy of the savants, which does not accommodate the partial intellect. As Piran had once importuned the child, just so the man is "mad," and as Afrasiyab had then observed, "his mind isn't set on its seat."

Kay Khosrow is a prophet[59] and like all prophets is in league with an angel or deity that is a messenger from the beyond. He was found and saved thanks to the Sorūshaic Siavash's guidance. He saw Sorūsh— whose sight even Fereidun was deprived of— in a dream, and by virtue

---

58. Corbin, ed., *Rūzbihān Baqlī*, 46.

59. Hamza Esfahani, *Payāmbarān*, trans. Shoā'r, 36.

of his grace reached God (M5: 409, 412). That deity who guides father and son is their point of convergence; they become one in him and recover their unity: "As if he were one with him in skin and mien" (M3: 240). Kay Khosrow's end is like Siavash's beginning except that in the interim the earth has been rid of Afrasiyab.

> The blessed Kay Khosrow who established sanctity and worship received word from the Hallowed One and conversed with Him in an occult state and his soul soared to the upper world and was decked with God's wisdom and the Lights of God radiated upon and manifested in him and converged in him. He grasped the purport of *Kian Kharreh*, which is that light that appears in the dominating soul, and by the power of God subdued the miscreant friend of enmity, his grandsire, the cruel Afrasiyab who rose against justice and refuted God's blessings, who negated sanctity, who, leading an army that those able to count were incapable of counting, was killed near Qaznai . . . And because the soul-wise king revived the mores in the world and paid reverence to the Lights of God and decreed that everyone on earth submit to God Almighty, lights for beholding the splendor of God streamed upon him in His Holy Presence. *He called Him the Proclaimer of Love, and He affirmed. The command of the Lord of Ardor was issued, and he advanced to sovereignty.* The Father called him, and he heard that He was calling him; he consented and departed toward God, abandoned the realm that he ruled and in concert with divine love, took leave of his kin and country and people. The ages had not witnessed such a sovereign and recall no other king like him. Divine power moved him, and he departed from his country. Salutations to the day he severed himself from his country, the day he united with the celestial realm.[60]

---

60. Corbin/Nasr, eds., *Sheikh-e Ishrāq*, 186–8.

SHAHNAMEH KING LIST

Note: *Figures who did not rule as kings appear in italics, as does Zahhāk, who was not a Pīshdādi, but the son of Merdās, a Tāzī (Arab) ruler.*

MYTHOLOGICAL AGE

Pīshdādiān Dynasty

Kiumars

Siyāmak
|
Hūshang
|
Tahmuras

Jamshīd

Zahhāk

Fereidūn

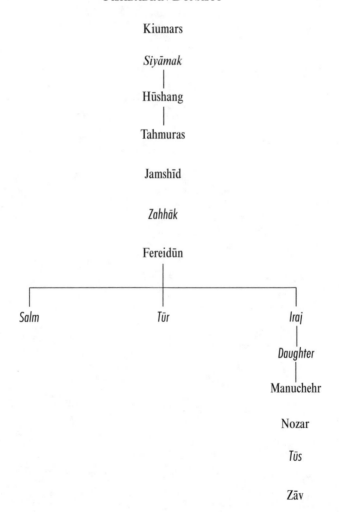

Salm   Tūr   *Iraj*

Daughter
|
Manuchehr

Nozar

Tūs

Zāv

HEROIC AGE

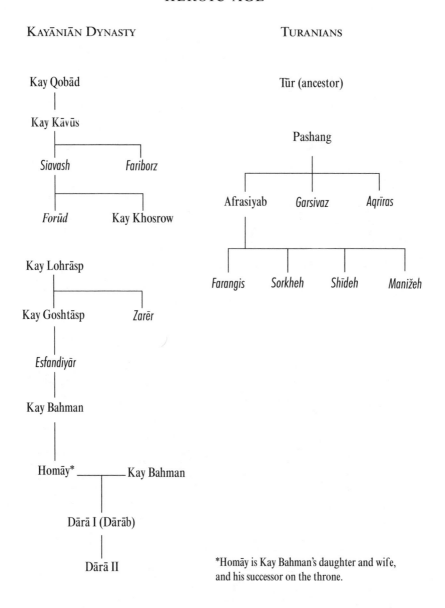

KAYĀNIĀN DYNASTY

Kay Qobād
|
Kay Kāvūs
├─────────────┐
Siavash   *Fariborz*
├─────────────┐
Forūd   Kay Khosrow

Kay Lohrāsp
├─────────────┐
Kay Goshtāsp   *Zarēr*
|
Esfandiyār
|
Kay Bahman
|
Homāy* ————— Kay Bahman
|
Dārā I (Dārāb)
|
Dārā II

TURANIANS

Tūr (ancestor)

Pashang
|
┌──────────┼──────────┐
Afrasiyab   *Garsivaz*   *Aqrīras*
|
┌──────┬──────┬──────┐
Farangis *Sorkheh* *Shīdeh* *Manižeh*

*Homāy is Kay Bahman's daughter and wife,
and his successor on the throne.

187

GLOSSARY OF NAMES

In the following, cross-references to other glossary entries are in bold type. For the use of diacritics here and in the translation, see the "Translator's Note," p. xiii.

Āb Zareh: "Waters of Zareh," refers to the Gulf of Oman (Makran), the sea route taken to reach Kangdež via the river Sindh (Persian derivative of *sindhu*, "river," in Sanksrit).

Ābtin: Av. *Āptya*, a descendant of **Jamshīd** and the father of **Fereidūn**.

Afrāsiyāb: Av. *Frangrasiiān*, "destroyer, vanisher." Son of **Pashang** and king of the Turanians (Av. *Tūirya*), an Iranian line descended from **Tūr**, **Fereidūn**'s second son. In the **Avesta**, he has an underground fortress that is lit by a sun and a moon through sorcery. In the *Shahnameh*, he builds *Behešt-kang*, "paradisical fortress," a massive, fortified city in Turkestan/Chorasmia. After many wars of vengeance for **Siavash**, he is killed by **Kay Khosrow** when he emerges from Lake **Chīchast** in Azarbaijan into which he had escaped after the hermit Hōm dragged him out of a cave (*"hang"*) in a nearby mountain-top.

Ahriman: Av. *Angra Mainyu*, the Evil Spirit who created all that is noxious on earth and will be annihilated at the end of time. His six chief demons are *Aešma* (Wrath), *Aka Manah* (Evil Mind), *Bušyasta*

(Sloth), *Apaoša* (Drought), and *Nasu* (the germ of death), and *Yatu*s (sorcerers) and *Pairika*s (spirits).

Ahura Mazdā: MP *Ohrmazd/Hormozd*, NP *Hormoz*, "Wise Lord," or "Lord Wisdom," depending on whether his name is read as an adjective or a noun. The uncreated god and the chief adversary of **Ahriman**, he created the good world in six stages: sky, water, earth, plants, animals, and humankind. He maintains cosmic law, *aša,* on earth with the aid of the six **Ameša Spentas** and the *yazata*s.

Alborz/Harborz: See **Harā Berezaiti.**

Ameša Spentas: MP *Amahraspands*, NP *Ameshāspands*, "Bounteous Immortals," the seven divine powers of Righteousness (*Aša Vahišta/ Arta*); Good Mind (*Vohu Manah*); Desirable Kingdom (*Xšathra Vairya*); Bounteous Devotion/Obedience (*Spenta Āmraiti*); Wholeness/Health (*Haurvatāt*); Immortal Life (*Amertāt*), and Bounteous Spirit (*Spenta Mainyu*). As children and emanations of their creator, **Ahura Mazdā**, each is assigned to one of his seven creations.

Anūshirvan: "Immortal Soul," epithet of the Sasanian king Khosrow I, called "the Just," *dādgar* (r. 531–79 CE). Counselled by his sagacious minister Bozorgmehr, a nobleman from the Parthian House of Kāren and military commander of Khorasan, he established a new administrative and political structure across the Sasanian empire (see **Espahbad**).

Aqrīras: Brother of **Afrāsiyāb** and **Garsīvaz**, a pacificist who is sympathetic to the Iranians and is killed by Afrāsiyāb.

Ārash: Legendary archer who shot an arrow from a mountain top in **Mazandaran** that travelled for several days and landed on a tree across the Oxus River in Greater Khorasan, demarcating the Iran-Turan border and demolishing his body in the process.

Aredvī Sūrā Anāhitā: MP *Aredvīsūr*, NP *Nāhīd*, the "Moist, Strong, Undefiled" *yazata* who is the source of all the waters that flow down from the peak of **Harā Berezaiti** into the **Farākhkart Sea**. She also guards Zoroaster's seed in Lake Kasaoya (NP *Kayānsih*).

Ashkāniān/Arsacid: A **Parthian** dynasty founded by Ashk/Arsaces I that ruled Iran from 247 BCE to 224 CE and reached its imperial peak under Mithridates I (r. *c.*165–132 BCE). Despite a nearly 500-year-long rule, Arsacid history was forgotten under the Sasanians, but their heroic exploits were preserved by Parthian minstrels, the *gōsān,* and integrated into the Kayāniān epic cycle. Ferdowsi (M7: 116) recognizes Ashk "from the line of **Kay Qobād**" and names a few others such as **Gūdarz** and **Bīžan**, but devotes only a short passage to the Ashkānian, saying their chieftains were scattered throughout petty kingdoms and that "their history is not chronicled."

Ashkbūs: A Turanian warrior at the Battle of **Hamāvan** who kills Rohhām and is in turn killed by **Rostam**.

Āturpāt/Ādurbād: Ādurbād ī Mahraspandān, Sasanian high priest patronized by Shāpūr II (r. 309–79 CE). According to legend, he edited and enlarged the **Avesta**, establishing Mazdayasna as the state religion with Jews and Christians in charge of their respective legal domains. In Pahlavi prophetic literature, Ādurbād undergoes a fire ordeal—molten metal poured onto his chest—to prove the truth of Mazdayasna vs. Buddhism and Christianity and to refute Manichaean and other sectarian traditions.

Avesta: MP *abestāg,* "chants of praise," a term used since the ninth/tenth century CE for the Mazdean canon that according to legend had been destroyed by Alexander *c.*334 BCE. The orally transmitted tradition was compiled and translated from Avestan into Pahlavi under the Sasanian Ardeshīr I (r. 224–42 CE), codified under Shāpūr II (see **Āturpāt**), and revised under Khosrow I (see **Anūshirvan**). The extant Avesta comprises the *Yasna,* liturgies that include the *Gāthā*s, seventeen hymns attributed to Zoroaster himself (believed to have lived in the thirteenth, eleventh, or sixth century BCE); *Visprad,* invocations of the divinities; *Khordeh* ("Little") *Avesta,* prayers; *Sīrōzeh* ("Thirty Days"), enumeration of the calendrical divinities; *Yašht*s, twenty-one hymns to the main deities; *Vidēvdād,* rules; and over twenty fragments, *Nīrangistān, Aogemadāēčā* and *Hādōxt Nask* among them. The oldest surviving manuscripts of the Avesta date from 1288 CE.

Āzar Goshasp: Arabized NP form of MP *Ādur Gušnasp,* a Zoroastrian fire temple in Shīz, western Azarbaijan, that housed *Ātash Bahrām,* the most sacred Mazdean fire dedicated to the *arteštār* "warrior" class and a site of pilgrimage, sacred festivals, and the coronation of kings.

Sitting sixty meters above a green valley and called *Takht-e Soleiman* ("Throne of Solomon") following the Timurid conquest of Iran in the late 14th c., the temple encircled a calcium-rich pool eighty meters in diameter formed during a volcanic eruption. Three kilometres to the west, *Zendan-e Soleiman* ("Prison of Solomon") features a hollow crater about a hundred meters deep. The other prominent fire temples were *Ādur Burzēn Mehr* at Rēvand near Neishapur dedicated to the farmer/laborer class, and *Ādur Farnbāg* at Kāriān in Pārs dedicated to the priestly class.

Bābak Khorramdin: Born *c.* 795/798 CE in Ardabil, Azarbaijan, Bābak (MP *Pābag*) joined the Kārinid revolutionary Māzyār, **Espahbad** of Tabarestān, and later led the anti-Islamic, neo-Mazdakite Khorramdin movement that aimed to restore Iranian traditions in the land. Starting in 817, and for over two decades, Bābak led numerous revolts against the caliphs al-Ma'mun and al-Mu'tasim. He was eventually defeated and betrayed by Afshīn, a Central Asian commander in al-Mu'tasim's service, and executed in 838 at age forty or forty-three.

Bahman: Son of **Esfandiyār**, husband of Homāy Chehrāzād, father of Dārāb, and successor to his grandfather **Goshtāsp**. In the *Shahnameh*, he is the ancestor of Ardeshir I (r. 224–42 CE), a lineage fabricated by the Sasanians to identify him with the Achaemenid Artaxerxes I (r. 465–424 BCE). He is not named in the **Avesta** but appears in *Zand ī Vohuman Yasn (Bahman Yašt)* and other ninth to eleventh century Zoroastrian texts.

Bahrām: Av. *Verethragna*, MP *Warahrām*, "Overcoming Obstacles," the god of victory who protects warriors in battle and in close association with Mithra and Rašn (*Yt* 14:47), deals justice and punishes oath-breakers. He appears in ten incarnations to Zoroaster, as wind, a boar, horse, camel, bird of prey . . . and a fifteen-year-old youth.

Bārmān: Son of the Turanian Vīseh and brother of **Pīrān**. He and **Hūmān** led Sohrāb's army to Iran and caused his tragic death by preventing him and his father **Rostam** from recognizing each other. Bārmān is killed by **Gūdarz'** son **Rohhām** in single combat in the Battle of the Twelve Rokh.

Behzād: "High-born," epithet of Siavash's black stallion **Shabrang**.

Bisotūn: OP *Bagastāna,* "Place of the Gods" (anglicized as *Behistun*), an Achaemenid rock relief on a cliff in Kermanshah province in western Iran depicting the triumph of Darius I (r. 522–486 BCE) over Gaumāta, the Median Magus imposter. In inscriptions in OP, Elamite, and Babylonian, Darius describes his royal lineage from his father **Goshtāsp** back to his ancestor Achaemenes, and recounting his successful exploits, attributes his kingship to the "grace of **Ahura Mazdā.**"

Bīžan: Son of **Gīv** and Bānū Goshasp, **Rostam**'s daughter, and grandson of **Gūdarz**. He and his wife **Manīžeh**, **Afrāsiyāb**'s daughter, are the subject of a romantic tale in the *Shahnameh* that is replete with heroic exploits.

Bundahišn: "Primal Creation," the name given to a Pahlavi text of uncertain date about Zoroastrian cosmogony, cosmography, and **Ērānshahr**. The text is extant in an Indian and an Iranian recension, the Iranian/ *Greater Bundahišn* (*GBd*) being twice as large and less corrupted. Its brief coverage of the **Kayāniān** (*GBd* 35:31–2) derives from the lost parts of the *Zand*, the Pahlavi commentary on the **Avesta**.

Būyeh: A fisherman in Dailamestan whose clan, the Āl-e Būyeh, resisted conversion to Islam before adopting Nizari Isma'ilism. The Būyid Empire dominated Iran in the mid tenth century. Their power struggle against the Abbasid Caliphate ended with the invasion of Iran by the Oghuz Seljuk Turks in 1037 CE.

Čagād i dāidīg: See **Harā Berezaiti**.

Chīchast/Čečast: Av. *Čaēčasta*, a mythical lake located in eastern Iran. In Pahlavi sources, it is described as "having warm water," "free from animals," and "saline." In *Yt* 9:21–3, **Kay Khosrow** begs **Druvāspa** by the lake to let him overcome **Afrāsiyāb** and is granted his wish, an account close to the *Shahnameh* (M4: 354) where Afrāsiyāb is first forced out of a cave (*hang*) then out of the lake and is killed by Kay Khosrow, who establishes the **Āzar Goshasp** fire temple on its shore. In Sasanian times, the lake was "relocated" to Azarbaijan (so also in the *Shahnameh*) and identified with Lake Urmia.

Chin and Māchin: China and Greater [from *Mā*/*Mahā* "Great"] China—
that is, southern China and bordering regions in India, vs. Khotai/
Khotan, northern China.

Chinvat Bridge: In Zoroastrian eschatology, the bridge crossed by the soul
of the deceased that, after a reckoning based on their past conduct,
leads them to heaven, hell, or purgatory, where they will await universal
resurrection at the end of time.

Daēnā: MP *dēn*, "faith, creed, conscience." As conscience personified,
she appears to dead souls at the **Chinvat Bridge** in the shape of a
beautiful maiden or an ugly hag, depending on the deceased person's
moral conduct in life.

Darius I: See **Bisotūn inscription**.

Dastān: An epithet of **Zāl**.

Dēnkard/Dēnkart: "Religious Acts/Chapters)," a post-Islamic, encyclo-
paedic exposition of Mazdean beliefs, practices, and legends, compiled
by Ādurfarnbag ī Farroxzādān in Pahlavi in the ninth century, edited
and expanded by Ādurbād Ēmēdān in the tenth century (three of the
original nine books are lost). Book 3 mentions the destruction of the
written **Avesta** after Alexander's conquest of Iran, and its translation
into Greek, among other legends.

druj/*Druj*: "lie," the evil principle personified as a demoness that is opposed
to *aša*/*arta* "truth."

Drvāspā: Av. *Druvāspā*, "Possessing Sound Horses." A *yazata* of cattle
and horses, she is venerated in *Yt 9*, which is dedicated to **Gēuš Urvan**.

Ērānshahr: the "Dominion of Iran" in X^w**anīras** at the centre of the
world, Av. *Xšathra*, NP *shahr* meaning "dominion/kingdom/country".
In Avestan literature, *Airyanem Vaējah*, "Land of the Aryans" (NP
Ērānvēj), is the homeland of the Iranians. The earliest archaeological
evidence for the name is the investiture scene of the founder of the
Sasanian dynasty, Ardeshir I, "Shahanshah-e Ērān," in 224 CE and the
inscription on Ka'be-ye Zartošt by his son Shāpūr at Naqš-e Rostam.

Esfandiyār: Av. *Spenōdhāta*, MP *Spentōdād*, the righteous son of **Goshtāsp**
and **Katāyūn**, and grandson of Lohrāsp. Unwilling to pass the throne

to his son, Goshtāsp orders **Esfandiyār** to go on a mission to spread the Mazdean faith, and then to rescue his sisters Homāy and Beh-āfarīd from Arjāsp's captivity, a perilous ordeal known as The Seven Labors, *Haft Khān*. Goshtāsp finally sends him to his death by ordering him to capture **Rostam** who, aided by the mythic bird **Sīmurgh**, shoots a double arrow at Esfandiyār's only vulnerable spot, his eyes, and kills him. (See also **Espahbad**).

Espahbad/Sepāhbad: One of the seven great Parthian clans that traced their lineage to **Esfandiyār** son of **Goshtāsp**. During Sasanian times, the House of Espahbad governed Ray (which included Qom and Esfahan), possibly together with the House of Mehrān, while Kāren ruled Māh Nehāvand, and Sūren, Sistan. Espahbad is also the official title of militaɪy commanders of the four administrative divisions, *kusts*/*pazgou*s, established by Anūshiravan the Just (531–79 CE). The divisions encompassed the federation of twenty some countries under Sasanian rule and recalled the Achaemenid concept of the "Four Corners" of the world: Khorasan; Azarbaijan; Pars and Khuzestan; Iraq, Syria, and Anatolia.

Farākhkart Sea: Av. *Vourukaša*, MP *Varkaš*, a mythical sea that covers a third of the earth and into which waters flow from the peak of **Harā Berezaiti**.

Farangīs: Daughter of **Afrāsiyāb**, wife of **Siavash**, and mother of **Kay Khosrow** who, thanks to Siavash's prescient guidance, knows how to safely bring Kay Khosrow to Iran. In *GBd*, she is named Vīspān-fryā, and in older *Shahnameh* MSS, *Farīgīs*.

Fariborz: Son of **Kay Kāvūs** and brother of **Siavash**. He marries **Farangīs** as decreed by **Kay Khosrow** when he ascends the throne. He follows the king into the mountain when the latter abdicates and along with other companions, disappears in the snow.

Farr/Farreh: Av. *Xᵛarenah*; MP *Xᵂarrah*, "glory," a term likely related to *xᵂar*, "sun," is a numinous force that manifests as *Farreh-ye īzadi* ("divine glory") in divinities, Zoroaster, and other luminaries, and as *Farreh-ye Kiani* ("Kianid glory") in kings, whose legitimacy and hold on power is contingent on possessing it. Ordinary humans may also be endowed with *Farr*.

Fereidūn: Av. *Thraetaōna*, MP *Frēdōn/Farēdōn*, a mythical figure who in the **Avesta** vanquishes the dragon Aži Dahāka. In the *Shahnameh*, he is a **Pīshdādiān** king who overcomes the evil, serpent-shouldered king **Zahhāk** and divides the world among his three sons, **Iraj** (Iran), Salm/Sarm (**Rūm**), and **Tūr** (**Tūrān**).

Forūd: Son of **Siavash** and **Pīrān**'s daughter **Jarireh**. He is killed in battle when **Tūs** defies **Kay Khosrow**'s orders not to harm his brother.

Fravāk/Frawāg: Together with his female twin Frawāgēn, the grandchildren of the first human couple, Mašyā and Mašyaneh. They bear fifteen pairs of twins who in turn generate the human races that populate the earth.

Gang/Gangdež: See **Kang/Kangdež**.

Garōdmān: Av. *Garō.demāna*, "House of Song," Paradise, also called the House of the Good Mind and of the Best Existence.

Garsīvas: Av. *Keresavazda*, the jealous brother of the Turanian king **Afrāsiyāb** who turns the king against his son-in-law **Siavash** and causes his death. He is avenged by Siavash's son **Kay Khosrow**.

*Gāthā*s: See **Avesta**.

Gerūy/Gorūy: The Turanian warrior who, prompted by **Garsīvas**, volunteers to behead **Siavash** on **Afrasiyāb**'s orders.

Geuš Urvan: MP *Gōš*, the Avestan guardian spirit of animals, later called the Uniquely Created Bull. He is invoked in *Gōš Yašt* (*Yt* 9) and is closely related to **Drvāspā**.

Gīv: Son of **Gūdarz** who finds **Kay Khosrow** in **Tūran** after a seven-year search and safely escorts him and **Farangīs** to Iran on the back of Siavash's stallion, **Shabrang-e Behzād**.

Golzarriun: City and river in Chāch (Tashkant) in northeast Uzbekestan.

Gordāfarid: Valorous daughter of Gaždaham, the governor of *Dež-e Sepīd*, the "White Fort." She dons chain mail and takes on Turanian warriors in single combat, her identity being exposed only when **Sohrāb** defeats her and removes her helmet.

Gordiyeh: A **Parthian** noblewoman of the House of Mehrān. She is the wife of her brother Bahrām Chūbin until he dies in battle against Khosrow II, then marries the king's uncle, Vistahm of the House of **Espahbad**, and when he dies after a rebellion, marries the Sasanian Khosrow II (Khosrow Parviz, r. 590–628 CE).

Goshtāsp: Av. *Vištāspa*, MP *Wištāsp*, Gk *Hystāspēs*, the fifth and last of the **Kayāniān/Kianid** kings in the *Shahnameh*. In the *Gāthās*, he is a venerated patron of Zoroaster opposed by the Daēva-worshipping *kavi*s (rulers) and *karapan*s (priests) (*Yasna* 28:11). In epic, he is a king reviled for sending his son **Esfandiyār** to certain death by ordering him to vanquish **Rostam**. He is succeeded by his grandson **Bahman**.

Gostahm: Son of **Nozar** and the younger brother of **Tūs**, one of the five men who disappear in the snow when they follow **Kay Khosrow** up the mountain.

Gūdarz: Head of the House of Gūdarz, one of the great **Parthian** dynastic clans during the **Ashkāniān/Arsacid** period whose heroic exploits became infused with Avestan mythology and celebrated in epic. Gūdarz loses his seventy sons battling the Turanians (see **Tūr**) and kills **Pīrān** in the Battle of the Twelve Rokh.

Hallāj: Mansur al-Hallāj (*c.* 858–922), a Persian mystic born in Pars. As a Sunni Muslim, his declaration "I am the Truth" (*Haqq*, an epithet of God) and other Sufi teachings conflicted with the Abbasid court's religious tenets and political interests and led to his execution.

Hamāvan: A mountain where the exhausted Iranian army, led by **Tūs**, **Gūdarz**, and **Gīv**, resorts to as a last defense against the Turanians who are led by **Pīrān**. When **Rostam** finally comes to their aid, he enters the battlefield on foot and shoots a fatal arrow at the mounted **Ashkbūs**, the killer of **Gūdarz**' son Rohhām.

Hāmāvarān: Yemen, the kingdom subjugated by **Kay Kāvūs**, who marries the king's daughter, **Sūdābeh**.

Haoma: (Vedic *soma*), MP and NP *Hōm*, a *yazata* of plants who protects and empowers the living. It is also the name of the plant, "The Golden One" (*zairi-*), whose juice is consumed by priests to gain mantic wisdom and by warriors to induce battle fury. In the **Avesta**, the

White Haoma grows in the **Farākhkart Sea** or on mountain tops. In the *Shahnameh*, Hōm is a cave-dwelling hermit of inordinate strength who binds **Afrasiyāb** with his sacred girdle and drags him out of the *hang*, or cave, near Lake **Chīchast** where he has taken refuge.

Harā Berezaiti: MP *Harborz*, NP *Alborz*, "High Watchpost," a mountain range whose peak, **Hukairya/Hukar** or Čagād ī dāidīg, is at the centre of the earth from where all waters descend. One end of the **Chinvat Bridge** rests on its peak.

Hasanak-e Vazīr: A native of Neishāpūr from the noble Mīkālī family of west Khorasan that descended from the Sasanian king Bahrām V (d. 438 CE). A Sunni, Hasanak was chief minister of Sultan Mahmud Ghaznavi from 1024 until the latter's death in 1030. In the ensuing civil war, Hasanak supported the sultan's younger son Mohammad. Upon the latter's defeat, he was imprisoned in Balkh, tried, accused of being a Shi'a Qarmati, and executed by the older brother Masu'd I in early 1032. A memorable account of his trial is given in *Tārīkh-e Bayhaqi*.

Hōm: See **Haoma**.

Hormozd/Ohrmazd: MP for Av. **Ahura Mazdā**.

Hukairya/Hukar: Literally, "of good activity," the highest peak in the world atop **Harā Berezaiti** from where **Aredvī Sūrā Anāhita** streams all the waters down to earth.

Hūmān: Brother of **Pirān**, the Turanian general.

Hūshang: Av. *Haošyangha*, titled *Paradhāta*/Pīshdād, a culture hero who promoted civilization in the primordial age, established the laws of sovereignty, and in some sources, founded the **Pīshdādiān** dynasty. In the *Shahnameh*, his grandfather **Kiumars** is named the dynastic founder.

Hūshidar: Av. *Uxšyat.ereta*, MP *Ōšēdar*, the first of three messianic sons born to Zoroaster posthumously, each at the beginning of the last three millennia of world history (see **Sūshiyāns**).

Hūshidar-Māh: Av. *Uxšyat.nemah*, MP *Ōšēdar-Māh*, the second of the three messianic sons of Zoroaster (see **Sūshiyāns**).

Iraj: Av. *Erēc*, "Aryan," the youngest son of **Fereidūn** from his wife Arnavāz, he is granted Iran (Av. *Airyanem Vaējah*) when his father divides his realm among his three sons. Iraj is killed by his envious brothers **Salm** and **Tūr** and is avenged by his grandson **Manuchehr**.

Īzad: Deity in NP. See *yazatas*.

Jamshīd: Av. *Yima Xšaēta*, a king of the mythological age who builds the underground *var* in the **Avesta**. When his royal glory (*farr*) abandons him because he speaks a lie, he is overcome by the dragon **Zahhāk**, who cuts him in two and ascends the throne. In the *Shahnameh*, he is the fourth **Pīshdādi** king and possesses the world-revealing cup.

Jarireh: Daughter of **Pīrān**, the first wife of **Siavash**, and mother of **Forūd**.

Kāmūs-e Kashani: A chieftain in Transoxiana and leader of an army in the Battle of **Hamāvan**. Uncommonly strong, when he is about to overcome **Gīv** in single combat, **Tūs** comes to his help and the three fight to a draw. The next day, **Rostam** uses a ruse to bind his arms and takes him to Iran where he is cut to pieces.

Kang/Kandež: *Gang/Gangdež*, from Av. *kang/kangha*, "pit" (NP *kandan*, "to dig") and *dež*, "fortification," in Avestan mythology, a celestial fort that Siavash builds on a sacred mountaintop beyond the China Sea. Kangdež is where the immortal Pashūtan is king and from where he will arise to prepare the end time. In the *Shanhameh*, Siavash builds the fortress minus any magical qualities before he moves back to Turan and builds **Siavashgerd**, his earthly residential city.

Katāyun: Also known as Nāhīd, the daughter of the king of **Rūm** and mother of **Esfandiyār**. Having seen **Goshtāsp**, a farmer and the future **Kayāniān/Kianid** king in a dream, she chooses him from among all the nobles and heroes gathered by his father as marriage prospects.

Kay Kāvūs: Av. *Kavi Usan*, son of **Kay Qobād**, and the second **Kayāniān/Kianid** king who commits many follies and whose wife **Sūdābeh** falsely accuses her stepson **Siavash** of having tried to violate her. He is succeeded on the throne by his grandson **Kay Khosrow**.

Kay: Av. *Kauui/Kavi*, "seer" and "ruler" in the **Avesta**, and the title of Zoroaster's patron Kavi Vištāspa (**Goshtāsp**). In epic, it is the title of the kings of the **Kayāniān/Kianid** dynasty.

Kay Khosrow: Av. *Kavi Haosravah*, MP *Husrōy*, son of **Siavash** and **Farangīs** who is saved by **Pīrān** at birth and reared by shepherds. He later avenges his father upon his grandfather **Afrāsiyāb** and rules Iran for sixty years in unprecedented peace and prosperity, then abdicates, appoints Lohrāsp king, and goes into occultation on a mountaintop.

Kay Lohrāsp: A descendant of **Kay Qobād**, he is crowned king by Kay Khosrow against the objections of several champions, in particular **Zāl**. He has two sons, Zarēr, and Vištāsp (**Goshtāsp**) who follows him on the throne as the last Kianid king.

Kay Qobād: Founder of the **Kayāniān/Kianid** dynasty, a descendant of **Manuchehr** and the father of **Kay Kāvūs**.

Kayāniān/Kianid: Dynasty founded by **Kay Qobād** that initiates the heroic age, which is dominated by wars between Iranians and Turanians (see **Tūr**) before the historic age.

Khotan: A Turanian province ruled by Pīrān in N. China where Siavash eventually resides. See **Chin and Māchin**.

Kiumars: Av. *Gayō.maretan*, "Mortal Life," the mythical First Man and founder of the **Pīshdādiān** dynasty in the *Shahnameh*.

Malkūs: Av. *Mahrkūša*, "The Destroyer," a demon who brings a calamitous winter at the end of the millennium of **Hūshīdar**, which drives **Jamshīd** to build the underground *var* to save the creation.

Mani: Founder of a dualistic gnostic religion, an Aramaic-speaking Iranian born in southern Babylonia near Ctesiphon in 216/7 CE and raised in a Jewish–Christian community. A prolific writer, painter, and proselytizer, he proclaimed a universalist prophethood surpassing the 'local and limited' teachings of Adam, the Buddha, Zoroaster, and Jesus. He was patronized by the Sasanian king Shapur I to whom he dedicated his *Dō bun ī Šābuhragān* in 242 CE. Fiercely opposed by the Magi, he died in prison *c.*274 in Gondishāpur after a trial administered by the chief *mobed* Kerdīr under Bahrām I. Manicheism spread in different languages in the Persian and Roman empires, Egypt and N.

Africa, southern Gaul, and Spain through his missionary zeal and survived his death. In the eighth century, it became the state religion of the Uighur kingdom of Qocho and continued in China until the fourteenth century.

Manīžeh: Daughter of **Afrāsiyāb** who seduces the Iranian prince **Bīžan** and marries him against her father's wishes. The couple are the subject of an adventurous romance in the *Shahnameh*.

Manuchehr: Av. *Manuščithra*, grandson of **Iraj**, and the eighth **Pīshdādi** king. He kills his jealous uncles Salm and **Tūr** to avenge the death of his father **Iraj**.

Mazandaran: See **Rūyān**.

Mazdak: A Zoroastrian religious revolutionary who was a gnostic, ascetic, anti-clerical, and pacifist promoter of wealth-sharing, and a vegetarian. Having gained a large following and converted the Sasanian Kavād I (r. 488–531 CE), the priesthood labelled the king heretical and deposed him in 496 CE. When Kavād regained the throne, his son and heir, **Anūshiravan**, hanged Mazdak (*c.*524–8) and according to the *Shahnameh,* buried three thousand Mazdakites alive.

Mehr: Av. Mithra (Vedic Mitra), the *yazata* and watchful guardian of covenants who rides his chariot across the sky with one thousand eyes and one thousand ears. His close associate in punishing oath-breakers is **Bahrām**, the god of victory. Mithra (Vedic Mitra) was closely associated with the sun and was later identified with it. For more on Mehr, see "Dawn," n. 26.

Nāhīd: See **Aredvī Sūra Anāhitā**.

Nakhshab: City in southern Uzbekestan, southwest of Tashkent (Chāch in the *Shahnameh)*, on the route between Balkh and Bokhara.

Nēryōsang: Av. *Nairyō.sangha*, a messenger between God and humans, he guards the seed of **Kiumars** and helps the immortal **Pashūtan** bring about universal resurrection at the end of time.

Nīmrūz: See **Zābolestan**.

Nozar: Son of **Manuchehr**. As a king, he loses his glory due to his oppressive rule and is killed by **Afrāsiyāb**.

Oshnar: Av. *Aoš.nara*, titled "learned [*dānā*]," **Kay Kāvūs'** wise counsellor. Kāvūs, misguided by demons, orders him killed.

Parthians: A north-eastern Iranian tribe infused with the Parni of Dahae who formed the **Askhāniān/Arsacid** dynasty in *c.*247 BCE when their eponymous founder, Arsaces I, proclaimed himself king in Aršak near Qūčān. In *c.*238 BCE, they defeated the Seleucid satrap of Parthava, captured Hyrcania and repulsed Antiochus III two decades later and moved their capital to Ctesiphon. Parthian noble clans, including the House of Sūren, Kāren, **Espahbad/Spahbad**, Mehrān, Warāz, and Kāmsarakān continued to hold regional power under the Sasanians after the Arsacids were overthrown by Ardeshir Bābakān in 224 CE.

Pashang: Father of **Afrāsiyāb**. His ancestor is **Fereidūn**, followed by Tūr, Dūrōšab, Spaenyasp, Tūra, and his father, Zādšam.

Pashūtan: Av. *Pešōtanu*, the immortal son of **Goshtāsp**. He will rise from **Kangdež** a thousand years after Zoroaster and aided by a group of divinities and 150 righteous men, prepare the world for the birth of the first of three *Sūshiyāns*.

Pilsam: The son of the Turanian Vīseh and brother of **Pīrān**. Brave and ambitious, he requests permission from **Afrāsiyāb** to fight **Rostam** in the second war of vengeance for **Siavash** and is speared to death.

Pīrān: Afrāsiyāb's commanding general and wise counsellor from the House of Vīseh and lord of **Khotan** where he takes **Siavash** and gives him his daughter Jarireh in marriage. He later saves the infant **Kay Khosrow's** life but ultimately fights him during the wars of vengeance for **Siavash** out of loyalty to Afrāsiyāb and **Tūrān**. He is killed by **Gūdarz** and mourned by Kay Khosrow.

Pīrūz: MP *Pērōz*, "Victorious," son of the Sasanian king Yazdgird II. Early in his reign (459–84 CE), Iran suffered from a drought that lasted seven years while he had to contend with the Hephthalites, and later on with revolts in Armenia and Iberta. It was during the third war with the Hephthalites, who had captured Neishapur, Herat, and Marv while **Zābolestan** had been seized by the Huns, that he was defeated and killed.

Pīshdādiān: Av. *Paradhāta*, the dynasty of primordial culture hero-kings. See **Hūshang**.

Qaznai/Ghazni: City in eastern Afghanistan and a major centre of Buddhism until the seventh century. In 867 CE, the coppersmith Ya'qūb Laith, founder of the Saffarid dynasty of Sistan who aspired to reviving Iran's ancient identity, sent the Abbasid Caliph a poem he had composed that said: "With me is the *Derafsh-e Kaviani* [the **Kayāniān/Kianid** banner] through which I hope to rule the nations." He besieged Qaznai in 870 and drove out the Hindu Shahis. In 962, Qaznai became the capital of the Qaznavids under Sabuktakin.

Rakhsh: "Luminous," **Rostam**'s legendary red stallion of unique strength, intelligence, and fealty, and the only horse that could bear Rostam's weight. After a life of epic length, horse and rider die when they fall into a pit dug by Rostam's half-brother Shaqād that is filled with poisoned arrows.

Rašn: Av. *Rašnu*, the "Very Righteous" *yazatalīzad* of justice and part of a trio with **Mehr** and **Sorūsh** who judge the souls of the dead.

Rohhām: Son of **Gūdarz**. He kills the Turanian **Bārmān** in the Battle of the Twelve Rokh and is among the group of heroes, including his brother **Gīv** and his nephew **Bīžan**, who disappear in the snow when they follow **Kay Khosrow** up the mountain at the end of his reign.

Rostam: "Big and Brawny," from Av. *road*, "growth" (NP *rūyeš*), and *taxma*, "brawny," he is a native of **Zābolestan**, the son of **Zāl** and **Rūdābeh**, married to Tahmineh, the daughter of the king of Samangān, and the father of Sohrāb. A hero of unique strength and loyalty to the king, he wears a tiger skin over his armor that makes him invincible. Among his singular exploits are The Seven Labors, *Haft Khān*, which he performs to rescue **Kāvūs** from prison in Mazandaran. Rostam and his legendary red stallion, **Rakhsh**, are killed when he is aged six hundred.

Rūdābeh: Daughter of Sindokht and Mehrāb, the king of **Kābol** who is a descendant of **Zahhāk**, she is the wife of **Zāl** and the mother of **Rostam**.

Rūm: The western territories granted by **Fereidūn** to **Salm** (Sarm), who is his first son from his wife Shahrnāz.

Rūyān: A mountainous region of western Mazandaran in northern Iran from where **Ārash** shot an arrow to demarcate the border between Iran and **Tūrān**.

Sakastān/Sistan: See **Zābolestan**.

Salm/Sarm: Av. *Sairama*, the oldest son of **Fereidūn**, he is granted **Rūm** when his father divides his dominion among his three sons. **Salm** and **Tūr**, who are of the same mother, **Shahrnāz**, band together and kill their youngest brother **Iraj** who is allotted the choicest land, Iran.

Satavēs/Sadvēs: Av. *Satavāesa*, is the leader of the constellation of the west (Antares), as Vanant is of the south (Vega), Teštar/Tīr (Canis Major) of the east, and Haptōk-ring/Haftōrang (Ursa Major) of the north.

Shabrang-e Behzād: "The Black High-born One," **Siavash**'s stallion that first takes him through the fire and later hides in **Tūrān** for seven years on his master's orders until **Gīv** finds him. Equipped with Siavash's saddle and riding gear, Shabrang then carries **Kay Khosrow** to Iran, accompanied by **Gīv** and guided by **Farangīs**.

Shīdeh: Son of **Afrāsiyāb**, also called Pashang in the *Shahnameh*. He is killed by **Kay Khosrow** during the last war of vengeance for **Siavash**.

Siavash: Av. *Siiāuuaršan*, MP *Siyavaxš*, "Having a Black Stallion," son of **Kay Kāvūs** and father of **Kay Khosrow**. He spurns his step-mother **Sūdābeh**'s love, undergoes a trial by fire, then takes refuge with **Afrāsiyāb** in **Tūrān**, who eventually orders him killed. A plant continues to sprout from the spot where his blood spilled on the earth.

Siavashgerd: City built by **Siavash** in **Khotan** at Afrasiyab's invitation after he has built **Kangdež** in outlying territories.

Sīmurgh: Av. *Saēna meregha*, MP *Sēn murv*, a gigantic, falcon-like mythical bird that in the Avesta (*Yt.* 12:17) nests on the Tree of All Seeds. In the *Shahnameh*, she rescues the infant **Zāl** and rears him in her perch atop Mount Qāf and imparts wisdom to him. She assists in the difficult birth of **Rostam** and later helps him when he is in dire straits.

Sistan: See **Zābolestan**.

Sohrāb: Son of **Rostam** who is born and raised in **Tūrān** and faces his father for the first time when they meet in battle. The two are unaware of their relationship until the victorious Rostam recognizes his son's armband after he has struck the fatal blow.

Sorūsh: Av. *Sraoša*, a divinity of prayer and a judge of the souls at death, he appears to **Siavash** and **Gūdarz** in their dreams to guide their actions.

Spandārmaz: Av. *Ārmaiti*, "Devotion/Obedience," a female **Ameša Spenta**, and a deity of the Earth.

Sūdābeh: Daughter of the king of **Hāmāvarān** and beloved wife of **Kay Kāvūs** whose unrequited love for her stepson **Siavash** leads to his eventual death.

Sūshiyāns: Av. *Saošyant*, "Benefactor," a term applied especially, but not exclusively, to the last of the three messianic sons of Zoroaster to be born posthumously from his seed, which is miraculously preserved in Lake Kašaoya (*Yt* 19.92). In *Yt* 13.128-29. The three are named *Uxšyat.ereta*, *Uxšyat.nemah*, and *Astvat.ereta* ("embodying righteousness"), and in Pahlavi texts, **Hūshidar, Hūshidar-Māh**, and Sōšyāns, the latter being the one who brings about Renovation (*Frašō.kereti*) at the end of time.

Tahamtan: "Strong-bodied," an epithet of **Rostam** and an alternative name for the hero; from Av. *taxma*, "strong, brawny," and *tan*, "body."

Tahmineh: Daughter of the king of Samangān, she boldly enters **Rostam**'s tent and declares her love for him and marries him. Their son, **Sohrāb**, is born after Rostam returns to his homeland.

Tahmuras: Av. *Taxma Urupi*, the third king of the **Pīshdādiān** dynasty after **Hūshang**, and a vanquisher of demons.

Tūr: Av. *Tūč* (**Tūr(a)ca*), "Brave," the second of **Fereidūn**'s three sons who is granted lands north and east of Iran, later known as **Tūrān**. The Turanians (Av. *Tūirya*) came to be identified with the Turks in the early seventh century and are so called in the *Shahnameh*.

Tūrān: Lands in Central Asia and China inhabited by Iranian peoples under the rule of **Afrāsiyāb**, who in the *Shahnameh* is identified as a Turk (see **Tūr**).

Tūs: Son of the **Pīshdādi** king **Nozar**, who causes the death of **Kay Khosrow**'s brother **Forūd** by dismissing Kay Khosrow's order not to harm him.

Vayu: MP *Vāy*, the Avestan wind (NP *bād*) god who in later traditions is a dual beneficent/deathly figure. The duality survives in the healing ceremonies of **Zār** in southern Iran where the patient is said to be afflicted either by the "good" wind, which is considered a Muslim, or the "evil" wind, an infidel, the latter being harder to exorcise.

Vištāsp: See **Goštāsp**.

Xʷanīras: In Avestan and Pahlavi literature, the greatest country (*kešvar*, *shahr*) among the seven concentric climes that were formed at creation (MP *būm ī haft kišwar*). Xʷanīras lies at the centre and is as large as the six others combined; it is where **Sūshiyāns** will rise at the end of time.

Ya'qūb Laith Saffari: See **Qaznai**.

Yasna: See **Avesta**

yazatas: NP *īzadān*, "Venerable Ones," prominent deities that rank below the **Ameša Spentas** and oversee special domains. They include **Mehr** (Av. *Mithra*)/covenants; **Aredvī Sūrā Anāhitā** (NP *Nāhīd*)/water and fertility; **Ātaš** (Av. *Ātar*)/fire; **Bahrām** (Av. *Verethragna*)/victory; **Rašn** (Av. *Rašnu*)/justice; and **Sorūsh** (Av. *Sraoša*)/discipline and obedience.

Zābolestan: Alternative term used in the *Shahnameh* for Sistan/Sakastān, and Nīmrūz, covering the eastern Iranian region of Sistan-Baluchestan/ SW Afghanistan. It is **Rostam**'s homeland and as decreed by **Kay Qobād**, under his rule.

Zahhāk: Av. *Aži Dahākā*. In the Avesta, he is a formidable dragon who slays **Jamshīd** and ascends the throne until he is overcome by **Fereidūn**. In the *Shahnameh*, he is an evil king of Tāzi/Arab lineage: two serpents grow from his shoulders and are fed human brains every day until **Kāveh** the Blacksmith rises and hoisting his leather apron as the **Kayāniān/Kianid** banner, *Derafš-e Kāviāni*, topples him.

Zāl: Son of Sām and grandson of Narīmān. Born with white hair (hence, *Zāl-e Zar*, "golden"), he is abandoned in open country to die but is rescued and reared by the fabulous bird **Sīmurgh** in her mountain-top nest. He later marries **Rūdābeh** and fathers **Rostam**, the greatest hero of the *Shahnameh*.

Zand: Also known as Zand-Avesta, exegetic literature collected in the Sasanian period to translate, explicate, and interpret the orally transmitted Avesta in Middle Persian/Pahlavi.

Zāv/Zav: Also called *Zāv-e Tahmāsp* and *Zou*, a descendant of **Nozar** and the tenth king of the **Pīshdādiān** dynasty.

Zurvan: "Time," or *Zurvan Akarana*, "Unbounded Time," the progenitor of the twins **Ahura Mazdā** and **Ahriman**. Zurvanite cosmology promoted a fatalistic vision of life that grew popular in the early Sasanian period.

BIBLIOGRAPHY

Anklesaria, B.T., trans. *Zand-Ākāsīh: Iranian or Greater Bundahišn.*
Bombay: Rahnumae Mazdayasnan Sahbha, 1956. Facsimile ed.
Tehran: Iranian Cultural Foundation No. 88, 1971.

Corbin, Henry. *Corps spirituel et terre céleste.* Paris: Buchet/Chastel,
1960.

———, ed. *Rūzbihān Baqlī, Sharh-e Shathiyāt.* Tehran: Institut
Franco-Iranien, 1966.

Darmesteter, James, trans. *Le Zend-Avesta.* 3 vols. Paris: Adrien
Maisonneuve, 1960.

Duchesne-Guillemain, Jacques. *La religion de l'Iran ancien.* Paris:
Presses Universitaires de France, 1962.

———. " Espace et temps dans l'Iran ancien. " *Revue de Synthèse*,
3:55–6 (1969): 259–80.

Dumézil, Georges. *Les dieux souverains des Indo-Européens.* Paris:
Presses Universitaires de France, 1952.

———. *L'idéologie tripartite des Indo-Européens.* Brussels: Latomus,
1958.

———. *Mitra-Varuna.* Paris: Gallimard, 1948.

———. *Mythe et Epopée.* 3 vols. Paris: Gallimard, 1968, 1971, 1973.

Eliade, Mircea. *Le mythe de l'éternel retour.* Paris: Gallimard, 1949.

———. *Le sacré et le profane.* Paris: Gallimard, 1965.

————. *Traité d'histoire des religions*. Paris: Payot, 1964.

Guerber, H.A. *Myths and Legends of the Middle Ages*. New York: Dover, 1983.

Massignon, Louis. *The Passion of al-Hallaj, Mystic and Martyr of Islam*. Translated by Herbert Mason. Princeton: Princeton University Press, 1982.

————, trans. *Akhbar al-Hallaj*. Paris: Librairie Philosophique J. Vrin, 1975.

Minorsky, Vladimir. "La domination des Dailamites." *Société des études iraniennes et de l'art persan*. Issue 3. Paris: E. Leroux, 1964: 12–30.

Molé, Marijan. *Culte, mythe et cosmologie dans l'Iran ancien*. Paris: Presses Universitaires de France, 1963.

————."La naissance du monde dans l'Iran préislamique." *Sources Orientales*. Vol. 1. Paris: Seuil, 1959: 299–328.

Sachau, Eduard, trans. *Chronology of Ancient Nations: An English Version of Āthār'ul-Bāqiya*. Frankfurt: Goethe University Press, 1998.

Widengren, Geo. *Hochgottglaube im alten Iran: eine religionsphänomenologische Untersuchung*. Uppsala: Almqvist & Wiksell, 1938.

————. *Les religions de l'Iran*. Paris: Payot, 1968.

Wikander, Stig. *Der arische Männerbund*. Lund: Gleerupska Univ.- Bokhandeln, 1938.

Zaehner, R.C. *The Dawn and Twilight of Zoroastrianism*. London: Weidenfeld & Nicolson, 1961.

————. *Zurvan: A Zoroastrian Dilemma*. New York: Biblo & Tannen, 1955.

Sources in Persian

Afifi, Rahim, trans. *Ardāvirāf-nāmeh*. Mashhad: Mashhad University Press, 1369/1990.

Afshar, Iraj, ed., *Eskandar-nāmeh of Pseudo Callisthenes*. Tehran: Bongah-e Tarjomeh va Nashr-e Ketab, 1343/1965.

Bahar, Mehrdad. "Joqrāfiyā-ye Asātiri-ye Jahan va Iran." *Bonyad-e Farhang*, 1:1 (1347/1968): 11–24.

Bahar, Mohammad-Taghi, Malek ul-Shoa'ra, trans. *Tarjomeh-ye Chand Matn-e Pahlavi*. Tehran: Sepehr, 1347/1968.

———. *Sabk-Shenāsi*. 3 vols. Tehran: Tūs, 1337/1958.

———, and M. Parvin Gonabadi, eds. *Tārikh-e Bal'ami: Tarjomeh-ye Tārikh-e Tabari.* Tehran: Zavvār, 1341/1962.

Biruni, Abu Rayhan. *Āthār ul-Bāghiya*. Translated by Akbar Dānāseresht. Tehran: Amir Kabir, 1386/2007.

Carnoy, Albert J. *Asātīr-e Irani*. Translated by A. Tabatabaie. Tehran: Franklin, 1341/1962.

Christensen, Arthur. *Kiāniān*. Translated by Zabihullah Safa. Tehran: Bongah-e Tarjomeh va Nashr-e Ketab, 1343/1964.

———. *Iran dar Zamān-e Sāsāniān*. Translated by Rashid Yasami. Tehran: Ibn Sina, 1332/1953.

Corbin, Henry, ed. *Majmu'eh-ye Mosannafāt-e Sheikh-e Ishrāq*, Vol. 3, *Persian Treatises*, edited by Hossein Nasr. Tehran: Anjoman-e Shahanshahi-ye Falsafeh-ye Iran, 1397/1977.

D'yakonov, Mikhail M. *Ashkānian*. Translated by Karim Keshavarz. Tehran: Payām, 1378/1999.

Fayyāz, Ali-Akbar, ed. *Tārīkh-e Beyhaqi.* Mashhad: Ferdowsi University Press, 1356/1977.

Forouzanfar, Badi'ul-Zaman, ed. *Kolliyāt-e Dīvān-e Shams*. 2 vols. Tehran: Rād, 1375/1996.

Hamza Esfahani. *Tārikh-e Payāmbarān va Pādeshāhān (Tārikh sini mulūk al-arz wa'l-anbiyā).* Translated by Jafar Shoā'r. Tehran: Bonyad-e Farhang-e Iran, 1346/1967.

Hedayat, Sadegh. "Tarānehā-ye Āmiyāneh-ye Farsi." *Majalleh-ye Musīghī*, 1:7 (1318/1939): 17–28.

———, trans. "Yādgār i Jāmāspi (Jāmāsb-nāmeh)." *Sokhan*, 1 (1322/1943).

———, trans. *Zand-e Vohuman Yasn (Bahman Yašt).* Tehran: Amir Kabir, 1342/1963.

Jayhounabadi, Hāj Ne'matullah. *Shahnameh-ye Haqiqat*. Edited by Mohammad Mokri. 2 vols. Tehran: Tahouri, 1361/1982.

Kashefi, Hossein Va'ez. *Rawzat ul-Shuhadā.* Edited by Mohammad Ramezani. Tehran: 1341/1962.

Minovi, Mojtaba, and Mohammad-Ali Rezvani, eds. *Nāmeh-ye Tansar be Goshnasp*. Tehran: Khārazmi, 1354/1975.

Nafisi, Saeed, ed. *Dīvān-e Anvari*. Tehran: Sanā'ie, 1337/1958.

Narshakhi, Mohammad ibn Jaʿfar. *Tārīkh-e Bokhārā*, abridged and edited by Mohammad ibn Zofar ibn Omar. Edited by Modarres Razavi. 2nd ed. Tehran: Tūs, 1363/1984.

Nasafi, Azizuddin. *Kitāb al-Insān ul-Kāmil*. Edited by Marijan Molé. Tehran: Institut Franco-Iranien, 1962.

Nicholson, R.A., ed. and trans. *The Mathnawī of Jalāl'uddīn Rūmī*. Vol. 1. Cambridge: Cambridge University Press, 1925.

———, and Guy Le Strange, eds. *The Fārs-nāmeh of Ibn ul-Balkhi*. London: Luzac & Co., 1962.

Pazhdo, Zartusht Bahram. *Zarātusht-nāmeh*. Edited by Mohammad Dabir-Siaghi. Tehran: Tahouri, 1338/1959.

Pourdavoud, Ebrahim, trans. *Gāthā*. Tehran: Tehran University Press, 1354/1975.

———, trans. *Yasnā, Jozvi az nāmeh-ye minovi-ye Avesta*. Vol. 1: Bombay: Society of the Iranian Zoroastrians of Bombay, 1312/1933. Vol. 2: Tehran: Tehran University Press, 1337/1958.

———, trans. *Yaŝthā*. 2 vols. Tehran: Tahouri, 1347/1968.

Rohani, Seyyed Hossein, trans. *Tārīkh-e Kāmel-e Ibn Athīr*. 14 vols. Tehran: Asātir, 1369/1991.

Soheili Khansari, Ahmad, ed. *Khosrow-nāmeh-ye Fariduddin Attar-e Neishabouri*. Tehran: Zavvār, 1355/1976.

Suri, Mashallah, trans. *Soroudhā-ye Dīni-ye Yārsān*. Tehran: Amir Kabir, 1319/1940.

Yaqmaie, Habib, ed. *Tarjomeh-ye Tafsīr-e Tabari*. 7 vols. 2nd ed. Tehran: Tūs, 1356/1977.

Ferdowsi and Other Cited Poets

Quotations from Ferdowsi's *Shahnameh* are sourced from the critical edition published in Moscow (M), with volume and page number (e.g. M3: 63), and exceptionally from the Borukhim (B) edition.

M   Bertels, E.E., ed. *Shahnameh*. 9 vols. Moscow: Institute of Oriental Studies, USSR Academy of Sciences, 1960–71.

B   Vullers, Joannes A., ed. *Shahnameh.* 10 vols. Tehran: Borukhim, 1315/1936.

All references to other poets provided by the translator (Trans.) in the footnotes are sourced from ganjoor.net (e.g. Hafez/Ganjoor, *Qazal* #105).

ABOUT THE AUTHORS

Shahrokh Meskoob was an Iranian writer and intellectual, who was born in Babol, on the Caspian coast, in 1924 and died in Paris in 2005 at the age of eighty-one. Imprisoned in Iran for three years in the mid 1950s for leftist activities, he was forced to leave the country following the Islamic Revolution of 1979, after publishing two articles in the *Ayandegan* newspaper in Tehran that criticized the new regime.

Meskoob authored seventeen books, including seminal works on Ferdowsi's *Shahnameh, Moghaddame-i bar Rostam o Esfandiyar* (1963) and *Sūg-e Siavash* (1971). Three of his works have been translated into English, *Iranian Nationality and the Persian Language* (1992), and posthumously, *In the Alley of the Friend: On the Poetry of Hafez* (2018), and *The Ant's Gift: A Study of the Shahnameh* (2021). His translations into Persian include Steinbeck's *The Grapes of Wrath* (1949) and five Greek tragedies by Aeschylus and Sophocles (1956-1973). Surveys of his literary output include *Shahrokh Meskoob: A Commemorative*, an *Iran Nameh* Special Issue (2006), and *A Scholar for Our Times: A Celebration of the Life and Work of Shahrokh Meskoob* (2022), Stanford Iranian Studies series.

Mahasti Afshar Ziai was born in Tehran. She studied Drama and Classical Music Production at the BBC/London and ORTF/Paris and served as technical director at the Shiraz Arts Festival before pursuing academic studies in the U.S. She earned a Ph.D. (1988) in Sanskrit and Indo-European Folklore and Mythology at Harvard; her dissertation was titled *The Immortal Hound: Genesis and Transformation of a Symbol in Indo-Iranian Traditions*. In 1989, she joined the Getty Conservation Institute in Los Angeles where she produced numerous documentaries and museum exhibitions around the world on humanity's cultural heritage.

Her publications include *Art and Eternity: Nefertari Wall Paintings*; *The Ecology of Conservation*; *Landmarks of a New Generation*; *Festival of Arts, Shiraz-Persepolis 1967-77*; and translations of Shahrokh Mesbook's *Notes by a Traveler*, Majid Lashkari's *The Theatre and Cinema of Arby Ovanessian*, and an extensively revised version of Saeed Habashi's *Final Sequence* about the father of Iranian cinema Esma'il Kushan.

Abbas Milani is the Hamid and Christina Moghadam Director of the Iranian Studies program at Stanford University. In his book, *Lost Wisdom: Rethinking Modernity in Iran* (2004), he provides evidence that Iranian modernity dates back at least 1,000 years. He is the author of many books, including *The Persian Sphinx: Amir Abbas Hoveyda and the Riddle of the Iranian Revolution* (2000), and *The Shah* (2012). His biography of Reza Shah is forthcoming.

INDEX

OTHER TITLES FROM MAGE

PERSIAN GULF SERIES BY WILLEM FLOOR

A Political and Economic History of 5 Port Cities, 1500–1750

The Rise of the Gulf Arabs, The Politics of Trade on the Persian Littoral, 1747–1792

The Rise and Fall of Bandar-e Lengeh, The Distribution Center for the Arabian Coast, 1750–1930

Bandar Abbas: The Natural Trade Gateway of Southeast Iran

Links with the Hinterland: Bushehr, Borazjan, Kazerun, Banu Ka'b, & Bandar Abbas

The Hula Arabs of The Shibkuh Coast of Iran

Dutch-Omani Relations: A Political History, 1651–1806

Muscat: City, Society and Trade

Karkh: The Island's Untold Story (with D.T. Potts)

The Persian Gulf: Bushehr: City, Society, & Trade, 1797-1947

The Rebel Bandits of Tangestan

IRANIAN HISTORY BY WILLEM FLOOR

Agriculture in Qajar Iran

Public Health in Qajar Iran

The History of Theater in Iran

A Social History of Sexual Relations in Iran

Guilds, Merchants, and Ulama in Nineteenth-Century Iran

Labor & Industry in Iran 1850 -1941

The Rise and Fall of Nader Shah: Dutch East India Company Reports 1730-1747

Games Persians Play: A History of Games and Pastimes in Iran from Hide-and-Seek to Hunting

History of Bread in Iran

Studies in the History of Medicine in Iran

Salar al-Dowleh: A Delusional Prince and Wannabe Shah

Kermanshah: City and Province, 1800-1945

History of Hospitals in Iran, 550–1950

The Beginnings of Modern Medicine in Iran

History of Glace and Ceramics, 1500–1925

Transportation & Technology in Iran, 1800–1940

History of Paper in Iran, 1501–1925

Willem Floor and Amélie Couvrat Desvergnes

ANNOTATED TRANSLATIONS BY WILLEM FLOOR

German Sources on Safavid Persia

Russian Sources on Iran: 1719–1748

Exotic Attractions in Persia, 1684–1688: Travels & Observations

Engelbert Kaempfer:

A Man of Two Worlds: Pedros Bedik in Iran, 1670–1675
translated with Colette Ouahes from the Latin

Astrakhan Anno 1770
Samuel Gottlieb Gmelin

Travels Through Northern Persia 1770–1774
Samuel Gottlieb Gmelin

Titles and Emoluments in Safavid Iran: A Third Manual of Safavid Administration
Mirza Naqi Nasiri

Persia: An Area Study, 1633

Joannes de Laet

translated with Colette Ouahes from the Latin

WILLEM FLOOR IN COLLABORATION WITH HASAN JAVADI

Persian Pleasures
How Iranians Relaxed Through the Centuries
with Food, Drink and Drugs

Awake: A Moslem Woman's Rare Memoir of Her Life and Partnership with the Editor of Molla Nasreddin, the Most Influential Satirical Journal of the Caucasus and Iran, 1907–1931
Hamideh Khanum Javanshir

The Heavenly Rose-Garden: A History of Shirvan & Daghestan
Abbas Qoli Aqa Bakikhanov

Travels in Iran and the Caucasus,
1652 and 1655
Evliya Chelebi

Persia Observed Series

The Strangling of Persia:
A Story of European Diplomacy and Oriental Intrigue
Morgan Shuster

The Persian Revolution of 1905-1909
Edward Brown / Introduction by Abbas Amanat

In the Land of the Lion & Sun:
Experiences of Life in Persia from 1866-1881
C. J. Wills / Introduction by Abbas Amanat

A Man of Many Worlds:
The Diaries and Memoirs of Dr. Ghasem Ghani
Ghasem Ghani / Edited by Cyrus Ghani

Cinema

The Films of Makhmalbaf: Cinema, Politics, and Culture in Iran
Eric Egan

Masters & Masterpieces of Iranian Cinema
Hamid Dabashi

My Favorite Films
Cyrus Ghani

FICTION

My Uncle Napoleon
Iraj Pezeshkzad / Translated by Dick Davis

Savushun: A Novel about Modern Iran
Simin Daneshvar / Translated by M.R. Ghanoonparvar

Daneshvar's Playhouse: A Collection of Stories
Simin Daneshvar / Translated by Maryam Mafi

Sutra and Other Stories
Simin Daneshvar / Translated by Hasan Javadi & Amin Neshati

Stories from Iran: A Chicago Anthology 1921-1991
Edited by Heshmat Moayyad

Garden of the Brave in War
Terence O'Donnell

Seven Shades of Memory: Stories of Old Iran
Terence O'Donnell

King of the Benighted
Houshang Golshiri / Translated by Abbas Milani

Black Parrot, Green Crow: A Collection of Short Fiction
Houshang Golshiri / Translated by Heshmat Moayyad et al.

COOKBOOKS BY NAJMIEH BATMANGLIJ

*Food of Life: Ancient Persian and
Modern Iranian Cooking and Ceremonies*

Joon: Persian Cooking Made Simple

Cooking in Iran: Regional Recipes and Kitchen Secrets

Silk Road Cooking: A Vegetarian Journey

From Persia to Napa: Wine at the Persian Table
With: Dick Davis and Burke Owens

Memoir and History

Discovering Cyrus: The Persian Conqueror
Astride the Ancient World
Reza Zarghamee

The Persian Sphinx:
Amir Abbas Hoveyda and the Iranian Revolution
Abbas Milani

Tales of Two Cities:
A Persian Memoir
Abbas Milani

Lost Wisdom:
Rethinking Modernity in Iran
Abbas Milani

Tarikh-e Azodi, Life at the Court of the Early Qajar Shahs
Soltan Ahmad Mirza Azod al-Dowleh,
Edited and Translated by Manoutchehr M. Eskandari-Qajar

The Artist and the Shah: Memoirs of Life at the Persian Court
by Dust-Ali Khan Mo`ayyer al-Mamalek,
Edited and Translated by Manoutchehr M. Eskandari-Qajar

Crowning Anguish: Taj al-Saltana
Memoirs of a Persian Princess
Introduction by Abbas Amanat / Translated by Anna Vanzan

French Hats in Iran
Heydar Radjavi

Father Takes a Drink and Other Memories of Iran
Heydar Radjavi

The Persian Garden: Echoes of Paradise
Mehdi Khansari / M. R. Moghtader / Minouch Yavari

Closed Circuit History
Ardeshir Mohassess, foreword by Ramsey Clark

Mosaddegh: Ahead of Their Time, Book 1
Nicolas Gorjestani

Shadman Diaries, 1926–1928, Book 1
Fakhr al-Din Shadman

Persia Portrayed : Envoys to the West, 1600–1842
D.T. Potts

A Nook in the Temple of Fame: French Military Officers in Service of Persia,
1807–1826
D.T. Potts

Albert Houtum Schindler:
A Remarkable Polymath in Late-Qajar Iran
D.T. Potts

POETRY

Faces of Love: Hafez and the Poets of Shiraz – Bilingual Edition
Translated by Dick Davis

The Mirror Of My Heart:
A Thousand Years of Persian Poetry by Women – Bilingual Edition
Translated by Dick Davis

Pearls That Soak My Dress: Elegies for a Child
Jahan Malek Khatun/ translated by Dick Davis

Layli and Majnun
Nezami Ganjavi / Translated by Dick Davis

Khosrow and Shirin
Nezami Ganjavi / Translated by Dick Davis

Shahnameh: the Persian Book of Kings
Abolqasem Ferdowsi / Translated by Dick Davis

Rostam: Tales of Love and War from Persia's Book of Kings
Abolqasem Ferdowsi / Translated by Dick Davis

Borrowed Ware: Medieval Persian Epigrams
Introduced and Translated by Dick Davis

At Home and Far from Home
Poems on Iran and Persian Culture
Dick Davis

When They Broke Down the Door: Poems
Fatemeh Shams / Introduction and translations by Dick Davis

The Layered Heart: Essays on Persian Poetry
In Celebration of Dick Davis
Edited by Ali-Asghar Seyyed Ghorab

Another Birth and Other Poems – Bilingual edition
By Forugh Farrokhzad
translated by Hasan Javadi and Susan Sallée

Obeyd-e Zakani: Ethics of Aristocrats and other Satirical Works
translated by Hasan Javadi

Milkvetch and Violets
Mohammad Reza Shafi'i-Kadkani/ translated by Mojdeh Bahar

Song of the Ground Jay, Poems by Iranian Women, 1960–2022
Bilingual Edition
translated by Mojdeh Bahar

Audio Books

Faces of Love: Hafez and the Poets of Shiraz
Translated by Dick Davis / Penguin Audio / Read by
Dick Davis, Tala Ashe and Ramiz Monsef

The Mirror of My Heart:
A Thousand Years of Persian Poetry by Women
Translated by Dick Davis / Penguin Audio / Read by
Dick Davis, Mozhan Marno, Tala Ashe and Serena Manteghi

Layli and Majnun
Nezami Ganjavi / Translated by Dick Davis
Penguin Audio / Read by
Dick Davis, Peter Ganim, Serena Manteghi and Sean Rohani

Vis and Ramin
Fakhraddin Gorgani / Translated by Dick Davis
Mage Audio / Read by
Mary Sarah Agliotta, Dick Davis (introduction)

My Uncle Napoleon
Iraj Pezeshkzad / Translated by Dick Davis
Mage Audio / Read by
Moti Margolin, Dick Davis (Introduction)

Savushun: A Novel about Modern Iran
Simin Daneshvar / Translated by M.R. Ghanoonparvar
Mage Audio / Read by
Mary Sarah Agliotta, Brian Spooner (Introduction)

Crowning Anguish: Taj al-Saltaneh
Memoirs of a Persian Princess
from the Harem to Modernity, 1884–1914
Introduction by Abbas Amanat / Translated by Anna Vanzan
Mage Audio / Read by
Kathreen Khavari